SEÁN O'FAOLÁIN

Seán O'Faoláin

Literature, Inheritance and the 1930s

PAUL DELANEY

IRISH ACADEMIC PRESS

First published in 2014 by Irish Academic Press
8 Chapel Lane
Sallins
Co. Kildare, Ireland

www.iap.ie

British Library Cataloguing in Publication Data
An entry can be found on request

ISBN: 978 0 7165 3266 8 (Paper)
ISBN: 978 0 7165 3267 5 (Cloth)
ISBN: 978 0 7165 3268 2 (PDF)

Library of Congress Cataloging-in-Publication Data
An entry can be found on request

Printed in Ireland by SPRINT-print Ltd

In memory of my mum,
Joan Delaney

Contents

Acknowledgements

Many people have helped me see this book through to print. Lisa Hyde at Irish Academic Press has been an enthusiastic supporter of the project, and I am deeply grateful to her for her encouragement and patience. I am also grateful to Helen Pockett, for her scrupulous attention to the text. Many thanks to Julia O'Faolain, who responded kindly to the idea of a book about her father's early work. Librarians and staff at Trinity College Dublin, the National Library of Ireland, and the British Library have been of tremendous assistance; Simon Lang and Helen McGinley in the Department of Early Printed Books in Trinity have been particularly helpful, and I am indebted to them for their expertise. Like any scholar, I am also indebted to the work of those who have gone before, as well as to contemporary critics who are engaging with the work and legacy of Seán O'Faoláin; any difference of opinion is grounded in respect for their accomplishments and insights.

Lyn Innes and George O'Brien each read substantial sections of this book in typescript, and their responses proved stimulating and enriching. Separate chapters have also been read and enhanced by the thoughts of Joe Cleary, Brian Cliff, Gerry Dawe, Nicky Grene, Heather Ingman, Anne Markey, Eve Patten and Eibhear Walshe. I am extremely grateful to all for their generosity, time and wisdom. I am also thankful to Brad Kent, Eoin Mac Cárthaigh, Máire Ní Bháin and Michael Parker, for advice and assistance along the way, and to Eugene McNulty and Michelle Keown, for the opportunity to present parts of this study to colleagues at St. Patrick's College, Drumcondra, and the University of Edinburgh. I am also obliged to Cheryl Alexander Malcolm and David Malcolm, Daithí Ó Corráin, Julia M. Wright, and the editors of *Irish Studies Review*, for the chance to explore other aspects of O'Faoláin's work in print. Above all, I am indebted to my colleagues and friends in the School of English, Trinity College Dublin, for nurturing a space that remains very precious, and to my students who have complicated, encouraged and extended my understanding of literary texts.

This book was completed in the months after my mother's death; but for the support of my father, Tony, and brother and sisters, Ciarán, Karen, Niamh and Lisa, this would not have been possible. My deepest debt is to my wife, Finola, who is my love and inspiration, and to our children, Katie Rose and Joe. The book is dedicated to my mum, who would have been proud.

A Note on the Text

This study follows the idiosyncratic spelling of Seán O'Faoláin's name throughout (with *fadas* and an apostrophe); this is the spelling preferred by O'Faoláin and used by his principal publishers, Jonathan Cape, in the 1930s. Other spellings of the writer's name are retained in the endnotes, since books, essays, articles, reviews and stories were published under 'Sean O'Faolain'(without *fadas*), 'Seán Ó Faoláin'(without an apostrophe), and 'Sean O Faolain'(without either) over the course of his life. Variations in the spelling of O'Faoláin's name are also respected in quotations from other scholars, and in the titles of critical studies in the endnotes and the bibliography. References to the following list of books are included in the main body of the text, and are indicated by abbreviation; in each instance, page references are to first editions published in Britain or in Ireland. References to all other texts by O'Faoláin, including later editions and books published in the USA, are included in the endnotes.

BA	*Bird Alone*
CM	*Constance Markievicz, or The Average Revolutionary*
DV	*De Valera*
KB	*King of the Beggars: A Life of Daniel O'Connell, the Irish Liberator, in a Study of the Rise of the Modern Irish Democracy (1775–1847)*
LS	*The Life Story of Eamon De Valera*
MNM	*Midsummer Night Madness and other stories*

NSF	*A Nest of Simple Folk*
PC	*A Purse of Coppers: Short Stories*
TWT	*The Autobiography of Theobald Wolfe Tone*
VM	*Vive Moi!: An Autobiography*

INTRODUCTION

Contexts and Early Criticism

'I have in my time written too much.'[1] So Seán O'Faoláin commented late in his life, in the revised edition of his autobiography *Vive Moi!*, published posthumously in 1993. Even the most committed admirer would find it hard to disagree. Over the course of a long publishing career, O'Faoláin wrote eight volumes of short stories, four novels, three travel books, six biographies, a play, a memoir, a history book and a so-called 'character study'. He published critical studies of the novel and the short-story form, introduced texts of historical, artistic and literary merit, and contributed scores of articles, reviews and uncollected stories to periodicals in Ireland, Britain and America. Most famously, he co-founded (with Peadar O'Donnell) and edited the influential journal *The Bell* from 1940 to 1946, and played a leading role in the fight against censorship in Ireland. For decades his work was widely read and discussed, and his fiction and non-fiction was praised and critiqued in equal measure. A divisive, dissident, middle-class liberal, O'Faoláin was banned but also canonical in his own lifetime. Generations of teenagers in Ireland engaged with his short stories as part of the school curriculum from the mid-1960s, and the writer they were introduced to was at one with the self-image that O'Faoláin liked to present to the world. Urbane and sophisticated, he was described by the late Gus Martin as 'a writer of great breadth and versatility' and an international artist of pressing significance.[2] Nearly half a century later, his writings are almost entirely out of print.

Few surveys of twentieth-century Irish history neglect to mention O'Faoláin, with Diarmaid Ferriter, for instance, categorizing him as 'one of the country's most influential writers' who contributed to the shape of modern Irish culture in a progressive and meaningful way.[3] Roy Foster has similarly reflected on his importance, characterizing *The Bell* as 'that essential journal' in post-revolutionary Irish culture and remarking that O'Faoláin's work 'stands as the record of an alternative' perspective in de Valera's Ireland.[4] If O'Faoláin is duly referenced in most historical studies, it is principally in the role of campaigner and figurehead; he has been similarly remembered in many overviews of Irish literature. By contrast, the texts that he produced have received relatively little detailed attention from commentators on Irish writing. This may be in the process of change, as a few interventions in recent years have suggested the beginnings of a reassessment of his *oeuvre*. Kelly Matthews's comprehensive survey of *The Bell*, published in 2012, is particularly notable in this respect, and adds to the modest attention that was given to O'Faoláin at the turn of the twenty-first century, which coincided with the centenary of his birth.[5] Niall Carson's recent work on O'Faoláin's relationship with the BBC is also critically significant (not least because it is a topic that has been ignored by scholars until now), while Brad Kent's forthcoming edition of O'Faoláin's cultural criticism should introduce a new readership, as well as re-introduce an older one, to a diverse range of O'Faoláin's concerns.[6] Such studies also build on earlier reflections by Conor Cruise O'Brien, Paul A. Doyle and Maurice Harmon, amongst others.[7]

Although these interventions are generally agreed on O'Faoláin's larger importance, they have nonetheless extrapolated very different messages from the work he produced. Thus, for some critics O'Faoláin was an archetypal pluralist who challenged proscriptive definitions of Irish culture, but for others he was an inverted snob or a self-serving polemicist who actually restricted the development of Irish literature. George O'Brien has described O'Faoláin's short fiction as 'a consistent exemplification of the alternatives to narrow-mindedness', for example, while Mark McNally has read O'Faoláin's cultural criticism as illustrative of a commitment to an inclusive, counter-hegemonic politics.[8] However, in a scathing assessment of the same body of material, Joe Cleary has suggested that O'Faoláin's work offers little more than 'a seriously limited, indeed quite conservative conception' of the possibilities available to the creative artist in a post-revolutionary context.[9] Similarly, in his study of post-Civil War republican writing in Ireland, Nicholas Allen has criticized O'Faoláin for being resistant to the 'constructive friction' or multiplicity of opinions that were expressed through the conflicts of the early 1920s, opinions that were re-articulated in key journals of the period, such as *The Irish Statesman* and, a decade later, *Ireland To-Day*. (O'Faoláin wrote a few articles for the former periodical; he was also a contributor to and served as the first book editor of the latter journal.) He is consequently taken to task by Allen for pursuing the 'wrong turn in the years to follow'.[10]

Regardless as to whether recent interventions have been supportive or critical of O'Faoláin, the corpus of engagements with his work remains comparatively small, particularly as it engages with texts published outside of *The Bell* and beyond the genre of the non-fiction essay. Various reasons might be supposed for this. For one thing, as O'Faoláin himself suggested, his output though extensive was uneven, and was often driven by market forces and the misplaced belief that he could master all literary forms as a self-styled 'Man of Letters'. It was only in his middle age that he began to train his interests more specifically, and to focus primarily, though not exclusively, on those genres that he was best suited to – especially the essay and the short story. In addition, it has been argued that O'Faoláin's writings have not aged well, and that much of his work is over-determined by the context in which it was first produced. The grounding of his texts in their period of publication, where the focus is often on such themes as nationalist mystification, provincial intolerance, post-revolutionary malaise and subservience to the Catholic Church, can appear leaden or dated to contemporary eyes. Fittingly, when a special issue of *The Cork Review* was published to mark the occasion of his death in 1991, the editor defined O'Faoláin's legacy in terms of loss and oversight. 'O'Faoláin left a mark on Ireland which will take years to measure', the late Seán Dunne lamented, and for all of his achievements he 'has not received real credit for what he did'.[11] The situation has scarcely changed in the intervening years, with the late Ruth Sherry suggesting that O'Faoláin is more likely to 'be remembered in future generations for the variety of his commitments' than for the quality of his writing.[12]

Further reasons might be advanced to account for O'Faoláin's relative eclipse from contemporary critical discourse. It is significant that his work is principally associated with forms which are vulnerable to the vicissitudes of taste and time – journalism and short fiction, most notably – and that each of these forms occupies a precarious existence in the academic marketplace. Short stories, in particular, are routinely considered the preserve of emerging writers in the publishing world, and O'Faoláin's alleged failure as a novelist has often been taken as evidence of his shortcomings as a fiction writer. It is equally telling that O'Faoláin favoured a stance that has become increasingly unsustainable in recent decades. A defining feature of his work, in fiction and non-fiction, is an assurance of tone and subject matter that was already outmoded by the time of its writing, and his use of seemingly traditional modes of narration can appear jaded in today's world. This apparent obsolescence is compounded by the fact that O'Faoláin expressed a preference for realist storytelling practices which require, or seem to require, little explication, and it has sometimes been argued that his *oeuvre* contains little evidence of the formal experimentation or existential or linguistic crises which characterized literature as a result of the modernist movement. Quite simply, one could forget that he was a compatriot and contemporary of Samuel Beckett, Flann O'Brien and Elizabeth Bowen.

If such claims have become commonplace, they are not always borne out by a close analysis of O'Faoláin's textual practice. For one thing, such criticism often relies upon an understanding of 'realism' that is reductive, simplistic or underdeveloped. As Pam Morris has observed, 'there is not one unified form of realism but many', which encompass a wide variety of authors, strategies and texts. If these many forms share the primary principle that realism is mimetic (that is to say, it imitates or mirrors a reality which exists beyond language), this is complicated by the fact that literary realism is mediated through language, and is organized by conventions which are rhetorical as well as representational. Realist fiction has not always been blind to these complexities, as many authors have creatively engaged with their art, exploring formal devices and linguistic styles which are anything but transparent or simply reflective. 'If we accept too quickly or unquestioningly the assumption that realist texts copy reality,' Morris has counselled, 'we tend to overlook a long, impressive tradition of artistic development during which writers struggled and experimented with the artistic means to convey a verbal sense of what it is like to live an embodied existence in the world'.[13] O'Faoláin's relationship with 'realism' is certainly more textured than many lazy assessments would suggest and, in some respects at least, bears witness to the complexities alluded to by Morris. His work frequently mixes romantic, realist and naturalist modes with experimental techniques such as perspectivalism, indirection, open-endedness and irony. It also routinely reflects upon its own act of narration, engaging with the ways in which stories are narrativized or told, and playing with the use of structures, generic forms, intertextual references and the processes of memory.

What is more, and notwithstanding claims for O'Faoláin's apparent obsolescence, it would be misleading to suggest that his work is entirely removed from today's writers and readers. Individual stories continue to be included in most anthologies of Irish short fiction, with Anne Enright recently incorporating some of his work into her edited collection *The Granta Book of the Irish Short Story* (2010). O'Faoláin's importance to that collection is underscored by Enright in her introduction to that anthology, where she describes him as one of the two 'pillars' of twentieth-century short fiction in Ireland (the other is Frank O'Connor), and many of her reflections on the short-story form testify to his ongoing influence as a practitioner and theorist.[14] Individual stories are also reprinted in other anthologies of Irish prose fiction, edited by fellow writers such as William Trevor, Dermot Bolger, Benedict Kiely and Colm Tóibín, and samples of his non-fiction can be found in various collections and readers, including David Pierce's *Irish Writing in the Twentieth Century* (2000) and Sean McMahon's much-reissued *The Best from 'The Bell'* (1978).[15] The structure of such texts demands that only a glimpse is ever given of O'Faoláin's *oeuvre*, however, as only a tiny fraction of his work is reproduced. Indeed, certain types of narratives are necessarily privileged in such collections (discrete short stories and stand-alone critical essays), and this is invariably at the expense of longer prose pieces. Interestingly, at the time of writing, only one full-length book by O'Faoláin is still in print, his biography of the sixteenth-century Gaelic chieftain Hugh O'Neill, first published in 1942, and reprinted by the Cork-based publishing house Mercier Press in 1997.[16] This is at odds with the fate of many of his contemporaries whose work remains readily available to local and international audiences.

Notwithstanding these difficulties, O'Faoláin is justifiably recognized as a key figure in the evolution of a post- or counter Revival aesthetic. In many respects the familiarity of his name can be taken as evidence that his work, if no longer widely read, nonetheless appears 'always already read' to many commentators and readers. In his literary study *The Political Unconscious*, Fredric Jameson used this formulation – 'always already read' – to suggest that readers 'never really confront a text immediately, in all its freshness as a thing-in-itself', since the idea of a text, or an author, is already invested with a series of associations that suit the interests or preconceptions of those who come to it. Because readers approach texts 'through sedimented layers of previous interpretations', Jameson surmised, the act of reading often involves less an engagement with the text itself and more an encounter with 'the interpretations through which we attempt to confront and appropriate' a text or an author.[17] O'Faoláin typifies this process, as his writings have frequently been referenced without being interrogated or discussed, and his legacy interpreted through a prism of pre-designed or conflicting interpretative paradigms. What is more, O'Faoláin's name has often been taken to signify a particular stance or style, and used as shorthand to describe issues and concerns which no longer seem relevant in a contemporary context. As one might expect this has sometimes led to simplifications and misreadings, as the received version of O'Faoláin – something which exists 'always already' in the popular imagination – is set against the historical reality of a man who wrote and lived. A case in point is provided by the online entry on O'Faoláin in the database, *The Oxford Dictionary of National Biography*, which is littered with factual inaccuracies.[18]

Whether O'Faoláin is labelled a liberal pluralist, an opinionated chauvinist, a proto-revisionist or a nascent postcolonial critic, the writer who is mentioned in most historical or literary surveys is usually a figure who fits the designs of the argument in question. Thus, commentators typically discuss a writer whose name is already familiar to them, someone who suits the expectations of a particular period in recent Irish history, and whose work exemplifies something readers had intended or presumed that they would find. The present study is partially a response to this 'already read' process, with the primary focus redirected towards a close reading of the principal texts that O'Faoláin wrote during the 1930s, the decade that was crucial for his emergence as a prose writer. It was during this decade that O'Faoláin produced some of his most important work, including his highly influential biography of Daniel O'Connell, *King of the Beggars* (1938), his first two collections of short stories, *Midsummer Night Madness* (1932) and *A Purse of Coppers* (1937), and the controversial novel *Bird Alone* (1936); it was also at this time that he laid the foundations for ideas that would prove central to the ethos of *The Bell*. Inevitably, the readings that are advanced in this study are indebted to other reflections on this major literary figure. Rather than approaching O'Faoláin's texts 'in all their freshness' as isolated literary artefacts, they feed into a received tradition that is identifiable today as 'Seán O'Faoláin'; it could not be otherwise. Since O'Faoláin has become such an uncertain subject, however – someone whose legacy signifies very different things, and whose work is often not read or deliberately misread despite his apparent canonicity – it is best to begin with a brief contextualization of his *oeuvre* and an overview of the early stages of his life and writing career.

Seán O'Faoláin was born John Whelan, in Cork city, in 1900. His parents were lower middle-class Catholics, who were keen to pass on a set of values and a desire for social respectability to their three sons. 'We were shabby-genteels at the lowest possible social level,' he reminisced in his autobiography, 'neither ever where we were or where we hoped to be, Janus-faced, throwing glances of desire and admiration upwards and ahead, glances of hatred or contempt downwards and behind' (*VM* 61).

Fiercely class-conscious and deeply pious, his parents were also assuredly conservative. His father was a political loyalist, a constable in the Royal Irish Constabulary (RIC), and a man who 'embodied all the accepted and respected values and conventions of what we would nowadays call the Establishment' (*VM* 28). His mother was extremely ambitious for her children, and her relationship with them – at least as O'Faoláin later described it – was governed by a complex mixture of parsimony, affectation, shame and religious fervour. These were the values John Whelan inherited as a youth, internalizing his mother's class and religious sensitivities, and fashioning himself 'in dutiful imitation' of his father, taking over 'holus-bolus, the accepted hierarchy of the imperial way of life' (*VM* 28). It is a way of life that was supported by much of his childhood reading, which included works by the popular Victorian writer for boys George A. Henty. Henty's derring-do novels, including *St. George for England* (1885), *Won by the Sword* (1900) and *With Kitchener in the Soudan* (1903), fed the imagination of the young John Whelan, and helped to inform his earliest loyalties; they also nurtured a fascination with a certain type of Englishness, fostering an appetite for pageantry, valour and ideas of high adventure. This imperialist inheritance was questioned in his teenage years, as it was for many of his peers, initially through contact with the spirit of Irish cultural nationalism and subsequently by the events of 1916.

Through the influence of a schoolteacher, Pádraig Ó Dómhnaill, O'Faoláin first became interested in the Irish language, attending classes of the Gaelic League in his early teens, later travelling to the Gaeltacht regions of West Cork, and eventually, like other young men and women of the age, gaelicizing his name. His interest in Irish was romantically inspired and nourished by the widely-held belief in the *fíor Gael* or 'true Irish'. Looking back in *Vive Moi!*, O'Faoláin recollected that remote, Irish-speaking areas such as West Cork were sacralized for many city-born people of his generation and seen as 'a wonderland where the star of Eden never died' (*VM* 103). Invested with numinous qualities, the poverty of these regions was frequently overlooked, with physical spaces transformed into the realm of the imaginary and referenced by such epithets as 'the wonderful country, the far-off country, the Free Country' (*VM* 109). Such places allowed for a return to a lost origin, it was supposed, and enabled a holistic and integrated sense of self to be posited. As O'Faoláin memorably explained in his travel book *An Irish Journey* (1940), 'nobody who has not had this sensation of suddenly "belonging" somewhere – of finding the lap of the lost mother – can understand what a release the discovery of the Gaelic world meant to modern Ireland'.[19] The people who inhabited the Gaeltacht regions were also imaginatively recast, and valorized as the essence of all things 'Irish', while the language that they spoke was afforded a weight of significance exceeding its cultural and linguistic value. Interpreted as 'a symbol of the larger freedom to which we were all groping', O'Faoláin would later note that Irish was made to function 'both as a matrix to the tissues of our political faith and as its sign and password' (*VM* 108, 113). Daniel Corkery, a prominent Cork educationalist and prose writer, was a critical figure in the encouragement of these beliefs, as he was actively involved in the work of the Gaelic League and served as a mentor to many young people in the locale, including O'Faoláin.

The Abbey playwright Lennox Robinson was an additional influence. In later years, O'Faoláin often recalled the occasion when he happened to see one of Robinson's plays performed as a fifteen-year old youth in the nearby Cork Opera House. The play, *Patriots* (first produced at the Abbey Theatre in 1912, and seen by O'Faoláin three years later on tour), exerted an immediate impact on his sympathies while also releasing a more gradual, slow-drip influence that only began to become apparent when he started to write. Set in the early years of the twentieth century, *Patriots* tells the story of James Nugent, a Fenian rebel who is released from a long prison sentence in England. The country Nugent returns to has changed in the time he was in jail, as the heroic ideals of an earlier age are replaced by political lethargy and material self-interest. Nugent finds himself at odds with family and former friends as a result. Although Robinson's allegiances are clearly with the rebel, he nonetheless depicts Nugent succumbing to local pressures and abandoning his principles at the play's end. The challenge, it seems, is displaced to Robinson's audience, who are called to examine their own beliefs in the light of all that they have witnessed. The young John Whelan was affected in this way.

Part of the appeal of *Patriots* for O'Faoláin – or, perhaps rather, part of the appeal he afforded it in retrospect – is that it represented a world already known to him. Its interior setting was instantly recognizable, for instance, and resembled many rural Irish houses he was acquainted with as a child, including his mother's family home in Rathkeale, County Limerick; similarly, the fictional characters who inhabited the play were identifiable and familiar. For the mature O'Faoláin looking back, this verisimilitude was a crucial early step in the realization that literature could describe a world that was local and commonplace. Writing of the experience twenty years later, in an essay for *The Yale Review*, he claimed that Robinson's play was 'a complete revelation' for these reasons.[20] Intriguingly, O'Faoláin's representation of this experience is comparable to Robinson's own account of a very similar revelation, recorded in his autobiography *Curtain Up* (1942). Recalling the time he first saw *Cathleen Ni Houlihan* performed by the touring Abbey company, also in the Cork Opera House (in 1907), Robinson talked of experiencing a 'conversion [that] was immediate and instant', as he became aware 'that play-material could be found outside one's own door – at one's own fireside'.[21] The coincidence is striking. In addition, Robinson's play was important for O'Faoláin since it engaged with the legacy of Fenian politics, bringing to mind distant family members who challenged his father's imperialist loyalties. 'Had not a certain Uncle Paudh of mine, from County Limerick – it came back to me from some gossiping of my mother and Aunt Nan over the cottage fire – run off to Australia to escape arrest at the time of the Fenian uprising in '67?', he asked in his autobiography. 'I had also read about the Fenians, and I had heard my father utter harsh words about them' (*VM* 90). Robinson's play provided O'Faoláin with a glimpse into this other world – a world that was partially hidden or hushed from him, but that was part of his inheritance even though it was in conflict with all that he had been brought up to believe. 'I will not say that I was changed, when I left the theatre,' he acknowledged years later in his autobiography, 'But I know that I was dazed' (*VM* 90).

Change began to be realized the following year as a consequence of the 1916 Rising. O'Faoláin later claimed that his initial response to the insurrection was the same as that of his father and many of his contemporaries. 'I raged at its betrayal', he conceded, as the events of Easter Week were seen in the larger context of the First World War and the horrific battles that were being fought in Flanders and northern France (*VM* 105). His loyalties began to shift, he later suggested, when he learned more about the rebellion's leaders, and this change was intensified in the period that followed the Easter Rising, particularly as a result of the brutal treatment of the insurgents at the hands of the British military. 'When, in the following weeks, the British took out the leaders and shot them in ones, and twos, and threes, everybody and everything I had believed in began to tumble about me. Henty, my father, my home' (*VM* 105). O'Faoláin consistently represented this event as if it held an immediate, life-changing significance for him, and many commentators have concurred with this line of thought; his biographer, Maurice Harmon, for instance, has remarked that the Rising 'broke O'Faoláin's loyalist links', as 'feelings rose up in him of which he was previously unaware'.[22] While such assessments carry a grain of truth, it is nonetheless more likely that any such 'break' was protracted and hard-won, as the teenage John Whelan strove to overturn attitudes that he had inherited from his parents and a conservative worldview that he had interpellated as a child. The quasi-autobiographical Denis Hussey begins to make these kinds of changes at the end of O'Faoláin's first novel, *A Nest of Simple Folk* (1933), but these changes are not fully understood or actualized by the protagonist of that novel; nor is it clear that Denis will easily shed the allegiances into which he has been born. As O'Faoláin succinctly stated elsewhere in his autobiography, 'no man jumps off his own shadow' because the perceptions we inherit as children are so woven into our psyche that they become 'part of [our] way of seeing and feeling forever' (*VM* 125). Indeed, it is tempting to read O'Faoláin's retrospective account of instantaneous change with suspicion, since the impact that he placed on the execution of the leaders, and the effect that this had on the general public (as well as the way that he chose to represent this impact, personally and collectively), is such a widespread historical generalization.

In one of his earliest books, the biography *Constance Markievicz* (1934), O'Faoláin asserted that the contemporary reaction to the aftermath of the

Rising was grounded in impulses and loyalties that were primarily atavistic. 'The executions awoke old and forgotten emotions in the hearts of the people,' he contended, 'disturbed and aroused the sleeping racial memory in which every Irish patriot has his niche and his votive lamp' (*CM* 241–2). This claim was repeated in subsequent works and points towards a constellation of issues which were to remain of enduring concern to him as a writer, including the power of inherited or collective memories, the interleaving of nationalist and religious iconographies, and the fusion of Irish patriotic discourse with the language of the Catholic Church. They are also illustrative of his fascination with the pageantry of the Rising, and the rich symbolism which it intentionally provoked in the popular imagination. This interest was partially sparked by O'Faoláin's early love of the theatre – something which allowed the young John Whelan to indulge his fascination with make-believe and fantasy. Looking back, O'Faoláin explained that drama granted him access to a world rich in transformative potential, as it 'inflamed my imagination and fanned my senses', enabling 'the here constantly become elsewhere, the solid dissolve, the familiar become unfamiliar' (*VM* 16,14). In addition, though, his response to the Rising was indebted to the Church and the basic idiom of Catholic practice which is recorded in such detail in *Vive Moi!*. Thus, in the early pages of his autobiography, close attention is given to the resonance of Catholic rites and images, the value of self-sacrifice, the transfiguration of the body, and the possibilities of life through resurrection – ideas which were to become synonymous with the Rising through the writings of Patrick Pearse especially, and which led to the sanctification of the leaders in the aftermath of the executions. The spheres of Church and theatre are tellingly brought together in the same pages, when O'Faoláin described the nature of religious practice in the Ireland that he knew as a child, recalling how he 'luxuriated in the sacraments' as a youth and 'enjoyed the ceremonies as I enjoyed the play' (*VM* 18, 20).

The pronounced theatricality of the Rising also appealed to O'Faoláin's tendency to romanticize, which was enriched by his childhood reading of Victorian imperialist fiction. Residual Henty-like traces are discernible in O'Faoláin's accounts of the Rising, for instance, as attention is given to idealized exemplars of courage and chivalry, with O'Faoláin pausing to consider the colour, thrill and flair of Easter Week. This romantic impulse is apparent in each of his two biographies of the most famous survivor of the Easter rebellion, Eamon de Valera. Despite the many differences which distinguish the hagiographical *The Life Story of Eamon De Valera* (1933) from the more modulated *De Valera* (1939), both of these texts use the loaded phrase 'gallant adventure' to describe the insurrection, and on each occasion emphasis is placed on the valorous behaviour of those who were centrally involved in the action (*LS* 39, *DV* 38). Intriguingly, this is done at the expense of any mention of the rebels' objectives, with little space given in either text to the conflicting forces that led to the rebels' involvement in the fighting. If O'Faoláin tended to romanticize accounts of the Rising in his early work, this was something he revised in his later years. In 1968, for example, in Peter Lennon's *The Rocky Road to Dublin*, O'Faoláin voiced the familiar republican complaint that had the leaders of Easter Week seen 'the kind of Ireland' that had evolved out of independence 'they would have felt only that their efforts had been betrayed and their sacrifice had been in vain'. Significantly, in his contribution to this unofficially banned film, O'Faoláin replaced the vaguely-defined 'spirit of 1916' with more tangible assertions for the need for a society characterized by modernity, freedom of speech and social justice, identifying the latter goals as the motivating principles behind the insurrection.[23]

O'Faoláin joined the Irish Volunteers sometime in late 1918 and subsequently served in the Irish Republican Army (IRA) during the War of Independence (1919–21). By his own admission he saw very little fighting: 'In my six years as a rank-and-filer of the IRA,' he conceded, 'I shot nobody and I was briefly under fire once. I have no war memories to record' (*VM* 139). To O'Faoláin's mind, this was a direct consequence of his youth. As his biographer has since noted, it was more likely a result of his background – O'Faoláin had no military experience, after all, and his RIC parentage probably meant that he was regarded with suspicion by those in the movement.[24] His involvement in this conflict coincided with his undergraduate studies at University College Cork (UCC), and in his later reflections he often brought his memories of the War of Independence together with his time at UCC. Both provided formative, interconnected, if very different types of educational experiences for the late adolescent, and in a neat twist it was a fellow student at UCC who inducted him into the Volunteer movement. If O'Faoláin's engagement in military activity was slight, but not entirely atypical, his subsequent representations of the conflict frequently depicted it as a struggle for personal as well as national and generational autonomy. These experiences saw him participate in a range of activities – drilling at night, hiding weapons, gathering information, keeping watch for comrades – that brought him into conflict with the world of his parents and their desire for conformity and respectability. 'Never will I forget the first day I stood in a field, in a deep glen, somewhere to the southwest of the city,' he reminisced:

> with a score of other raw recruits, being given my first drill by some older student … It was an autumn day of sun and shower, and just as [our captain] began to speak to us a faint, gentle sprinkling rain began to fall on us, and then the sun floated out again and sparkled on every leaf and blade of grass as if some invisible presence had passed over us with a lighted taper, binding us together not only in loyalty and in friendship but in something dearer still that I am not ashamed to call love. In that moment life became one with the emotion of Ireland. In that moment I am sure every one of us ceased to be single or individual and became part of one another, in union, almost like coupling lovers … This extraordinarily heart-lifting revelation, this gaiety, this liberation of the spirit, was to stay with us all through the exciting years to come (*VM* 137).

Many of O'Faoláin's reflections of this period interleave the experience of life during these 'exciting' or turbulent years with a range of emotions not dissimilar to those evoked by William Wordsworth in his celebrated account of the French Revolution in *The Prelude* (1805).[25] For O'Faoláin, looking back, Ireland at war was transformed, as people and place were aligned and the natural world was felt imparting its blessing to all – but particularly the young – who committed themselves to the cause of independence.[26] Such transformations allowed for the most transcendent of experiences, with the lines of self dissolved into a richly-imagined homosocial, even homoerotic, sense of camaraderie and oneness. 'If any of the youths or young men of those days should chance to read these lines today,' he postulated years later, 'I am sure that he will make no wonder of them. He will acknowledge that I am describing something very simple that happened to us all when we were not bald or grey, paunching, tired or sceptical, when in our generous youth we lived and were ready to die for one of the most wild, beautiful and inexhaustible faiths possible to man – faith in one's fellows' (*VM* 137–8).

Not all of O'Faoláin's memories were rose-tinted, however. His second biography of de Valera contains numerous allusions to the campaign of state terror that was unleashed by Crown forces in the early 1920s, and is unequivocal in its assertion that 'nothing can resuscitate the full meaning of the Terror' of life in Ireland at this time (*DV* 75). Mention is made of summary executions, indiscriminate damage, reprisals, internment and the use of torture, for instance; and evidence is provided of the British establishment's attempts to cover up such atrocities – the censorship of Ernie O'Malley's account of the struggle, *On Another Man's Wound* (1936), by his London publishers, is cited to prove this point (*DV* 77).[27] In addition, attention is given to the exhaustion that was suffered by insurgents and civilians alike, as a population lived in a state of fear, under the threat of violence and curfew. Such conditions supply the background to many of the stories in *Midsummer Night Madness*, where a dominant motif in the collection – that of movement – is repeatedly set against the restrictions imposed by martial law; they are also vividly recreated in *Vive Moi!*, where O'Faoláin contemplated the consequences of surviving this 'war of nerves'. 'After forty years have blunted my worst memories [of the conflict],' he confessed, 'I … still frequently awake sweating from a nightmare that has whirled me back among them again' (*VM* 142). The terror that is registered in such a passage quickly gives way to nostalgia, however, as it is also recorded, on the same page, that 'the truth of it is that they were both wonderful times and nightmare times' (*VM* 142). This quasi-Dickensian conflation is characteristic of O'Faoláin's reflections on the War of Independence, more generally, and is perhaps attributable to the fact that his experiences of that conflict were episodic and often at some remove.[28] 'Sean could be a student by day, an IRA rebel in the evenings or on Sundays,' Harmon has noted; this part-time schedule afforded him opportunities to step outside the conflict, as he courted his future wife, the writer Eileen O'Faoláin, continued to attend classes of the Gaelic League, and became involved in literary activities in his hometown.[29]

Under Corkery's influence, O'Faoláin rejected the Treaty which concluded the War of Independence. He subsequently took the anti-Treaty side in the Irish Civil War (1922–3), outraged by the perceived betrayal of republican ideals and indignant that anything less than total freedom had been secured. He was deeply affected by this bitter conflict, hinting in *Vive Moi!* that it continued 'to oppress me traumatically for many years' (*VM* 145). Like many of his peers, O'Faoláin was reluctant to write about this conflict at length, alluding to it instead for the most part in short sketches and occasional pieces. Ten years later, for instance, in the slight essay 'About Myself' (1932), he described the Civil War in one suitably convoluted sentence as 'a miserable business, men unwilling to fight and without the character to throw in their guns, much cruelty and brutality, politicians manoeuvring for position while young boys and young men were being executed or murdered for murdering one another by the score'.[30] Similar sentiments were expressed in the short story 'The Patriot', which was published the same year in *Midsummer Night Madness*, and also inform the essay 'Letter from a Novelist to an Idealist' (1933), where O'Faoláin sought to account for his generation's cynicism and loss of belief:

> We grew up in a period when the patriots broke into bits the dreams that had so long supported the poets and them and all of us. As Joyce was born into unreason [*sic*] in the awful years when Parnell was battered through the towns of Ireland; as O'Casey was born into reason when the Dublin employers were trying to starve the poor of Dublin through the winter of 1913, so we

> came when the lovely and the noble and the proud was dragged through a shambles.[31]

In the latter essay, O'Faoláin urged his imagined reader – a narrow-minded 'idealist' or 'Irish Ireland' exclusivist – to remember that this was the case, and so 'have more patience with Irish writers of the day'. At the same time, he refrained from expanding on what he meant by the euphemistically-described 'shambles'.

O'Faoláin worked as a bomb-maker and then as a propagandist during the Civil War, contributing to several Munster republican papers such as *An Phoblacht (Southern Edition)* and the short-lived *An Lóng*, as well as the *Cork Examiner* after it was seized by republican forces. Despite his youth, he held senior posts in publicity and propaganda, including that of Director of Publicity for the First Southern Division from late 1922. He was appointed Assistant Director of Publicity for Sinn Féin in mid-1923, following de Valera's proclamation for a ceasefire (partially because so many of his comrades were either in jail or dead), and was Director of Publicity when Mary MacSwiney was arrested by Free State authorities. From the summer of 1923 through to January 1924, he was heavily involved in the production of the Dublin-based republican newspapers *An Phoblacht* and *Sinn Féin*, serving for a time as editor of both papers. This coincided with a period in his life when, he would later claim, 'we were all idealists, self-crazed by abstractions, lost in the labyrinths of the dreams to which we had retreated' (*VM* 169). He soon grew tired of the scope of these 'dreams', quitting his position in early 1924 and returning to Cork, 'a more than disillusioned and embittered young man' (*VM* 171). Several months later, he briefly reprised his association with one of these papers, when he became embroiled in one of his earliest published disputes after submitting a disgruntled letter to the new editor of *Sinn Féin*.

In the early to mid-1920s *Sinn Féin* was an eight-page weekly newspaper (it was briefly a four-page daily) driven along clear ideological lines, with links to Arthur Griffith's newspaper of the same name, which had been suppressed by the British government in 1914. The newspaper consisted of anonymous partisan reportage, sympathetic readers' letters, and feature articles by prominent republicans of the day, such as Patrick Ruttledge, Constance Markievicz, Mary MacSwiney and Dorothy Macardle. It also contained advertisements from like-minded businessmen, occasional photographs of recent events, a serialization of *Principles of Freedom* by the martyred hunger striker Terence MacSwiney (Mary MacSwiney's brother), and haunting images of young volunteers who had died during the Civil War. In September 1924 O'Faoláin wrote the first of three letters to the paper, objecting to a series of articles by Frank Gallagher, the future editor of de Valera's *The Irish Press*, on the so-called 'Volunteer Spirit'. The attitude behind these articles was 'wearisome and disheartening to the people', O'Faoláin protested, as it recycled old arguments and indicated a lack of leadership in the contemporary republican movement. 'The reiteration of principles is unnecessary,' he argued, and 'the reiteration of Propaganda is offensive'. What is needed instead is a critical interrogation of the principles of Irish republicanism, and a serious analysis of its expectations and aims, for 'one might read *Sinn Féin* for a long time before one's faith warned one to a suspicion that Republicanism was an intellectual movement'.[32] O'Faoláin's comments provoked criticism from several quarters, including a response from Gallagher himself, and prompted O'Faoláin to submit a second letter to the newspaper a few weeks later, where he expanded on his original complaint.

'All propaganda represents a low plane of thought,' the erstwhile editor of *Sinn Féin* declared, and even when 'the things said in propaganda be true, the whole attitude which impels its writing and publication is a false one'. This is because propaganda is by definition doctrinaire, and eschews any mode of thought that does not fit within its pre-determined boundaries. To illustrate the point, O'Faoláin alluded to the bitter legacy of the Civil War. Rather than raking over the coals of this recent conflict, he suggested that it was time for Irish republicanism to formulate an integrated policy and expend its energies on issues of pressing concern, such as poverty, schooling and the language revival. It was also time to engage constructively with the achievements of the Free State in the hopes of creating an inclusive and genuinely synthetic republican politics:

> The Irish people are at this moment fit to climb any height or plane where we shall not sneer at everything the Free State population may attempt, irrespective of good intention; a plane where we shall not be afraid to say that [Michael] Collins and [Arthur] Griffith were men of noble qualities; a plane where we shall encourage actively a Gaelic tradition as well as a Republican one; and achieve a tradition of Republican culture instead of Republican sentimentality.[33]

This drew a response from the hard-line Mary MacSwiney. 'To talk of propaganda being "unnecessary and offensive" while the Irish people return to a Parliament a majority of men pledged to subvert National Independence, shows a lack of commonsense without which all intellectualism is a snare and a delusion', MacSwiney wrote in the same issue of *Sinn Féin*. She also asked what O'Faoláin was doing to 'preach the gospel' of the Irish language.[34]

A short reply in Irish appeared a fortnight later, in which O'Faoláin, apparently, chose not to engage any further in the dispute. '*Is é is lúgha is gann dom a rádh i ndiaidh a bhfuil ráidhte agam i gcoinnibh do pháipéir ná an méid eile seo*' ('The least I can do, after what I have said against your paper, is to add the following'), he stated, before proceeding to commend *Sinn Féin* for its commitment to publish Irish-language material each week, marking out for particular praise its regular '*Leathnach na bhFilí*' or 'Poet's Page', and setting this against the anti-Gaelic bias of most Irish newspapers. An implied critique was buried within O'Faoláin's *plámás* or flattery, though, as he concluded the letter with the double-edged tribute that '*Táim cinnte ghur mór duine a cheannuighean "Sinn Féin" ar son a leathanaigh so do bheith ann*' ('I am certain that there is many a person who buys *Sinn Féin* because this page is in it') – the implication being that the paper was not always bought for its republican content or propagandist material.[35]

In response to MacSwiney, O'Faoláin might have also mentioned his recent authorship of several texts in Irish, including the short story 'Prendergast', about a seminarian's struggles to reconcile conflicting emotions, and an extended essay on the seventeenth-century poet Dáibhí

Ó Bruadair, both published in the UCC Gaelic journal *Éarna*.[36] He might have also added, on a personal note, that he had gone back to school to learn more Irish, re-enrolling at UCC to pursue a Master's degree in the subject in 1924. After a short spell as a schoolteacher in Ennis, County Clare (from where he wrote the third letter to *Sinn Féin*), he returned to the safety of UCC for a third time, the following year, to continue his postgraduate studies. By this time, O'Faoláin appears to literary history as a well-educated, opinionated but increasingly isolated young man, cut off from former comrades and questioning beliefs that he had previously held dear; what is more, despite his several degrees, he was out of work. 'This was no longer the romantic Ireland of little cottages and the hunted men', his friend Frank O'Connor recollected years later, but 'the real Ireland', a depressed economy with high unemployment and few opportunities, 'where everyone was frantically searching for a pension or a job'.[37]

O'Faoláin was disillusioned by the society that emerged out of independence, coming to believe that the Free State was characterized by lost promises and wasted potential. The revolution provided only the most superficial of transformations, he contended, encouraging narrow-gauged definitions of identity, self-congratulating myths of origin, cronyism, caution, and 'a new, native, acquisitive, middle class intent only on cashing in on the change of governments' (*VM* 165). Thus, in his first contribution to George Russell's *The Irish Statesman*, in the autumn of 1925, O'Faoláin kicked against conventional orthodoxy by questioning one of the pillars of that society, the contemporary Irish-language movement. The occasion for this polemic was a recent review of an anthology of Irish love poetry, *Laoíthe Cumainn*, edited by Tomas Ó Rathile. In his review of Ó Rathile's collection, Daniel Corkery had waxed lyrical about the current state of literature in Irish, rejoicing in its links with the past and claiming that 'even already it has become the dominant factor in the culture of this country'.[38] O'Faoláin's mordant response came in the form of an open letter to the editor of *The Irish Statesman*. 'Those who go digging in the Gaeltacht to-day will only get a tradition about the fag-end of a fag-end of a culture', he argued:

> and if they go there seeking culture they will waste much time. But, it is another matter if the educationalists and the revivalists should attempt to force this uneducated peasant tradition on a country like ours, which is already in the European current, and whose literature in Irish, as in English, will be part and parcel of Europe's gift to the world.[39]

O'Faoláin's interest in Irish was not the issue in this letter, rather, his concern was with the romanticization of the Irish-language heritage and its use as political capital. As Nicholas Allen has observed, these comments were gratefully received by Russell, chiming as they did with his own beliefs that post-Independence Irish culture needed to embrace its many diverse elements, including its English- and Irish-language inheritances.[40] For all its criticism, though, O'Faoláin's comments belonged to a stage in his life when he was only beginning to reassess the possibilities of language revival, and when he was 'only mildly pessimistic' about the project, as Philip O'Leary has noted. This pessimism would increase in the years to follow; however, at this time periodicals like *Iris an Fháinne* still included O'Faoláin amongst the lists of people giving lectures on the Irish language to interested audiences in Cork.[41] O'Faoláin's criticisms also carried a contemporary edge, as they coincided with the work of a powerful government commission (established in early 1925) charged with determining which areas of the country might be designated Gaeltacht or Irish-speaking, and fed into a larger debate concerning the place of Irish in the educational system and its importance to the cultural life of the emerging state.

The points raised were extended in two subsequent essays, both of which were commissioned by Russell and advertised as 'special articles' in *The Irish Statesman*. In the first of these, 'A Plea for a New Irish Scholarship', O'Faoláin considered the status of contemporary Irish-language scholarship and its relationship to the educational curriculum. In particular, he bemoaned the tendency to focus on rote-learning and pedantic exercises in schools, advancing instead the need for a culture of critical engagement that would encourage students 'to handle Irish, not as a dead, but as a living language'. 'Surely there needs to be some progression [from the early ambitions of the Gaelic League],' he remarked, 'a mental development such as takes place with every other subject that forms a liberal education in itself – namely, a deepening of the mind, a widening of the outlook, a sense of proportions, not merely an exercise of memory'.[42] This concern with 'widening outlooks' was further developed in the second essay, 'The Gaoltacht [*sic*] Tradition', where O'Faoláin argued against received wisdom by contesting the supposed purity of the Irish-language heritage, criticizing what he termed 'the poverty and the degenerate nature' of Gaeltacht culture.

Part of the motivation for 'The Gaoltacht Tradition' arose from the belief – a belief O'Faoláin himself had espoused only a few years earlier, as a member of the Gaelic League – that remote Irish-speaking areas were 'the real Ireland' because of an imagined link between these regions, their inhabitants, and the culture of pre-nineteenth-century Gaelic Ireland. Writing against the grain, and in the shadow of Corkery's recent *The Hidden Ireland* (1924), he claimed that eighteenth-century Gaelic culture was merely 'the death-wail' of a once vibrant living heritage that did not survive the defeats of the seventeenth century, it 'died of senility, and is to-day a mere memory'. 'The sole surviving representative of the great past is an illiterate peasant', he posited, resident in the Gaeltacht and celebrated only by parties with a vested interest, such as language revivalists and opportunistic politicians. In addition, and more contentiously, he suggested that if the Gaeltacht was to be perceived as that which was most purely Irish, it followed that Gaeltacht culture was, at the very least, wary of external influences and, at worst, full of 'fear and hate for the culture and traditions of Europe'. This claim is flatly contradicted by an entire body of Irish-language literature. O'Faoláin conveniently chose to overlook this fact, however, as he stressed the need for a reconsideration of Ireland's links with Europe (a Europe which included England), and acknowledged the importance of international pressures and influences for any understanding of Irish history and the contemporary scene. This point, however awkwardly phrased, provided a central strand of this early polemic, as he concluded:

> We must borrow in great handfuls from Europe at the same time borrowing in great handfuls from the pre-1607 Ireland, and though we can never hope to recover the old power of assimilation, we might spare the children learning Irish in the schools at this moment the discovery that 'Ireland-free' is ignorant of both the culture of Ireland and of the world, having bartered both for the sham-Irish traditions of a semi-illiterate Gaoltacht.[43]

O'Faoláin's contributions to *The Irish Statesman*, and his letters to *Sinn Féin*, suggest that a defining feature of his criticism at this time was an assertiveness of tone combined with a willingness to challenge prevailing orthodoxies, to court controversy, and to pontificate on a variety of topics. In the wide-ranging essay 'Style and the Limitations of Speech' (1928), for instance, he turned his attention to James Joyce's 'maltreatment of language' in the recently-published *Work in Progress* (1927). In a hostile review for T.S. Eliot's journal *The Criterion*, O'Faoláin attempted to read *Work in Progress* through a jumble of references to medieval Irish poetry, rhetoric, philology, the Elizabethan poets, Carlyle, the Romantics, Hardy and the artist J.M.W. Turner. The result was unfavourable. Joyce's recent writing 'comes from nowhere, goes nowhere, is not part of life at all', he complained, and only results in 'many circles of nothing'. 'It may be that Joyce wishes these meaningless scrawls to have a place in his design and if so nobody will grudge him his will of them. But we cannot be expected to understand them as language for they are as near nothing as anything can be on this earth'.[44] O'Faoláin was not the only contemporary reader to express doubts about Joyce's experimental text; however, he did go to considerable lengths to ensure that his misgivings were circulated to as wide an audience as possible – reprinting sections of his critique verbatim in an essay for *The Virginia Quarterly Review* (also in 1928), and rehashing the central charge in a correspondence article, 'Anna Livia Plurabelle', for *The Irish Statesman* in early 1929.[45] His critique proved controversial, as intended, upsetting Joyce personally, and inspiring responses from sympathetic readers.[46] Eugene Jolas, for instance, who was responsible for the publication of instalments of *Work in Progress* in the

Parisian review *transition*, wrote to *The Irish Statesman* in defence of Joyce, attacking O'Faoláin's unduly historicist approach, and commenting that a primary condition of language is that 'it is not static. It is in a constant state of becoming'. Joyce's work, Jolas contended, provided an exemplary instance of this.[47]

A comparable note was struck in the beautifully-produced *Lyrics and Satires from Tom Moore, selected by Seán O'Faoláin*, published by Elizabeth Corbet Yeats and the Cuala Press in 1929. In his preface to that slim anthology, O'Faoláin chose to tell the reader very little about his subject, but revealed a lot about his own preferences and biases. Thus, Moore was described as 'a charming and graceful songster' twice within a few pages; 'the emotive quality of his music' was traced to something as indistinct as 'the delicacy and fragility of his sentiment'; and his 'heart' was tellingly – but remarkably, given O'Faoláin's later impatience with such modes of thinking – praised for having 'opened to his own country' and allowing 'her charm [to breathe] vitality in his frail muse'. 'He appealed to all sorts of people,' O'Faoláin claimed, 'but he endeared himself forever to the simple, and it is curious and pleasing that to-day the simple alone still read him with complete delight – the simple who do not know that *fashion* is a word applicable to literature'. The assurance which characterizes such passages is compounded by the casual inclusion of several untranslated French phrases in the preface, a decision which smacks of elitism and a desire to impress, but which also betrays a self-conscious anxiety.[48] In addition, though, the inclusion of these phrases can be considered illustrative of O'Faoláin's commitment to extend the terms of reference in Ireland, and to describe a literary culture that is 'already in the European current,' as he had previously claimed in *The Irish Statesman*. This perhaps accounts for the wide range of references in the short preface to *Lyrics and Satires*, as Ireland's most famous nineteenth-century 'national poet' is placed in a tradition that is resolutely internationalist and pan-European. That each of these interpretations is possible suggests an implicit tension in O'Faoláin's enterprise, as much-needed arguments in favour of the revision of the Irish cultural heritage are presented in a style which is simultaneously inclusive and patronizing. This tension speaks to a fundamental ambivalence at the heart of O'Faoláin's critical project, and is one of several issues explored in this study.

O'Faoláin's early formation as a loyalist then a nationalist, middle-class, Catholic subject, and his critical writings of the mid-to-late 1920s, provide the context for the book that follows. This book focuses on O'Faoláin's work in the 1930s, a decade of international volatility and fear, and a period marked by capitalist crises, the rise of totalitarianism, and the drift towards the Second World War. Closer to home, the decade is often associated with the rise to power of one of O'Faoláin's greatest but most ambivalent influences, Eamon de Valera. In his biography of de Valera, Tim Pat Coogan characterized the 1930s as, roughly speaking, 'de Valera's decade', since it covers a period of high drama in this revolutionary-turned-statesman's long political life.[49] Just as the 1930s are associated with this crucial figure in modern Irish history, so are they frequently considered in terms of insularity and cultural stagnation. The prevailing ideologies of the day were restrictive and conservative, Terence Brown has noted, and 'to cultural and religious protectionism at their most draconian in the censorship policy was added the official encouragement of economic nationalism as a force sustaining the structure of an essentially rural society'.[50] 'The decade appears to inaugurate a form of cultural meltdown,' Alan Gillis has agreed, and seems like 'an almighty comedown' from the creative energies of the Literary Revival and the movement towards independence.[51] Such comments provide a salutary reminder of the hardships that were felt by many at this time, as an enervated state struggled to cope with the realities of poverty, unemployment and mass emigration; they also suggest the pressures that were exerted on many to conform, as well as the very real consequences of censorship for Irish writing, the publishing industry, and the reading public. However, as Gillis has also contended, such comments can be exaggerated to the point of nullity, as the achievements of an entire decade of creative artists are overlooked for the sake of a neat historical symmetry: Revival highs versus post-Independence blues. Many talented writers produced exceptional works during this decade (even though most did so in a state of exile), not all of these books were suppressed, and many of the books that were banned still circulated and were read.

Several recent historical and literary studies have followed this line of thought, seeing 1930s Ireland as a place where vital debates about identity, art, censorship and politics were produced, notwithstanding official pressures and institutional hypocrisies. If the popular perception of this period is that of a time when a narrowly-defined identity was posited (when to be Irish meant to be Catholic, Gaelic and not from Dublin), Joost Augusteijn has pointed out that many people responded to such proscriptive labels 'in a very diverse and often outward looking way, and that at this time the Free State was not just the insular, self-obsessed and culturally barren society it has often been portrayed' to be.[52] Neil Corcoran has similarly claimed that many writers of this period responded to such constraints by fashioning a body of literature built upon uncertainty and contradiction, a literature 'in which ideas of Ireland – of people, community and nation – [were] both created and reflected, and in which conceptions of a distinctively Irish identity [were] articulated, defended and challenged'. Corcoran consequently suggested that post-Independence Irish writing might best be characterized as 'a literature of process and becoming'.[53] This redolent phrase – 'process and becoming' – encapsulates a core aspect of O'Faoláin's thinking, as he engaged in discussions over what is now termed the politics of identity formation, and revised the ways in which we think about cultural inheritance in Ireland, seeing this as a messy, open-ended process rather than as something fixed, immutable or essentialist. In the essay 'Pigeon-holing the Modern Novel' (1935), for example, he remarked that 'it is the essence of a tradition that it grows with the times', and that it is always changing and in a state of flux.[54] For O'Faoláin, such fluidity allowed for a freeing up of possibilities, as unexpected patterns of influence could be supposed. It also enabled him to reflect upon the ways in which certain modes of 'being' are officially preferred, or sanctioned, and to consider the status that is granted to particular types of 'Irishness' through selective interpretations and narratives of history. This accounts, at least in part, for O'Faoláin's interest in biography as a form during the 1930s, as the writing of biographies allowed him the opportunity to reflect on the process by which the past is recorded and remembered.

Such reflections are sometimes represented as if they were somehow impartial or value-free, with O'Faoláin afforded a space beyond that of his contemporaries. Such claims obviously underestimate the strength of O'Faoláin's liberalist politics – something which carries its own ideological agenda. In addition, they fail to appreciate the extent to which his work was influenced by the context that he inhabited. As Frank O'Connor noted in his introduction to the anthology *Modern Irish Short Stories* (1957), 'O'Faoláin, O'Flaherty, and I wrote in the period of disillusionment which followed the Civil War, though with considerable respect for the nationalism that gave rise to it'.[55] More recently, with respect to *King of the Beggars*, Fiona Dunne has similarly argued that O'Faoláin's critique of Irish republicanism emerged from within that body of knowledge, 'and not, as is commonly imagined, from the position of dispassionate, or cynical, alienation from it'. Consequently, there were 'narrow enough limits' to his critique, as O'Faoláin sought to revise this political tradition and make it relevant for a contemporary context, rather than abandon it entirely, or write from a different, and supposedly impartial, perspective.[56] This can be evinced in a passage in his second biography of de Valera, which includes the following appraisal of the pro-Treaty leader Michael Collins:

> Even men so realistic as Collins, so ready to meet the hard facts of life and to create with them a new heroism, a finer heroism because demanding more complexity of effort, and making greater recognition of the nature of all created things, seemed to be still caught in the webs of the old dream (*DV* 100).

O'Faoláin's correlation of 'realism' with 'a new heroism' is intentionally provocative here. Equally significant is his observation that a hard-headed 'realist' such as Collins was 'still caught in the webs of the old dream'. For not only does this suggest the seductive power of that particular 'dream' (the independent republic), it also testifies to the force of ideas that were absorbed by Collins in his youth, and that continued to inform his thinking as a mature subject. The power of such forces is something that O'Faoláin was well aware of, as he returned to the subject over and again in his fiction and non-fiction; it is a subject that is explored at length in the pages that follow.

If O'Faoláin's work engaged with the tradition of Irish republicanism from within, it also considered the conflicting legacies of Irish Catholicism and loyalty to the Crown. In the opening pages of *Bird Alone*, the first-person narrator, Corney Crone, seeks to recreate the late nineteenth-century Cork that he knew as a child. Buried within Corney's tender reminiscence is an observation on two particular buildings, Cork's North Cathedral and the local military barracks. 'All [of] Ireland, and we knew it even as children, is in those two buildings,' he reflects years later as a sixty-something year-old man, 'the cathedral … and the Fort' (*BA*, 11). The careful use of the present tense 'is' insists that both buildings were not only important then, and that what they stand for retains significance in the post-Independence context from where Corney narrates his story. What they signify, of course, is the formative significance of the Catholic Church and British imperialism, respectively, and in many respects O'Faoláin's importance as a nascent postcolonial writer stems from his interrogation of the ongoing impact of both of these ideologies. This dual inheritance perhaps explains the ambivalent and often admiring portrait of Anglo-Irish society in the early pages of *Constance Markievicz*, as well as in the stories 'Midsummer Night Madness' and 'A Broken World'; it also accounts for the writer's nostalgic recreation of his early life as a loyalist subject in his autobiography, reaffirming the strength of his observation that 'no man jumps off his own shadow' (*VM* 125).

In addition, it testifies to the influential codes of the Catholic Church in the post-Independence state, and their internalization by O'Faoláin as an Irish subject. As he humorously explained in the retrospective essay 'A Portrait of the Artist as an Old Man' (1976), that is the 'one dye, one pigment, one stain, scar or mark that no soap in the world can wholly eradicate'.[57] O'Faoláin's response to such codes was equivocal, however. 'Far from being an insubordinate child and boy,' he later wrote, 'I was, it is more than evident, most dutiful. If I questioned at all, it was a mild and groping sort of business ending always in a lapse into the old submissiveness' (*VM* 93). This remarkable self-admission gestures towards O'Faoláin's complex relationship with each of these ideologies, as he challenged but simultaneously sought to reconcile himself with certain modes of thinking in his writing; his double description of himself as 'a mild rebel' in *Vive Moi!* reinforces this sense of acquiescence, a self-diagnosis that is redolent and deeply revealing (*VM* 28, 93).

This is a text of two parts: the first concentrates on O'Faoláin's work as a biographer during the 1930s; the second examines his earliest novels and collections of short fiction. The focus in each instance is on O'Faoláin's 'major' texts, and this is supplemented by references to other material, including essays, articles and reviews by O'Faoláin and some of his contemporaries. Each of the two parts begins with a short essay, which explores O'Faoláin's use of and reflections on the generic forms of biography and fiction respectively; and the study concludes with a brief postscript which considers his only published and performed play, *She Had to Do Something* (1938). The study does not aim to provide a biographical reading of O'Faoláin at a particular stage in his career, since such readings have already been produced by Maurice Harmon and Marie Arndt. Rather, the stress is on the texts that O'Faoláin published during this decade, texts which are contextualized, in turn, with respect to his life, times, reception and *oeuvre*. Once again, this study is motivated by the desire to refocus attention on a body of work that appears 'always already read' to many commentators and readers.

Some of these texts will be more familiar than others. *King of the Beggars*, for instance, is often cited as a key revisionist work in Ireland and the short-story collections are consistently referenced in general surveys of the form. His novels, by contrast, are largely forgotten, while his early biographies have been gently overlooked, with most critics agreeing with Paul A. Doyle's fifty-year-old assessment that these texts belong to 'the minor phases in his career'.[58] F.S.L. Lyons similarly chose to forget *The Life Story of Eamon De Valera* in his analysis of O'Faoláin's *oeuvre*, justifying this omission with the assertion that since O'Faoláin 'dismissed it himself as "arrant tripe", the critic need do no more than signal his agreement by a discreet silence'.[59] Conversely, however, it might be argued that the *Life Story* is of particular interest since O'Faoláin was so keen to dissociate himself from it, and that it gains in value when it is read alongside the ostensibly more critical *De Valera* – not least because the latter text quietly repeats while appearing to refute many aspects of the earlier study. The often-neglected *Constance Markievicz* is also worth serious consideration, not only for what it says about Markievicz as an historical subject, but also for what it reveals about O'Faoláin's own attitudes, including his casual male chauvinism and his willingness to trade in conventional gender stereotypes.

Any assessment of O'Faoláin's work needs to engage with such issues, traditionally ignored by commentators whether supportive or critical of his enterprise. However, it would be wrong to focus solely on these shortcomings, since O'Faoláin equally, and consistently, challenged many tired or reactionary modes of thinking in his writing. Over and again, he attacked those who championed the cause for a narrowly-defined essence of 'Irishness', for instance, advancing instead the thesis that national identities are historically produced and culturally hybrid. He also denounced those who promoted sentimental images of the so-called 'peasant', seeing in this an ignorance of the harsh realities of rural life and a denial of the changing conditions of Irish society. Crucially, O'Faoláin saw himself as someone who was living through a transitional point in time, and understood that his responsibility as a writer – which he took to include the roles of social commentator and public intellectual – entailed his participation in many key debates of the day. This necessitated interventions on such topics as decolonization, freedom of expression, historiography, the relationship between Church and State, and the importance of traditional practices in a modernizing environment. Post-Revival, post-partition and post-Independence, he explicitly drew a distinction between his generation and that of W.B. Yeats, testifying to the impact of the Troubles, and particularly the Civil War, on his contemporaries' attitudes and codes of belief.[60] 'The whole social picture is upside down,' he despaired in an article for *The Fortnightly* in the mid-1930s, 'and we do not know where we are or what is real or unreal, what clashes are arising in it, what values are being followed in the lives of the people. Every Irish writer of to-day over thirty is a spiritual *déraciné*'.[61]

Despite this uncertainty, though, or perhaps because of it, O'Faoláin hoped to initiate a new agenda in Irish writing – one that would be realist, pluralist and socially committed – and worked throughout the 1930s to position himself in the vanguard of such a movement. One of the most striking things about O'Faoláin during this decade is his sheer productivity, as he wrote an impressive number of texts across a variety of genres while contributing to Irish, British and American periodicals; he also participated in many innovative artistic projects of the day, such as the journal *Ireland To-Day*. Such activities meant that O'Faoláin was soon perceived as a central figure by many of his contemporaries. The elder Yeats, for instance, paired him with Frank O'Connor as two of the country's leading lights when he supported their nominations to the newly-formed Irish Academy of Letters in 1932.[62] A few years later, Elizabeth Bowen singled him out as one of 'the younger Irish writers [who] have almost all carried arms' and who have breathed new energy into the short-story form in *The Faber Book of Modern Stories* (1937).[63] Meanwhile, for the young Flann O'Brien, O'Faoláin was already an established figure in Dublin literary circles by the late 1930s (one of the mischievously-dubbed 'corduroys'), since he was important enough to caricature in a series of irreverent letter exchanges in *The Irish Times*.[64]

O'Faoláin, in turn, was quick to capitalize on this new-found centrality, promoting a group of Irish writers (O'Connor, Peadar O'Donnell, Sean O'Casey, Liam O'Flaherty and himself, especially) whom he considered representative of a 'brutal literature of despair'.[65] This attempt at canon-formation proved deeply influential and helped to shape the ways in which subsequent generations of readers viewed the cultural history of the Free State. As Joe Cleary has observed, this was only possible through a careful process of selection, as some writers were favoured, others were sidelined, and all were interpreted along very specific lines.[66] The shape of that canon, of course, reflected O'Faoláin's own interests and biases – not only was it 'realist' and largely prose based, it was also regionally diverse, post- or counter Revivalist, and entirely male. This process of selection is particularly ironic given O'Faoláin's pluralist credentials as well as his contemporaneous critique of the ways that narratives of history are often produced to justify particular ends.

It is worth remembering, however, that the cultural power that enabled O'Faoláin to create this canon was only recently obtained, and that at the start of the decade he was an emerging writer himself, reliant upon the support of senior figures like Yeats and Edward Garnett, writing from England since he was unable to find work at home. Indeed, it is not without significance, although it is seldom mentioned by critics, that some of his earliest works were written when he was living outside of Ireland – in the USA until 1929 (having been awarded a Commonwealth scholarship to study at Harvard in the autumn of 1926), and then in England until 1933, when he finally returned to live in Ireland. It is likely that this experience impacted upon aspects of those texts – on the ways that they perceive the subject of 'Ireland', for instance, and on their engagement with political and cultural events of the day. It is equally probable that this had a bearing on the image that O'Faoláin constructed for himself during this period. In an impassioned essay in the Gate Theatre's magazine, *Motley*, in 1932, for example, he voiced the recognizable complaint of one of the great literary archetypes, the Irish writer in exile (even though that role was not entirely compatible with his position as a middle-class Harvard postgraduate, employed in a senior capacity at a teacher-training college in affluent Twickenham). 'It is natural that the Irish writer, ignored, or misunderstood, at home, should gravitate away from his own people,' O'Faoláin wrote:

> often in bitterness and disgust – even though he knows at the same time that all his interests and sympathies are for ever anchored deeply and firmly in their lives … all of us exiles [are] living on English hospitality because the Irish public, ungrateful as well as graceless, self-satisfied and aggressive in its priggishness, would rather kill off its writers than encourage and, if necessary, bear with them until they are certain in their craft and outlook.[67]

Garnett's influence might be discerned in this passage, since it echoes the elder writer's descriptions of the paucity of Irish cultural life, included in his acerbic introduction to *Midsummer Night Madness* (also published in 1932).[68] More importantly, however, this passage records one of the great sources of tension in O'Faoláin's work – namely, his attraction to, and simultaneous repulsion from, the codes of Irish life. It is a tension without resolution and is characteristic of O'Faoláin at his best, speaking to the strength of his interpellation as a turn-of-the-century Irish subject but also his desire to interrogate the many strands of this complicated inheritance. Part of the motivation for this book is an unease with critical studies which claim to resolve this tension, supposing an easy dichotomy between that which is international (signifying all that is good) and that which is national (which includes all that is bad) in O'Faoláin's work. Thus, for instance, one of his most prominent commentators, Marie Arndt, sought to summarize O'Faoláin's legacy, commenting upon his yearning 'for moral and intellectual freedom with an international outlook, which was hindered by his persistent attachment to his Irish roots'.[69] This book suggests otherwise, seeing O'Faoláin as a writer who was not simply restricted by a seemingly wilful 'attachment' to inherited allegiances, and who read Ireland in challenging, nuanced and often uncertain ways. The figure that emerges in consequence is far less confident, but also far more searching and pertinent, than he is often assumed to be.

NOTES

1. Seán O'Faoláin, *Vive Moi!*, revised edn., with an afterword by Julia O'Faolain (London: Sinclair-Stevenson, 1993), p.295. These comments are not included in the original edition of *Vive Moi!*, first published in Boston in 1964, and in London in 1965.
2. Augustine Martin, *Exploring English 1: An Anthology of Short Stories for the Intermediate Certificate* (Dublin: Gill & Macmillan, 1967), p.351. The tender coming-of-age story 'The Trout' and the withering excoriation of parental ambition 'Up the Bare Stairs', from *Teresa and other stories* (1947) and *The Stories of Sean O'Faolain* (1958), respectively, were the two stories included on the curriculum.

3. Diarmaid Ferriter, *The Transformation of Ireland, 1900–2000* (London: Profile, 2004), p.65.
4. R.F. Foster, *The Irish Story: Telling Tales and Making It Up in Ireland* (London: Allen Lane, 2001), p.151; R.F. Foster, *Modern Ireland 1600–1972* (London: Allen Lane, 1988), p.548.
5. Kelly Matthews, *'The Bell' Magazine and the Representation of Irish Identity: Opening Windows* (Dublin: Four Courts Press, 2012). The centenary of O'Faoláin's birth saw the publication of the following texts: Eibhear Walshe (ed.), 'Sean O'Faolain: Reassessments', *The Irish Review* 26 (Autumn 2000), pp.1–59; Marie Arndt, *A Critical Study of Sean O'Faolain's Life and Work* (Lewiston: Edwin Mellon Press, 2001); Donatella Abbate Badin, et al (eds), *Sean O'Faolain: A Centenary Celebration* (Torino: Trauben, 2001).
6. Niall Carson, 'The Barbaric Note: Seán O'Faoláin's early years at the BBC', *Irish University Review* 43: 2 (Autumn/Winter 2013), pp.398–413. Brad Kent's annotated edition of O'Faoláin's critical essays will be published by McGill-Queen's University Press in 2015.
7. Donat O'Donnell (Conor Cruise O'Brien), 'The Parnellism of Seán O'Faoláin', in *Maria Cross: Imaginative Patterns in a Group of Modern Catholic Writers* (London: Chatto & Windus, 1954), pp.95–115; Paul A. Doyle, *Sean O'Faolain* (New York: Twayne, 1968); Maurice Harmon, *Sean O'Faolain: A Critical Introduction* (Notre Dame: University of Notre Dame Press, 1966).
8. George O'Brien, 'Contemporary prose in English: 1940–2000', in Margaret Kelleher and Philip O'Leary (eds), *The Cambridge History of Irish Literature: Volume 2, 1890–2000* (Cambridge: Cambridge University Press, 2006), p.454; Mark McNally, 'Countering the hegemony of the Irish national canon: the modernist rhetoric of Seán O'Faoláin (1938–50)', *Nations and Nationalism* 15: 3 (2009), pp.524–55.
9. Joe Cleary, 'This Thing of Darkness: Conjectures on Irish Naturalism', in *Outrageous Fortune: Capital and Culture in Modern Ireland* (Dublin: Field Day, 2007), p.148.
10. Nicholas Allen, *Modernism, Ireland and Civil War* (Cambridge: Cambridge University Press, 2009), p.109.
11. Seán Dunne, 'Introduction' to *The Cork Review* (1991), p.3.
12. Ruth Sherry, 'Sean O'Faolain', in W.J. McCormack (ed.), *The Blackwell Companion to Modern Irish Culture* (Oxford: Blackwell, 1999), p.441.
13. Pam Morris, *Realism* (London: Routledge, 2003), pp.4, 47.
14. Anne Enright, 'Introduction' to *The Granta Book of the Irish Short Story* (London: Granta, 2010), p.xii.
15. William Trevor (ed.), *The Oxford Book of Irish Short Stories* (Oxford: Oxford University Press, 1989); Dermot Bolger (ed.), *The Picador Book of Contemporary*

Irish Fiction (London: Picador, 1993); Benedict Kiely (ed.), *The Penguin Book of Irish Short Stories* (London: Penguin, 1981); Colm Tóibín (ed.), *The Penguin Book of Irish Fiction* (London: Penguin, 1999); David Pierce (ed.), *Irish Writing in the Twentieth Century* (Cork: Cork University Press, 2000); Sean McMahon (ed.), *The Best from 'The Bell': Great Irish Writing* (Dublin: O'Brien Press, 1978).

16. Reprinted in 1997, the cover and spine of the Mercier Press edition of *The Great O'Neill* carry the impossible name 'Seán O Fáolain', and provide a ready example of the difficulties publishers, commentators and readers have had with the spelling of O'Faoláin's name. The title page, copyright notice and back cover of the same edition give his name as the *fada*-less and apostrophized 'Sean O'Faolain'. Such inconsistencies are a characteristic feature of O'Faoláin's publishing career. They were compounded when the book was reissued by Mercier Press a few years later, with the copyright still attributed to 'Seán O Fáolain' but the new cover and prelims listing the author's name as 'Seán O'Faolain'.
17. Fredric Jameson, *The Political Unconscious: Narrative as a Socially Symbolic Act* (London: Methuen, 1981), pp.9–10.
18. Adrian Room, 'Seán O'Faoláin', in *The Oxford Dictionary of National Biography* (Oxford: Oxford University Press, 2004–11), http://www.oxforddnb.com/. This entry neglects to mention one of O'Faoláin's major short-story collections, *A Purse of Coppers*, in the general outline of his *oeuvre*. Limited editions of stand-alone stories are instead given, including the British-issued *There's a Birdie in the Cage* and the American *The Born Genius*, published in 1935 and 1936 respectively – the latter is incorrectly listed as *A Born Genuis*, which is the title of the story included in *A Purse of Coppers*. The entry also provides the wrong publishing date for *Constance Markievicz* (given as 1939 rather than 1934), and misreads the plot of *Come Back to Erin*, confusing this novel with the earlier book *A Nest of Simple Folk* as well as the debut short-story collection *Midsummer Night Madness*. In addition, it misspells the surname of one of O'Faoláin's most prominent commentators Marie Arndt, listed as 'M. Arnt'.
19. Sean O'Faolain, *An Irish Journey*, specially illustrated by Paul Henry (London: Longmans, Green & Co., 1940), p.144.
20. Seán O'Faoláin, 'The Emancipation of Irish Writers', *The Yale Review* 23 (Spring 1934), p.494.
21. Lennox Robinson, *Curtain Up: An Autobiography* (London: Michael Joseph, 1942), p.18. O'Faoláin was aware of the coincidence, writing to Robinson in 1938: 'When you tell how *Cathleen* crystallized things for you in the Opera House, I remembered again how your *Patriots* did precisely the same for me, in the same theatre, and by the same players'. O'Faoláin chose not to mention this similarity

in *Vive Moi!*. O'Faoláin, letter to Lennox Robinson, qtd. in Maurice Harmon, *Sean O'Faolain: A Life* (London: Constable, 1994), p.26.

22. Harmon, *O'Faolain: A Life*, p.40.
23. Peter Lennon, director, *The Rocky Road to Dublin* (Victor Herbert Productions, 1968); cf. Clair Wills, *Dublin 1916: The Siege of the GPO* (London: Profile, 2010), pp.184–5.
24. Harmon, *O'Faolain: A Life*, p.50.
25. 'Bliss was it in that dawn to be alive, / But to be young was very heaven!' Wordsworth famously recollected in the tenth book of *The Prelude* (1805), when 'the meagre, stale, forbidding ways / Of custom, law, and statute, took at once / The attraction of a country in romance'. William Wordsworth, *The Prelude* (1805), Book X, ll. 692–696, in Jonathan Wordsworth, M.H. Abrams and Stephen Gill (eds), *The Prelude: 1799, 1805, 1850* (New York: W.W. Norton, 1979), p.396. The lines are repeated, with slight alteration, in Book XI of the 1850 edition of *The Prelude*, ll. 108–112.
26. In the late essay 'A Portrait of the Artist as an Old Man', for instance, O'Faoláin drew a further analogy between the two events. Aware of the obvious differences, he nonetheless described the period of the Troubles as 'those heavenly years [when] I dreamed of liberty, equality, fraternity'. On this occasion the analogy was forged through reference to O'Faoláin's beloved Stendhal. Seán O'Faoláin, 'A Portrait of the Artist as an Old Man', *Irish University Review* 6: 1 (Spring 1976), pp.15–6.
27. *On Another Man's Wound* was first published by Rich & Cowan in London in 1936. Seven pages of the text were deleted by the publishers, recounting the torture that Ernie O'Malley endured as a prisoner in Dublin Castle. These pages were restored in the American edition of O'Malley's memoir, which was published under a different title, *Army Without Banners: Adventures of an Irish Volunteer*, in 1937. Cormac K.H. O'Malley, 'The Publication History of *On Another Man's Wound*', *New Hibernia Review* 7: 3 (Autumn 2003), p.136.
28. O'Faoláin's comments recall the famous opening lines of Charles Dickens's *A Tale of Two Cities* (1859): 'It was the best of times, it was the worst of times, it was the age of wisdom, it was the age of foolishness, it was the season of Light, it was the season of Darkness, it was the spring of hope, it was the winter of despair'. The implied analogy further impresses the link between the Troubles and the French Revolution.
29. Harmon, *O'Faolain: A Life*, p.63.
30. Seán O'Faoláin, 'About Myself', *Now and Then* 41 (Spring 1932), p.35.
31. Sean O'Faolain, 'Letter from a Novelist to an Idealist', *Motley* 2: 7 (November 1933), p.5.

32. Sean O Faolain, 'A Letter to the Editor', *Sinn Féin* (20 September 1924), p.7.
33. Sean O Faolain, 'Principles versus Propaganda', *Sinn Féin* (11 October 1924), p. 2, ctd. p.8.
34. Mary MacSwiney, 'A Reply', *Sinn Féin* (11 October 1924), p.8.
35. Seán Ó Faoláin, 'D'fhear eagair "Shinn Féin"', *Sinn Féin* (25 October 1924), p.6.
36. Seán Ó Faoláin, 'Prendergast', *Éarna* 2: 5 (Meitheamh 1924), pp.12–6; Seán Ó Faoláin, 'Deich mBliana d'Fhás i mBeatha Fhile, Dáibhidh Ó Bruadair; 1670–1680', *Éarna* 2/3: 7 and 2/4: 8 (Féile Pádraig and Nodlaig 1925), pp.26–33 and pp.14–7.
37. Frank O'Connor, *My Father's Son* (London: Macmillan, 1968), p.49.
38. Daniel Corkery, 'Love Songs in Irish', *The Irish Statesman* 4: 24 (22 August 1925), p.762.
39. Seán O'Faoláin, 'The Best Irish Literature', *The Irish Statesman* 4: 26 (5 September 1925), p.816.
40. Nicholas Allen, *George Russell (Æ) and the New Ireland, 1905-30* (Dublin: Four Courts Press, 2003), p.182.
41. Philip O'Leary, *Gaelic Prose in the Irish Free State, 1922–1939* (Dublin: University College Dublin Press, 2004), p.537 n.58, p.625 n.99.
42. Seán O'Faoláin, 'A Plea for a New Irish Scholarship', *The Irish Statesman* 5: 10 (14 November 1925), p.297.
43. Seán O'Faoláin, 'The Gaoltacht Tradition', *The Irish Statesman* 6: 7 (24 April 1926), pp.175–6.
44. Sean O'Faolain, 'Style and the Limitations of Speech', *The Criterion* 8: 30 (September 1928), pp.83, 86–7.
45. Seán O'Faoláin, 'The Cruelty and Beauty of Words', *The Virginia Quarterly Review* 4 (April 1928), pp.222, 225; Seán O'Faoláin, 'Anna Livia Plurabelle', *The Irish Statesman* 11: 18 (5 January 1929), pp.354–55.
46. O'Faoláin's criticism of *Work in Progress* caused Joyce some upset since it was published under Eliot's editorship, leading Joyce to worry (wrongly) that this meant Eliot disliked his new work. O'Faoláin, it seems, was either oblivious of this anxiety or naive of the offence caused, sending Joyce a copy of *Bird Alone* for comment only a few years later. Joyce, unsurprisingly, declined to read the novel. Richard Ellmann, *James Joyce*, second edition (Oxford: Oxford University Press, 1982), pp.607, 700n.
47. Eugene Jolas, 'Style and the Limitations of Speech', *The Irish Statesman* 11: 21 (26 January 1926), p.414.
48. Seán O'Faoláin, 'Preface' to *Lyrics and Satires from Tom Moore, selected by Seán O'Faoláin* (Dublin: Cuala Press, 1929), np [emphasis as original].

49. Tim Pat Coogan, *De Valera: Long Fellow, Long Shadow* (London: Hutchinson, 1993), p.408. Coogan suggests that this period begins slightly earlier, with de Valera's decision to enter the Irish parliament in the late 1920s. 'High points' of the decade include de Valera's development of the Fianna Fáil party, his establishment of the newspaper *The Irish Press*, his political success of 1932 and election to Taoiseach, his subsequent 'economic war' with Britain, and his dismantling of much of the Anglo-Irish Treaty, culminating in the Irish Constitution, *Bunreacht na hÉireann*, in 1937.
50. Terence Brown, *Ireland: A Social and Cultural History, 1922–1985*, second edition (London: Fontana, 1985), p.151.
51. Alan Gillis, *Irish Poetry of the 1930s* (Oxford: Oxford University Press, 2005), p.1.
52. Joost Augusteijn, 'Preface' to *Ireland in the 1930s: New Perspectives* (Dublin: Four Courts Press, 1999), p.7.
53. Neil Corcoran, *After Yeats and Joyce: Reading Modern Irish Literature* (Oxford: Oxford University Press, 1997), p.vi.
54. Seán O'Faoláin, 'Pigeon-holing the Modern Novel', *The London Mercury* 33: 194 (December 1935), p.159.
55. Frank O'Connor, 'Introduction' to *Modern Irish Short Stories* (London: Oxford University Press, 1957), p.xvi. This anthology was retitled *Classic Irish Short Stories* in 1985, and the comments can be found on pp.xiii–xiv.
56. Fiona Dunne, '*King of the Beggars*: "A Perfect Onion of Worlds within Worlds"', *The Irish Review* 26 (Autumn 2000), pp.30, 36.
57. O'Faoláin, 'A Portrait of the Artist as an Old Man', p.13.
58. Doyle, *Sean O'Faolain*, np (preface).
59. F.S.L. Lyons, 'Seán O'Faoláin as Biographer', *Irish University Review* 6: 1 (Spring 1976), pp.95–6.
60. See, for instance: Seán O'Fáolain [*sic*], 'Yeats and the Younger Generation', *Horizon: A Review of Literature and Art* 5: 25 (January 1942), pp.43–54; see also Seán O'Faoláin, 'Ireland After Yeats', *Books Abroad* 26: 4 (Autumn 1952), pp.325–33.
61. Sean O'Faolain, 'Irish Letters: To-Day and To-Morrow', *The Fortnightly* 138 (September 1935), p.370.
62. R.F. Foster, *W.B. Yeats: A Life, Volume 2: The Arch-Poet* (Oxford: Oxford University Press, 2003), pp.448–9.
63. Elizabeth Bowen, 'Introduction: The Short Story', to *The Faber Book of Modern Stories* (London: Faber and Faber, 1937), p.11. O'Faoláin and Bowen had an affair in the late 1930s. For information on this, see Harmon, *O'Faolain: A Life*, pp.114–5; see also Victoria Glendinning, *Elizabeth Bowen: Portrait of a Writer* (London: Weidenfeld & Nicolson, 1977), pp.118–21. The relationship is discussed by O'Faoláin in the revised edition of *Vive Moi!*, expanded after his wife's death

in 1988; it and other affairs are also considered by Julia O'Faolain in her recent autobiography, *Trespassers: A Memoir* (London: Faber and Faber, 2013), pp.29–55.

64. Flann O'Brien, qtd. in Carol Taaffe, *Ireland Through the Looking-Glass: Flann O'Brien, Myles na gCopaleen and Irish cultural debate* (Cork: Cork University Press, 2008), p.141. For details on letter exchanges in *The Irish Times*, see Taaffe, pp.26–9.
65. O'Faolain, 'Irish Letters: To-Day and To-Morrow', p.369.
66. Joe Cleary, 'Distress Signals: Sean O'Faolain and the Fate of Twentieth-Century Irish Literature', *Field Day Review* 5 (2009), pp.69–70.
67. Seán O'Faoláin, 'Provincialism and Literature', *Motley* 1: 3 (August 1932), p.4. Those familiar with O'Faoláin's life story might detect a hint of sour grapes in this passage, explained by his unsuccessful application for the Chair of Literature at UCC the previous year. To make matters worse, the coveted job went to Corkery. For details of the UCC post, see Harmon, *O'Faolain: A Life*, pp.90–5; see also Patrick Maume, *'Life that is Exile': Daniel Corkery and the Search for Irish Ireland* (Belfast: Institute of Irish Studies, 1993), pp.118–20.
68. Edward Garnett, 'Introduction' to Seán O'Faoláin, *Midsummer Night Madness and other stories* (London: Jonathan Cape, 1932), pp.11–6.
69. Marie Arndt, 'Sean O'Faolain', in Brian Lalor, general ed. *The Encyclopaedia of Ireland* (Dublin: Gill & Macmillan, 2003), p.815.

PART I

BIOGRAPHY

Interpretation, Intervention, Revision

'Biography is not a neutral art,' Paula Backscheider has observed, 'in fact, of all the major literary genres it is probably the most political – the one most likely to influence how a nation and its history are defined'.[1] O'Faoláin's biographies of the 1930s and early 1940s illustrate the strength of this thesis, as they sought to intervene in received accounts of Irish history and offer significant reappraisals of the lives of revered nationalist figures: Eamon de Valera (twice), Constance Markievicz, Daniel O'Connell and Hugh O'Neill, as well as Theobald Wolfe Tone through the abridged edition of Tone's *Autobiography* (1937). In each of these texts O'Faoláin assumed the role of a demystifying critic, exposing expedient myths about his subjects and recording uncomfortable truths about the perceived reality of their lives. Not only did O'Faoláin challenge popular preconceptions of the past, however, he also used the occasion of his subjects' lives to comment on the current state of Ireland, as he revised standard historical narratives to fit the needs of present-day agendas and concerns. His biographies, that is to say, are deliberately interventionist, and were designed for all their stress on 'fact' and 'truth' to be neither innocent nor value-free.

In an essay for *The Criterion* in 1935, O'Faoláin sought to account for 'the recent popularity of certain kinds of books', amongst which he numbered 'the craze for biographies and autobiographies'. 'It is one kind of search for truth,' he supposed, a truth that might seem '"stranger" than fiction,' but that is necessary in order to satiate 'the thirst in the people for fundamental reality'.[2] He might have added, in a local context, that the appetite for life stories in Ireland was fostered by a public keen to make sense of its recent revolutionary past, and a publishing industry happy to cash in on this market. O'Faoláin's biographies partly speak to this need to articulate an historic truth or 'fundamental reality'. His texts are more nuanced in their appreciation of this subject, however, and gesture towards the ways in which historical material is selected, interpreted and finessed into a narrative which is then afforded the weight of 'fact' and objectivity. Each of the biographies declares its status as a published text, for instance, and each includes references to questions of structure, genre and writing. A case in point is supplied in his biography of O'Connell, *King of the Beggars*, when it is suddenly claimed – for no apparent reason – that 'chapter divisions lie' and provide 'a sop to one's love of perspective' (*KB* 214). Similar comments are repeated elsewhere in the same text – such as when it is said of O'Connell taking his seat at Westminster in 1829 that 'here, once more, every biographer will feel a natural temptation to close a chapter or a volume', or when the following self-reflexive note is folded into the narrative:

> Perhaps a dozen times, while writing this biography, I have come to some such point as this – a point where a formal account of the lives of the people seemed necessary; but having gathered and regathered the little, the terrible little, we know about the physical conditions under which our forefathers lived, I have thrown it aside each time as unrevealing and almost irrelevant, and I know, in the end, that to describe their daily lives is something I cannot do (*KB* 264, 153).

Analogous remarks are included in the other life stories. In the biography of Markievicz, to take a particularly striking example, it is abruptly conceded that 'frankly, to this biographer', Markievicz's activities in the years between 1918 and 1924 are 'of little interest'; and this diminution of interest is reflected in the narrative's representation of her life during this formative historical period (*CM* 254).[3] Such observations are knowingly self-referential and encourage readers to reflect on the strategies that are deployed in the telling of each of the biographies; they also suggest the role of the author in determining the shape of the life stories told.

As well as including references to genre and writing, O'Faoláin undermined many expectations which are traditionally associated with historical and biographical studies. Little or no archival research is conducted in these texts, no critical apparatus is provided, sweeping comments are made without documentation or substantiation, and many elementary features of good scholarship (such as footnotes, page references for quotations, and bibliographies) are omitted or overlooked.[4] *The Great O'Neill* (1942) is slightly unusual in this respect as it includes a rudimentary set of endnotes and an annotated bibliography, but any sense of original research is qualified by a set of disclaimers which bookend that text, with the preface claiming that the book is no more than 'a popular account of O'Neill's life and times', and the bibliography insistent that the text 'makes no pretensions to being an academic study'.[5] O'Faoláin's more general practice in the life stories seems to have been to avoid manuscript research and to focus instead on a close engagement with previously published biographies, historical commentaries, literary sources and anecdotal evidence. Indeed, in *Constance Markievicz*, O'Faoláin claimed that archival material on this subject barely existed in the first instance:

> I have written this biography from the published records of the period and from oral testimony. As far as concerns Constance Markievicz the printed material is small, the oral testimony copious as a legend. While this has had the advantage of giving life, colour, and verisimilitude to the popular memory it has also, very naturally (especially in a city like Dublin), been too often inimical to cold truth (*CM* 9).

As Karen Steele has since shown, this line of thinking is flatly contradicted by the texts that Markievicz herself saw to print at key periods in her life, most notably the essays she wrote for publication during the period of intense politicization between 1909 and 1915.[6] For some reason this body of material is not discussed in O'Faoláin's account of her life. Nor are her later contributions to the republican press, even though O'Faoláin edited some of this material for *Sinn Féin* in his early years as a republican propagandist.[7]

If O'Faoláin's comments in the preface to *Constance Markievicz* are suggestive of his attitude to the subject of that particular book, they also speak to a more general feature of his use of form and choice of style. 'The essence of his biographical style is a form of impressionism', F.S.L. Lyons once stated, and 'while what he gives us is always new, it is novelty of interpretation rather than of fact'.[8] Lyons's stress on interpretation is worth re-emphasizing, since the biographies are less important for the information that they disclose about their subjects and more revealing of the uses to which that information is put. At times this information is used to create an imagined idea of the past, at odds with received opinions and standard historiographic practices, an interpretation couched in the language of objectivity and 'cold truth' but carrying its own agenda. The biographies were also designed to suit a particular purpose – to write the past in order to comment on the present, as Marie Arndt has noted, and to speculate on future paths and things that might have been otherwise.[9] In addition, the texts were used to re-write versions of the past that were dominant or well-known in the 1930s and early 1940s, narratives which were used to justify contemporary measures and political ideologies. In *King of the Beggars* and *The Great O'Neill*, for instance, O'Faoláin used the form of the biography as a means to stress the international contexts of Irish history, and to draw attention to the hybrid state of the Irish cultural heritage. In each case this was done to deconstruct the logic of a narrowly-defined revivalist programme as well as to challenge the politics of introversion and cultural isolation. 'It is one of the most dismaying falsifications of history,' it is claimed in the biography of O'Neill, 'that this man who was a European figure … has been lost to European history, and made part of a merely local piety'.[10] Such comments were clearly directed against myopic nationalist policies and were grounded in the immediate context of neutrality and the Second World War. Their stimulus, in the words of O'Faoláin's contemporary, Patrick Kavanagh, was an 'Ireland that froze for want of Europe'.[11]

As works of the imagination, one might almost say works of fiction, a principal concern of the biographies is to give a sense of their subjects' interiority as well as to capture aspects of their personality, public acquaintances and private lives. David Novarr's comments on the relationship between biography and the novel are worth recalling in this respect, particularly his claim that both narrative forms are subtly interlinked, as novelists and biographers utilize similar modes of narrative and often exploit 'the inner life of thought and emotion' of their respective subjects. Both forms trace the development of their subjects' lives through relationships and chance encounters, suggest patterns or trajectories that might encompass the messiness of an individual life, and experiment in written form with 'the manipulation of point of view, distance and time'.[12] It is hardly incidental that O'Faoláin saw himself as a novelist above all at this stage of his career, downplaying his work as a short-story writer and essayist as a consequence. In an article for *The Dublin Magazine* in 1936, for instance, he grouped himself alongside his contemporaries Frank O'Connor and Liam O'Flaherty as writers 'who hoped one day to be novelists', and by the decade's end, in the biography *De Valera*, he was happy to identify himself first and foremost as 'a biographer and a novelist' (*DV* 181).[13] Nor is it coincidental that O'Faoláin's preferred mode of novel-writing was heavily influenced by historical fiction, since that genre has been considered instrumental in developing configurations of national identity and collective history.[14] Indeed, O'Faoláin's two novels of the 1930s, *A Nest of Simple Folk* and *Bird Alone*, are set against the backdrop of decisive historical periods – the years between the end of the Famine and the Easter Rebellion, and the Parnellite split, respectively – and reflect upon the representation of those periods.

A further concern of the biographies is to chart the part that specifically chosen figures played in determining the shape of particular events. In a caustic review of M.J. MacManus's laudatory biography *Eamon de Valera* (1944) for *The Bell*, O'Faoláin outlined the various options and stances that he thought were available to any writer of biography. 'Analysis, apology, or what one may call epic description' are positions that might be adopted, he remarked, along with the decision 'to consider the social significance of a man as a type'.[15] Each of these positions is taken in the biographies, with particular attention given to the 'epic' and 'social significance' models. In the same essay, O'Faoláin explained that the former position allows the subject of a biography to be represented as if inflated by the events of 'his', or presumably her (though this is not stated), time, and to become 'the noble embodiment of the Great Adventure if he has the dignity and stature to carry it off'. The latter stance, meanwhile, was said to testify to the ways in which 'public men' (or women) 'serve as models for the whole nation. They can disseminate a general philosophy of living, popularize certain attitudes of mind, set standards and create values'.[16] In both cases, emphasis was placed on the so-called 'enlarged' qualities of the subject, and O'Faoláin's choice of biographical subjects accords with this. Not only are they all larger-than-life figures – the rebel Countess, the United Irish leader, the Liberator, the last Gaelic chieftain, the surviving embodiment of 1916 – they are also individuals who were positioned at critical points in Irish history, who were inspired or 'dilated' by the circumstances in which they found themselves, and who responded to those circumstances in ways that led to significant shifts in politics and direction (*DV* 19). O'Faoláin's O'Connell is an exemplary instance of this, as he is said to have virtually willed a people into existence. 'He thought a democracy and it rose', it is claimed of him in *King of the Beggars*. 'He defined himself, and his people became him' (*KB* 368).

In many ways, this stress on transitional periods is the key which unites the various biographies, for in each of the texts O'Faoláin's subjects are pictured living through critical junctures and responding to changes in the world around them. In O'Neill's case, it is the collapse of the Gaelic order and the onset of imperial conquest; in Tone's *Autobiography*, it is the revolutionary potential of a new political order; in O'Connell's biography, it is the rise of a democratic populace and agitation for the repeal of the Act of Union; and in de Valera's and Markievicz's very different life stories, it is involvement in the struggle for independence. Not only are O'Faoláin's subjects depicted responding to these changes, however, they are also represented anticipating them, sometimes even determining them, through their convictions, personalities and actions. In part, this speaks to O'Faoláin's interest in public events and 'enlarged' figures, as his focus repeatedly turns to the received narratives of Irish history, and an interpretation of those narratives that fits a revisionist agenda. It is telling that in each instance the context for the biography is a decisive moment or a luminous incident – the Battle of Kinsale, the United Irish Rebellion, Catholic Emancipation, Easter Week. It is also significant that at no point does O'Faoláin move from the larger, 'inflated' register to offer anything like a history from below or the story of collaborative groups, marginal events or less well-known individuals. In this respect, his biographies display the influence of the Victorian idea of the hero, and in particular Thomas Carlyle's influential set of lectures and essays *On Heroes, Hero-Worship, and the Heroic in History* (1841). Carlyle's theories on the dramatic impetus of heroes, and their ability to create while remaining paradoxically conditioned by surrounding forces, certainly resonate with O'Faoláin's thinking; so too does his often-quoted assertion that history is ultimately the 'biography of great men'.[17]

If the stress on critical junctures is linked to O'Faoláin's interest in re-writing the received or 'official' national narrative (a narrative which he perceives to be full of fault-lines, complications, ambiguities and fractures), it nonetheless also speaks to the time in which the biographies were produced. For O'Faoláin was consciously writing in a period that was itself transitional. There is a sense throughout this body of work that the potential of the Irish revolution had not yet been realized, but neither had it (yet) been fully squandered. The stress on the transitional, that is to say, is partly self-reflective, and speaks to O'Faoláin's own belief in the 1930s that despite his growing disillusionment with the Irish state, things might still find purpose and a sense of direction. 'A young nation cannot possibly develop if … there is not to be at every point a reconsideration of traditional values', he wrote in *Ireland To-Day* in 1936, drawing upon an analogy of youth and the emerging nation-state that features in much of his writing of this period. 'Perhaps an old nation may for a long period fold its wings – though one may doubt it. A young one, scarcely fledged, can do so only at the peril of becoming moribund. We are at the threshold of life. We should be full of eagerness and the lust for discovery'.[18]

NOTES

1. Paula R. Backscheider, *Reflections on Biography* (Oxford: Oxford University Press, 1999), p.216.
2. Sean O'Faolain, 'It No Longer Matters, or the Death of the English Novel', *The Criterion* 15: 58 (October 1935), pp.51–2. O'Faolain made the same point, almost verbatim, in the contemporaneous essay, 'The Modern Novel: A Catholic Point of View', *The Virginia Quarterly Review* 11 (July 1935), p.343.
3. Interestingly, this comment was qualified, but also extended, in subsequent editions of the Markievicz biography, where it was suggested that her life during this period was 'of less interest than her life before the Rising'. Sean O'Faolain, *Constance Markievicz*, revised edition (London: Sphere, 1967), p.174.
4. An index is included in a later version of *King of the Beggars*, published by Poolbeg Press in Dublin in 1980. This was not included in the original edition; nor was the explanatory 'Historical Note' which is inserted into the preliminary pages of the later edition.
5. Sean O'Faolain, *The Great O'Neill: A Biography of Hugh O'Neill, Earl of Tyrone, 1550–1616* (London: Longmans, Green & Co., 1942), pp.v, 284.
6. Karen Steele, 'Constance Markievicz's Allegorical Garden: Femininity, Militancy, and the Press, 1909–1915', *Women's Studies* 29 (2000), pp.423–47.
7. Markievicz was an occasional contributor to the newspaper *Sinn Féin*, and it is likely that she is one of the women – along with Mary MacSwiney and Molly Childers – that O'Faoláin alluded to years later in *Vive Moi!*. Thinking back to his editorship of *Sinn Féin*, O'Faoláin made the astonishing claim that the republican women that he knew at the time were 'particularly disturbing' and 'were driven by that unfeminine animus which seems always to make the male constituent in women behave like the worse side of the feminine element in men. They were theatrical, self-dramatizing, power-hungry, temperamental but with few warm emotions, ruthless, abstract in discussion, and full of terrifying sentimentality' (*VM* 169).
8. F.S.L. Lyons, 'Seán O'Faoláin as Biographer', *Irish University Review* 6: 1 (Spring 1976), p.97.
9. Marie Arndt, 'Sean O'Faolain as Biographer and Commentator', in Karl-Heinz Westarp and Michael Böss (eds), *Ireland: Towards New Identities?* (Aarhus: Aarhus University Press, 1998), p.66.
10. O'Faolain, *The Great O'Neill*, p.277.
11. Patrick Kavanagh, 'Lough Derg', in *The Complete Poems* (ed.), Peter Kavanagh (Newbridge: The Goldsmith Press, 1984), p.117. 'Self-reliance has taken on the astonishing implication of estrangement from the world', O'Faoláin wrote the

following year, in a critique of isolationist policies. 'We have become, that is to say, alienated from Europe'. Sean O'Faolain, 'Ireland and the Modern World', *The Bell* 5: 6 (March 1943), p.423.

12. David Novarr, *The Lines of Life: Theories of Biography, 1880–1970* (West Lafayette: Purdue University Press, 1986), p.151. Frank O'Connor also recognized the relationship between O'Faoláin's work as a biographer and creative artist. 'His stories and novels are a commentary on his biographies, histories, and essays', O'Connor speculated, citing the representations of Anglo-Irish society in *Constance Markievicz* and 'Midsummer Night Madness' as a case in point. O'Connor, *Modern Irish Short Stories*, p.xv.
13. Sean O'Faolain, 'Daniel Corkery', *The Dublin Magazine* 11: 2 (April-June 1936), p.52.
14. Jerome de Groot, *The Historical Novel* (London: Routledge, 2010), p.94.
15. Sean O'Faolain, 'Eamon De Valera', *The Bell* 10: 1 (April 1945), p.10; M.J. MacManus, *Eamon de Valera: A Biography* (Dublin: Talbot Press, 1944).
16. O'Faolain, 'Eamon De Valera', pp.8, 10.
17. Thomas Carlyle, *On Heroes, Hero-Worship, and the Heroic in History*, with notes and introduction by Michael K. Goldberg (1841; Berkeley: University of California Press, 1993), p.26.
18. Sean O'Faolain, 'The Dangers of Censorship', *Ireland To-Day* 1: 6 (November 1936), p.60. For a discussion of O'Faoláin's use of the child-state analogy in *The Bell*, see Matthews, *'The Bell' Magazine*, pp.20–1.

1

'QUITE UNNECESSARY': THE EARLY BIOGRAPHIES

'It will be said now that I am writing as an apologist of De Valera, and I do not deny it. Heaven knows, the man needs an apologist – he has had his share of critics' (*LS* 95). The motivation behind *The Life Story of Eamon De Valera* (1933) might come as a surprise given that O'Faoláin is more often numbered amongst de Valera's detractors and critics. The truth, though, is that his relationship with de Valera, ever since taking the anti-Treaty side during the Civil War, was fluid and vexed. The *Life Story* was one of the earliest in a series of discussions which O'Faoláin penned during the 1930s and early 1940s which sought to make sense of this influence; it was easily the most supportive. Reflecting on the book twelve years later, in a disillusioned editorial for *The Bell*, O'Faoláin sought to distance himself from the project. 'Shamelessly pro-Dev and pro-Irish propaganda,' he remarked that it was written 'at a time when all of us who had stuck by de Valera from 1916 onwards at last saw our hero coming into power and all our dreams and ideals – as we foolishly and trustingly hoped – about to be realized'.[1]

The *Life Story* had its origins in a series of articles for the English newspaper *The Sunday Chronicle*, published in 1932. This series sought to account for de Valera's popular appeal, and was timed to coincide with Fianna Fáil's success in the Irish general election of that year. Ironically, it was also produced at a point when O'Faoláin had begun to question many of the principles which informed de Valera's politics as well as certain strands of republican thinking. *Midsummer Night Madness* was published and banned the same year, and led to disputes with several influential figures, including O'Faoláin's old mentor Daniel Corkery. In 1932, O'Faoláin also wrote a couple of essays for the magazine *New Statesman and Nation*, which raised concerns about de Valera's intentions and political abilities. In the first of these, 'Celts and Irishmen', O'Faoláin depicted de Valera as insular and intransigent, speculating 'whether he can make any practical contribution to the development of a genuine Irish civilization is doubtful'.[2] Similar concerns were repeated in the companion essay, tellingly entitled 'Mr. De Valera – Rebel or Reformer?', where de Valera's capacity for equivocation was identified as a cause for particular worry.

> To-day he will talk like another O'Connell – i.e., as a constructive reformer – and in that capacity he cannot fail to enlist the support and sympathy of every Irishman; but to-morrow he will talk like any ineffectual rebel who might lead the country into a turmoil for something which would leave the farmer and the worker precisely where they were before he was born.[3]

The fear for O'Faoláin was that de Valera was not the revolutionary figure he had once appeared to be and that an opportunity for real change was in danger of being lost. This opportunity was hinted at only a few months earlier, in *The Commonweal* essay 'The New Irish Revolutionaries' (1931), where O'Faoláin charted the emergence of the recently-established republican group Saor Éire, the crackdown on dissident IRA activities, and growing disgruntlement with the presiding Cumann na nGaedheal party, particularly amongst the rural poor. 'If out of the present unrest … should rise a new fervour of a nationalistic emotion,' he remarked, 'it will not help the present government; in fact the most likely thing to occur may well be a victory for Mr. De Valera at the polls'.[4] What such a victory might mean was something O'Faoláin avoided developing, however, and few of the anxieties that he subsequently articulated in *New Statesman and Nation* made their way into the *Life Story*, as a narrative was instead produced that appeared committed in its politics, concluding with an image of de Valera leading Fianna Fáil into government for the first time.

In many respects, the *Life Story* is a work of political hagiography, chronicling the first fifty years of de Valera's life in an extraordinarily idealized manner, and providing an impossible image of a man who appears the very epitome of heroism, gallantry, self-restraint and martial endeavour. One section is entitled 'The Cuchulainn of Easter Week', for instance, while another discusses the 'superhuman nature' of the tasks already achieved (*LS* 28, 71). This barely chimes with O'Faoláin's own statement in the short prologue to the study, that the book was intended as an attempt 'to see something of the humanity' of his subject (*LS* 9). According to O'Faoláin, this desire was frustrated by certain complexities in de Valera's character – he was such a guarded figure, O'Faoláin argued, it was difficult to see beyond the intrigue and reserve. 'Somehow or other, one never seems to be able to penetrate behind the brown mask of his lined features ... he eludes you and you leave him with his secret, as unsolved a riddle as the Sphinx' (*LS* 9). And not only was it the case that de Valera evaded the biographer's gaze, de Valera's stature was such that he had already become the stuff of myth and popular legend. The *Life Story* was advertized as an attempt to pierce the skin of this mythology, to reveal 'the man' who had recently been elected to power, and to explore the ways in which he had been transformed into one of the governing myths – 'a figurehead, a name, soon to become a legend' – for many people in modern Ireland (*LS* 10).

Rather than interrogating these processes, however, the *Life Story* contributed to them, as O'Faoláin collapsed the humanizing impulse behind his project and traded instead in the inflated vocabularies of romantic nationalism and historical melodrama. Repeatedly his text draws upon ideas of national progress, destiny and the cult of the leader, and offers an account of the recent past – and de Valera's involvement in the shaping of that past – which is reductive and propagandist. Certain idiosyncrasies in punctuation and vocabulary are deployed to support this representation, with O'Faoláin making liberal use of exclamation marks, capitalized nouns, weighted en dashes, inverted commas, random italicization, dramatic sound-bites and superlative adjectives to emphasize the point. O'Faoláin also organized his text as if it were a story of predestination and triumph, at one stage going so far as to suggest that 'Divine Providence' had rescued de Valera from execution in Kilmainham Gaol in the aftermath of the Easter Rising so that he could 'lead his people in the great struggle that was to follow' (*LS* 41). This sense of the prophetic partly explains the depiction of de Valera as some kind of super-historical or Moses-type figure, chosen by the fates to lead 'his people' out of bondage. Tenuous links with Parnell, O'Connell, Napoleon, Abraham Lincoln and, conversely, Robert E. Lee are drawn as a result. Analogies are also suggested between the life of the nation and the career of de Valera, and clichéd images are rhythmically supplied of a man who slowly comes to terms with 'the great future' that has been laid out before him, gradually realizing that in 'the fight to achieve [Ireland's] freedom he must for ever sacrifice all his own' (*LS* 16, 51).

The trope of self-sacrifice is ever-present in O'Faoláin's narrative, as is the related representation of Ireland as a defenceless mother or young woman (most often Cathleen Ní Houlihan) who calls her men to arms. O'Faoláin consistently looked to both images in the biography and used them, without any sense of qualification or irony, to position his text firmly within the fold of traditional nationalist expression. 'How dear and cruel is the price that Cathleen demands from her children!' the *Life Story* states in apparent sincerity, when it pauses to consider de Valera's activities during the Easter Rising (*LS* 32). Not only did O'Faoláin deploy such images to situate his book within this context, the imprint and design of the *Life Story* also placed it inside these parameters, as the biography was published by the then prominent Irish publisher Talbot Press, which included leading nationalist and republican writers like Corkery, P.S. O'Hegarty, Piaras Béaslaí and Aodh de Blacam in its stable. The Talbot Press was also responsible for such texts as David T. Dwane's near-reverential *Early Life of Eamonn de Valera* (1922) a decade earlier – a book completed just before the outbreak of the Civil War, and unequivocal in its admiration of de Valera's courage, integrity and devotion to the struggle for independence. 'The two greatest causes for which man can work are the love of God and the love of country,' Dwane enthused about his subject in this early biography, 'the soul that sighs alternately under the influence of these two loves is a soul pure at its foundation'.[5] It is likely that this association with the Talbot Press meant that some readers opening the *Life Story*'s pages had certain expectations about its ideological antecedents. These expectations might have been raised by the insertion of a photograph of de Valera in the frontispiece, and the fact that this photograph bears a copy of de Valera's signature presumably led some readers to the incorrect impression that the book had been authorized by its subject.

Nationalist associations were further strengthened by the spelling of the author's name 'Seán Ó Faoláin' on the spine and title page. In the context of his larger career, this spelling – though correct – is unusual since O'Faoláin generally preferred a more syncretic form of his surname which fused Irish and English-language elements. The *Life Story* carries the proper Gaelic spelling of the surname 'Ó Faoláin', with the apostrophe dropped and a *fada* inserted over the upper case 'O', and a space included thereafter; a conventional anglicized version would remove the second *fada* for consistency and spell the surname 'O'Faolain' or, alternatively, translate it to the author's birth name 'Whelan'. O'Faoláin was obviously aware of this, but generally preferred the idiosyncratic spelling 'O'Faoláin' – it is the name that most of his books were published under by Jonathan Cape in the 1930s, and it is the form that he would later use in his autobiography *Vive Moi!*. Recalling the events leading up to the changing of his name from John Whelan as a youth, he remarked that it was because of his love for Irish that he 'became and remain, as my children do, O'Faoláin' (*VM* 113). O'Faoláin never consistently followed this spelling to the letter, though, and sometimes played with other versions of his name as the occasion required. An essay in the newspaper *The Leader* in 1938, for instance, written as part of a dispute with the academic Michael Tierney following the publication of *King of the Beggars*, was pointedly signed 'John Whelan (By youthful sentimentality – Seán O'Faoláin)'.[6] The *Life Story* was one of the few occasions when he adopted the proper Irish-language spelling (some early essays in and on Irish are similarly signed), and is the only book he ever published under this name. As Frank Shovlin has observed, the decision to do this was almost certainly politically motivated, and was underscored by an attempt to locate the book within a particular tradition and sell it to a specific audience.[7]

Just as the *Life Story* depicts de Valera sacrificing himself to the cause of 'Cathleen [who] seemed bound tighter than ever in her chains' after the 1916 rebellion, so it argues that the sufferings of Ireland were reflected back onto de Valera and inscribed in the very fibres of his being (*LS* 39). A lot of attention is devoted to de Valera's appearance in this relatively short study, and – in a possible echo of Thomas Carlyle's reflections on the heroic – de Valera's face, in particular, becomes the focus for O'Faoláin's energies on numerous occasions.[8] The discourse of physiognomy is repeatedly used to trace the lineaments of this face, and if it is initially supposed that de Valera's visage (or his 'mask') reveals none of its secrets, it is nonetheless also suggested that his character can be ascertained though a close analysis of his features. 'Look at his face to-day', O'Faoláin directs the reader at one point:

> Every crisis in the history of Ireland during the past sixteen years has sculptured itself in lines upon his face – and that awful week [Easter 1916], among others, has left its indelible mark. Where else does he get that leanness of face, that brooding shadow, but from the inner fire that has been eating his heart since he heard the name – Ireland? (*LS* 28)

Hyperbole and melodrama aside, such comments are significant for their promotion of a particular way of reading de Valera, as subject and nation are aligned and de Valera's story is considered at one with national history. What is more, de Valera is seen to bear the weight of that history, as he is depicted absorbing and embodying the conflicts and changes which defined the recent past in Ireland.

Similar points are made elsewhere in the text, particularly with reference to the Civil War, where O'Faoláin was keen to offer justifications and respond to serious criticisms and controversies. 'There can be no Irish biographer of De Valera who would not wish to pass over the period of the Civil War,' he solemnly intones, '– not, one hastens to add, because there can be recorded a single action of his during those years of which any man could be possibly ashamed, but because that period of internecine strife, horrible for anybody, was for him a period of complete despair' (*LS* 91). Historians have since struggled over de Valera's 'actions' (for some, his vacillation, incoherence or inaction) at this especially fraught time, and many of the questions that energized O'Faoláin continue to provoke debate. Did de Valera's rejection of the Anglo-Irish Treaty precipitate the Civil War in Ireland, or was the Civil War at all inevitable following the Sinn Féin split over the Treaty debates? Were the pro- and anti-Treaty sides of Sinn Féin as homogenous or unified as is often supposed? What level of authority did de Valera exert across the anti-Treaty ranks, and did he do enough (or could he have done more) to prevent the fighting? Many commentators have sounded a note of caution over such questions, warning against the dangers of projecting contemporary assumptions onto past events. It has been pointed out, for example, that the Civil War marked a particularly low point in de Valera's public life, as he was frequently out of touch with what was happening on the ground. Time and again de Valera appears to have been frustrated, outmanoeuvred or simply bypassed by people on both sides of the conflict. Suspected as 'a temporiser' by some fellow republicans, according to Dermot Keogh, he was nonetheless also caricatured as 'an intransigent anti-Treatyite' by many supporters of the Free State.[9] As Diarmaid Ferriter has contended, de Valera often found himself in the position of 'being led rather than being the leader' as a result. If he privately expressed 'ambivalence about the side he was now stuck with', many of the more 'extreme' or 'incorruptible' republicans he was grouped alongside 'in turn were sceptical about his republican credentials and appetite for the fight'.[10]

The *Life Story* gestured towards some of these divisions and tensions. This was not done in the name of historical objectivity, though (the biography is anecdotal, subjective and unashamedly partisan), but rather to seek to explain de Valera's actions and add depth to the myth that was being created. If de Valera is described as the father of the nation and so-styled 'leader of his race', he is also represented as a selfless martyr or dove-bearer, 'thinking, as always, of peace and unity' rather than bearing any responsibility for an acutely divisive conflict (*LS* 96, 94). 'The blame of the Civil War has been unjustly thrown on De Valera', O'Faoláin declaimed:

> and since, as the leader of the people, he takes the glory of the fight against the British from 1916 onward, it may be supposed that he can carry the blame for 1922 also. It is the common lot of leaders. But in his case it is most cruelly unjust to blame him for the events of 1922 ... Over the militarists he had no control, and they avoided or rejected his influence (*LS* 94).

The image of de Valera suffering for his people runs like a seam through the 1933 biography. Attention is repeatedly drawn to his several stretches in prison, for instance, as well as to the many privations and humiliations experienced, the agonies endured over the brutal deaths of former comrades and friends, and the sacrifices made in the relationships with his wife and children. This stress on suffering is enforced in the above quotation through the emotive choice of adverbs, and is underlined by the loaded repetition of the word 'unjust' and the triple refrain 'blame'. A basic tenet of the *Life Story* is that de Valera freely assumed, and in turn came to embody, the distress of 'his people' at this time, and that he bore their suffering in an almost Christ-like fashion.[11] One Gethsemane-type scene depicts him in a prison cell late in 1923, 'knowing' and, crucially, accepting, 'that the blame of all this sorrow, and all these deaths, ... will be flung ponderous on his back, to bear as long as he lives'; thus it is remarked that 'it was from this time on that his face grew darker with furrowed lines, and the deeper marks of sorrow engraved themselves on his face' (*LS* 99). The *Life Story* is clear in its belief that collective sorrow was not only borne by de Valera, it was also internalized and intensified by him precisely because he was a born 'Mediator' and man of peace:

> Is it not this responsibility, above all, of keeping peace between extreme factions that has made of him at times of crisis the buffer between warring parties and brought down on his head

> the vituperation which the factions really deserved? It is his most ardent desire to keep peace between his fellow-countrymen. It is a thankless task. And it is a task that only a patriot would attempt, and a born leader achieve. … He is trying to maintain it to-day, and no man but can wish him well. He has sacrificed his entire life, his peace and comfort and happiness to that unselfish cause (*LS* 56).

The image of de Valera as a natural peace-maker is the image de Valera himself authorized in his official biography many years later, as he wanted himself to be remembered striving to hold together the competing factions of Sinn Féin in the period after the signing of the Treaty, represented by Michael Collins and Arthur Griffith on the one side and Cathal Brugha and militant anti-Treaty republicans on the other.[12] It is an image that has proved inevitably controversial. Tim Pat Coogan, for instance, in an unsympathetic biography, more recently ascribed him the role of 'Disturber' (with a capital 'D') rather than 'Mediator' (with an upper case 'M'), commenting that 'in the final analysis de Valera's record demonstrates that he was a unifier only when he could control the movements and personalities involved … when he could not exercise control he was prepared to wreak havoc'.[13] The theme of the *Life Story* runs contrariwise, with O'Faoláin toeing the party line, adamant that de Valera's commitment to peace and unity was absolute. Such was the depth of this commitment, according to O'Faoláin, that it left a lasting impression on his physical features, resulting in 'the tired and drawn face of De Valera to-day – the face, as has been so well said, that recalls the face of Dante – "the man who had descended into hell"' (*LS* 101).

O'Faoláin's reference to Dante is an unacknowledged rehearsal of the words of the veteran parliamentarian and agrarian campaigner William O'Brien. In *The Irish Revolution and how it came about* (1923), the former Irish Parliamentary Party MP recalled his first meeting with de Valera at an anti-conscription conference in Dublin's Mansion House in the spring of 1918. 'His transparent sincerity, his gentleness and equability captured the hearts of us all', O'Brien reminisced. 'His gaunt frame and sad eyes deeply buried in their sockets had much of the Dantesque suggestion of "the man who had been in hell"'.[14] O'Brien's allusion to Dante enforced the impression that de Valera was a significant witness to despair and suffering, and this significance explained, and was further enhanced, by the symbolic stature de Valera was afforded in nationalist circles following the Easter Rising. O'Faoláin's subsequent reference carries a similar suggestion, but encompasses the larger period of unrest from 1916 to 1923. In addition, though, O'Faoláin's mention of Dante gives notice of the consciously textual status of the *Life Story*. For just as de Valera is related to an iconic and much-written about figure who changed the shape of literary history, so his life is told as if it was a piece of writing – it is, as the title implies, a *story* – which is narrated with the aid of tropes, metaphors, analogies, intertexts and generic references. The latter are especially important to the design of O'Faoláin's biography, and the genre that is most often mentioned is curiously, given that the *Life Story* is a prose work, but revealingly theatre. 'It is possible … to tell the amazing story of his life', it is announced in the opening pages of the prologue:

> not of course as yet as a finished thing, but as a fully rounded story, with all its dramatic crises, all its tense excitement, its hopes and fears and dangers, crowned by this extraordinary climax, which, like the conclusion of one cycle of a play, is being even now enacted before our eyes, the ending of one great story, one fervently hopes, as 'harbingers preceding still the fates', to an even greater, if less exciting one (*LS* 11).

This is one of several instances in the *Life Story* where the generic form of theatre is referenced, and the value of this reference is magnified by the inclusion of a quotation from Shakespeare. O'Faoláin's use of this quotation is telling, as a brief comment from *Hamlet* is inserted into the world of early 1930s Ireland and Shakespeare's words are invested with an alternative meaning in consequence. In the opening scene of *Hamlet*, just before the second appearance of the figure of the Ghost, Horatio anxiously explains that the harbingers of fate serve as 'prologue to the omen coming on'.[15] Recycling these words in the *Life Story*, O'Faoláin proposed that the portents could be viewed positively as evidence of 'a new Ireland' which was in the process of being created by de Valera and his recently-elected Fianna Fáil colleagues (*LS* 50). O'Faoláin still seems to have believed that this 'new Ireland' could be a place of promise and potential (despite the ominous Shakespearean echoes), and this accounts for the general air of optimism which characterizes the closing sections of the *Life Story*. It is clear from contemporaneous and subsequent texts that this optimism was short-lived.

The allusion to theatre, and the extended metaphor of drama and the stage, speaks back to one of O'Faoláin's earliest influences, the Cork Opera House, and is something that he revisited over and again throughout his career. In the *Life Story*, this metaphor is primarily important insofar as it provides a defined frame though which 'the tragic drama' of de Valera's life and, most importantly, his involvement in the Civil War can be comprehended (*LS* 96–8). Indeed, the initial reference to de Valera's 'mask' gains in significance when it is read in this context, as does the repeated figuration of de Valera as a tragic hero who is acting out a life that has been preordained by the fates. The metaphor is also of critical worth, though, insofar as it permits a more flexible way of thinking about the subject of the *Life Story* and issues of identity more generally. For O'Faoláin's deployment of the idiom of the theatre meant that his narrative could adopt a motif that challenged predetermined, or essentialist, notions of identity and related configurations of 'blood', 'community' and 'race'. It also allowed him to talk about people performing aspects of their identity in public, and cultivating, fashioning or playing with a variety of personas or selves. This challenge to ideas of identity was neither uniform nor especially effective, as O'Faoláin simultaneously, and paradoxically, fell back into essentialist modes of thinking when considering de Valera's physical appearance and the consequences of his 'mixed' parentage. 'The fire of Spain and the warmth of Ireland were spilled into his blood', it is uncomfortably remarked at one point, as the author is drawn to comment on de Valera's supposed genetic inheritance (*LS* 15). Even still, O'Faoláin's deployment of this idiom enabled the *Life Story* to talk about – or, at least, to begin to talk about – ways of being in more fluid ways, and to gesture towards related ideas of role-play and performance.

Allusions to drama and playacting are also threaded through O'Faoláin's second work of non-fiction, a biography of the political activist Countess Markievicz (Constance Gore-Booth). This is perhaps to be expected since Markievicz was a keen supporter of the theatre, and, for a time, took an active part in amateur dramatics. Her husband, Casimir Dunin-Markievicz, was also an actor, dramatist and director. In *Constance Markievicz, or The Average Revolutionary* (1934), O'Faoláin duly recorded these points but appeared uninterested in exploring the consequent details. Markievicz's abilities on the stage, for instance, were summed up with the brusque assessment that 'everyone agrees she was a poor actress', and her later attempts at playwriting were said to have 'remained, and properly so', unpublished and not produced (*CM* 78, 306). What O'Faoláin was instead interested in was the idea that Markievicz brought performative qualities to her everyday life, and that this added a touch of glamour – but also, perhaps, a hint of illusion, even a charge of affectation – to the activities she undertook and the causes she championed. Thus, for example, the reader is informed that 'she saw things in the form of a drama in which she must always be the hero', that she 'had a good flair for dramatic effect,' and that she 'was always fond of dressing up' (*CM* 20, 40, 42). Such references are littered throughout *Constance Markievicz* and are linked to a larger vocabulary which is theatrically inspired, with words like 'role', 'play', 'costume', 'disguise', 'stage', 'audience' and 'drama' providing the basic idiom of O'Faoláin's biography. Theatrical references are supported by a series of photographs which accompanies the text, and are reinforced by comments from some of Markievicz's contemporaries, including her friend, the feminist and republican activist, Helena Moloney, who is quoted talking about the Countess's 'love of the limelight' and her preference for work which was of a singularly 'dramatic' kind (*CM* 111).[16]

O'Faoláin's stress on Markievicz's theatricality testifies to his subject's affinity for performing aspects of her identity in public. 'Her dramatizations aided, and did not interfere with, the work she chose to do', O'Faoláin stated, suggesting that this gave Markievicz the belief, and also the opportunity, to assume roles and intervene in debates which would have been otherwise off-limits for reasons of class and gender (*CM* 309). The point has become a familiar refrain in readings of Markievicz's life, and has been reiterated by other biographers and historians equally keen to comment on Markievicz's 'tendency to self-dramatization' (in the words of Anne Marreco), her 'love of flamboyant gestures' (according to Margaret Ward), her 'successful performances off stage' (to quote Jacqueline Van Vorris), her 'gift for disguise' (to recall Elizabeth Coxhead), and her 'characteristically theatrical fashion' (as Senia Paseta most recently remarked).[17]

In the third volume of his autobiographies, *Drums under the Windows* (1945), Sean O'Casey memorably seized on this theme in order to sketch an acidic portrait of Markievicz 'scintillating in the suit of a harlequin' and acting out the role of 'the lady of the ladle' in soup-kitchens during the 1913 Lock-out. In O'Casey's famously jaundiced account, Markievicz's theatricality was born out of the desire to be the centre of attention – her 'spotless bib and tucker' was only ever donned, he alleged, when a reporter visited Liberty Hall – and this was taken to signify a lack of commitment to any defined political praxis. O'Casey related these criticisms to intellectual laziness on Markievicz's part, and suggested that this allowed her to believe that she could skip freely between organizations in the period prior to the Easter Rising. (Markievicz's dual membership of the nationalist women's movement Cumann na mBan, with its links to the Irish Volunteers, and the socialist Irish Citizen Army infuriated O'Casey especially, and led to his resignation from the latter organization in 1914.) 'She looked at the names over the doors' of each of these groups, he sniped, 'and then thought she was one of the family. But the movements were no more to her than the hedges over which her horses jumped'.[18]

O'Faoláin's account of Markievicz's activities lacks the obvious bite of O'Casey's later autobiography, and appears more appreciative in its estimation of her accomplishments and abilities. There is little sense that Markievicz's commitment to the Dublin poor was not genuine, for instance, with O'Faoláin going so far as to claim – and then reinforce the claim by repeating the point verbatim – that her work with the labour leaders Jim Larkin and James Connolly, and her associations with the city's impoverished labourers and unemployed, constituted 'her true vocation' in life (*CM* 146, repeated 174). For O'Faoláin, this was only possible because of Markievicz's personal courage, as she repudiated a life of privilege and security, and unlearned a body of prejudices and beliefs that she had absorbed as a child. In effect, it involved a revolution in the ways Markievicz perceived herself and the world around her, something which was not easy to conceptualize or enact, with O'Faoláin adamant that it was 'only with great difficulty' that she managed to 'abandon the current of the life – that strangely divided life – into which she was born' (*CM* 20). Crucially, O'Faoláin believed that Markievicz realized this revolution and abandoned aspects of this inheritance in the course of her life; O'Casey, by contrast, was to remain unconvinced by what he termed 'the myth of her devotion to the poor'. 'For all that she was of the Ascendancy', O'Faoláin argued:

> for all that she was of the old landlord class of usurpers and undertakers, for all that she never came to know them as only one of their own number could know them, she did get to understand them far better than either [her husband] or even they themselves ever suspected (*CM* 86).

Not only did Markievicz reject the world she was born into by empathizing with the urban poor, she was also 'accepted by the common people' in ways that were 'extraordinary' for someone of her background, and it was this acceptance which marked the singularity of her achievement, according to O'Faoláin (*CM* 89). This was all the more impressive given that it involved a transgression of the boundaries of gender as well as culture, religion and class. 'If it was inadvisable', but not entirely exceptional, for men of the gentry 'to take part in that kind of politics', O'Faoláin asked, 'what word is there for … a woman, still more for a woman of the Gore-Booth class', to assume a prominent role in labour activism in the early years of the twentieth century in Ireland (*CM* 88).

Of course, this was not the only kind of politics that interested Markievicz. However, O'Faoláin was far less certain about the sincerity, or the wisdom, of her connection to other activities and organizations. Her commitment to the suffragette movement, for instance, was dismissed with the perfunctory comment that although 'she sympathized with them … their poison was not hers,' since there was 'nothing in her character to be moved at the thought of injustice to woman *qua* woman' (*CM* 80–2). (Interestingly, the word 'poison' was silently revised to read 'passion' in a later edition of this biography.[19]) And the rationale behind her involvement in nationalist politics of conflicting shades and varieties was treated with a measure of smug condescension. Reflecting on her associations with Arthur Griffith's moderate Sinn Féin group, O'Faoláin quipped that 'she did not join [it] – she never joined anything – she flung herself into it', while her subsequent involvement in advanced nationalist and republican circles was attributed, in no small part, to her love of action, danger and gesture (*CM* 109). According to O'Faoláin, such associations were less evidence of genuine ideological affinity on the part of Markievicz, and rather a case of attraction to, even absorption by, seductive and more powerful political forces. 'That has always been the fate of the Irish underdog,' he supposed, 'to be swallowed by the roaring hounds of Nationalism' (*CM* 146). Absorbed by the discursive energies of nationalist politics, Markievicz was depicted 'hypnotized by the same rich dream-colour of the Poor Old Woman' as some of her contemporaries, including Patrick Pearse, to the point where she 'could not see, for more than a little interval, that the poor old women of the Dublin slums were, in their rags, a dream beyond even that panoply of ancient vision' (*CM* 146).

A central question in O'Faoláin's biography is whether Markievicz's involvement in the politics of Irish nationalism came at the expense of her labour activities, and whether she unintentionally traded the pressing needs of the 'poor old women' on the street off against the abstract interests of the 'Poor Old Woman' (in capital letters) that is a personification of Ireland. In addition, O'Faoláin wondered whether Markievicz's participation in nationalist politics was in some ways representative – hence the text's subtitle, *The Average Revolutionary* – notwithstanding the fact that she was such an atypical rebel in terms of birth, profile and personality. The trajectory of Markievicz's life was certainly remarkable. Born into a landed Protestant family with imperialist loyalties, she played a courageous part in the struggle for independence; she served as a staff officer during the Easter

Rising and was sentenced to death for her involvement in that rebellion (this sentence was only commuted because of her gender); she subsequently spent large periods of the years between 1916 and 1923 in jail as a common prisoner; she was the first woman to be elected to Westminster (but did not take her seat) and was the only woman to serve as a Minister in de Valera's proscribed first Dáil.[20] Despite this extraordinary life, O'Faoláin argued that his subject was 'average' insofar as she was driven by emotion and ebullience rather than political philosophy or reasoned logic.

As O'Faoláin saw it, this was also true of many of her fellow revolutionaries (male and female) who were caught up in the excitement of 'a movement of emotion rather than of thought' (*CM* 284). 'One begins to wonder if revolutionary movements ever move towards defined ends,' he asked, 'whether all such movements are not in the main movements of emotion rather than of thought, movements arising out of a dissatisfaction with things as they are but without any clear or detailed notion as to what will produce satisfaction in the end' (*CM* 104). O'Faoláin's basic point – that most modern revolutionaries in Ireland have been inspired by discontent, latent energy and what he termed 'sleeping racial memory', but have tended to lack a clear sense of the society they wished to create – has sparked much debate, not least because it conflates the ambitions of very different individuals, ideologies and movements (*CM* 241). It also ascribes to revolutionaries an inherent lack of imagination or an implicit short-sightedness, as those who sought to implement change were routinely depicted thwarted by their own inherited impulses. This atavistic quality accounted for the absence of change in post-revolutionary Ireland, according to O'Faoláin, as a diverse body of genuinely motivated people became disillusioned or deflated by a listless reality and a politics of respectability and personal greed. In the words of Kevin Whelan, many of these people found themselves 'marooned between an unattainable golden age from which they were irrevocably severed', but to which they remained inexplicably drawn, and 'a future which they were incapable of embracing' – or, more to the point, incapable of visualizing and describing.[21]

This failure of vision was a characteristic feature of modern Irish history, according to O'Faoláin, and was something to which he returned in his fiction and non-fiction – in his novels *A Nest of Simple Folk* and *Come Back to Erin*, as well as in his historical studies *The Story of Ireland* (1943) and *The Irish* (1947). In the latter text, for instance, he argued that there are several archetypes in Irish history, one of which is 'The Rebel', who operates in 'two types or stages'. The first type 'rebels against an immediate injustice ... [and] sees no farther. The other sees beyond the immediate thing to the larger implications; he is the man who uses words like Emancipation, Liberty, Freedom'. The difference between the two is perhaps best explained by a conceptual distinction between rebels and revolutionaries. 'Rebels', O'Faoláin remarked, 'deprived themselves, and Ireland, of as much as they gave':

> they choked the critical side of their minds, they were good rebels in proportion as they were bad revolutionaries, so that their passion for change and their vision of change never pierced to organic change, halted dead at the purely modal and circumstantial. It had to be that way since they devoted their lives and all their beings to passion rather than thought.[22]

This distinction provides the basic structural logic of *Constance Markievicz*. A characteristic feature of its articulation in this text, though, is that it is presented in a casually sexist way, as it draws upon what is now – if it was not already then – a tired discourse of cliché and type.

For all O'Faoláin's suggestion that Markievicz shared in the revolutionary excitement of her contemporaries, a lot of space is given over to the predilections and emotional extremes of the 'ever-enthusiastic Madame' in the pages of this biography (*CM* 126). Time and again Markievicz is described as 'impulsive', 'scarcely at all reflective' and 'unthinking', and this is seen to account for many of her strengths and weaknesses as a biographical figure. O'Faoláin was not alone in delineating this aspect of his subject's personality, and some of the points he raised have also been articulated by subsequent and more sensitive commentators. Anne Marreco, for instance, in her authoritative biography, *The Rebel Countess* (1967), claimed that Markievicz 'always tended to live and act rather than reflect', while Anne Haverty more recently opined that 'at heart she was simple, fervent, spontaneous and responsive'.[23] In *Constance Markievicz,* O'Faoláin anticipated these comments but granted them an additional inflection, as Markievicz's personality was used to provide the occasion for a more general observation concerning women *per se*. Only a few lines after O'Faoláin's reflection on the shortcomings of revolutionary movements (quoted above), for example, he remarked that 'Constance Markievicz, in her woman's way, had no intelligible ideas but many instincts' (*CM* 105). Too much is implied by this passing generalization 'in her woman's way', and the offhand way in which it is injected into the sentence, and suspended between two commas, is suggestive of a fundamental assumption concerning supposedly 'natural' female characteristics.

This assumption runs through the biography and routinely leads to sexist inanities and textual irrelevances. A case in point is provided when the text blandly professes, for no apparent reason, that 'women are kinder (when they are kind), more immediately opportunist, and less suspicious (when they have decided not to be suspicious) than men' (*CM* 113). Similarly, in the context of a general discussion on quarrels and personal slights, it is claimed that readers 'will learn an immensity from such trifles, especially women, for whom trifles can mean a world of happiness and unhappiness' (*CM* 71). Or again, buried deep within a potted history of political activity in the 1880s, a parenthetical observation is included concerning the young Markievicz as a debutante in London: '– how lovely she must have looked at that time! –' (*CM* 91). Needless to say, no analogous interjections are made about any of her male contemporaries, as men, in the biography.

Such observations are part of the fabric of O'Faoláin's narrative and give the text a dated and frequently patronizing quality. They also reflect back onto, and restrict, the recurring allusions to performance and playacting in the text. For despite the many references to theatre, which include telling references to disguise and costume (Markievicz famously wondered what she should wear to the Rising, and whether she should wear breeches like her male comrades), O'Faoláin was reluctant to explore the extent to which Markievicz's pronounced performativity played with, and fundamentally challenged, established gender boundaries. Granted, O'Faoláin's intention was not to provide some form of proto-gender studies commentary in his biography, something which would use Markievicz to illustrate the ways in which gender roles are socially enacted, or which would demonstrate the potential of these roles to be transgressed, and so anticipating the work of recent literary theorists like Judith Butler.[24] O'Faoláin was a product of his time, after all, and, as Evelyn Conlon once observed, was part of a long line of Irish male writers who accepted the general idea that there is a natural distinction between the sexes, taking for granted the debilitating set of polarized expectations which stems from this.[25] Nonetheless, his reluctance to engage in the politics of gender identification is remarkable since the topic was germane to the subject of his biography. It is also noteworthy since O'Faoláin was otherwise so explicit about Markievicz's repudiation of conventional attitudes and prescribed modes of inheritance and social activity.

For the most part, O'Faoláin's representation of this defiance was channelled in predictable ways, and centred upon Markievicz's rejection of Anglo-Irish prejudices as well as her gradual identification with the so-called 'common people'. As the text traces the arc of her biography, it also recorded her rejection of the accepted idea of what a woman of her class could and should do with her life. Her decision to leave her family's home in Sligo to follow a bohemian path as an artist in London and Paris is noted, for example, as is the fact that she married relatively late, and despite her parents' reservations, only to reject the life of domesticity that she had established with her husband in Dublin, amicably separating from Casimir and distancing herself from their only child, Maeve. Although these details are dutifully recorded, they provide little cause for serious reflection, and their representation seems quirky when it is set against the depiction of the other revolutions that Markievicz staged.

These details are also presented in a surprisingly awkward prose style, as if O'Faoláin struggled to find an appropriate register with which to describe Markievicz's unorthodox behaviour. It is telling, therefore, that he resorted to the discourse of the grotesque to account for the more rebellious aspects of her life. Drawn to explain her unconventional or 'boyish' pursuits as a child, for instance, O'Faoláin stated that she must have seemed 'something of a freak' to the more respectable members of the Gore-Booth family (*CM* 27). This sense of grotesquery gains in value, and also in frequency, as the text develops, and is afforded particular significance when it is placed in relation to questions of gender construction and self-identification. At various points in the biography Markievicz is described in such terms as 'a boyish woman', 'half-boy herself', and an 'unwomanly woman', with O'Faoláin going so far as to lament 'the strange unwomanliness' that engulfed her later in her life, which was 'so alien to her nature' and upbringing (*CM* 116, 121, 204, 166). In such instances, the invitation is clearly there to read Markievicz as an embodiment of something unnatural or monstrous, as if she tested the limits of the supposedly secure referents 'male' and 'female', and sought to erode traditional expectations which are 'normally' associated with this binary.

Despite Markievicz's attempts to overcome these expectations, each of these referents remains intact in *Constance Markievicz,* and a fundamental distinction between men and women is invariably upheld by O'Faoláin. This distinction is partly achieved through O'Faoláin's stress on Markievicz's exceptionality (notwithstanding the fact that she is also considered 'average'), which is reinforced by his decision to minimize her associations with contemporary feminists, including Helena Moloney, Louie Bennett, Madeleine ffrench-Mullen, Hanna Sheehy Skeffington, Kathleen Lynn and Maud Gonne. Isolated from her peers, Markievicz's defiance of conventional gender roles loses much of its force and risks being seen as little more than a personal foray into a world of costume and make-believe. Her involvement in the women's organizations Inghinidhe na hÉireann and Cumann na mBan is accordingly downplayed, and her contributions to the feminist-nationalist newspaper *Bean na hÉireann* and the suffragette weekly *Irish Citizen* are all but ignored. This is done despite the fact that Markievicz routinely linked her feminism to her other political activities. In a 1909 lecture, for example, subsequently published in the pamphlet *Women, Ideals and the Nation*, she explicitly stated the case that '"A Free Ireland with No Sex Disabilities in her Constitution" should be the motto of all Nationalist Women. And a grand motto it is'.[26]

Markievicz's exceptionality is also articulated through the loaded accusation that she failed in her duties as a mother and a wife, as she is charged with having 'abandon[ed] her daughter gradually' and grown 'sexually cold' towards her husband soon after their marriage (*CM* 67, 50). Although these accusations are pivotal to the design of *Constance Markievicz*, information concerning the difficulties in Markievicz's domestic relationships is scrupulously (but not surprisingly) avoided. Indeed, O'Faoláin appears to have been unsure whether this information should be represented at all, or in what format it could be articulated, and he ultimately dodged this topic in preference to what he claimed was as 'a very shrewd remark' by an unnamed source 'who worked side by side with her in her revolutionary days'. According to this source, the writer and revolutionary P.S. O'Hegarty, Markievicz was 'a woman of great kindness but no natural affection' (*CM* 67). O'Faoláin's shying away from this topic is richly suggestive, as is his recourse, by way of O'Hegarty, to an idiom of the 'natural' to summarize her alleged shortcomings as a lover and a mother.

The issue remained of interest to O'Faoláin, though, as is clear from his foreword to a slightly revised edition of the biography, published without a subtitle in 1967. On that occasion, O'Faoláin returned to consider – in the most emotive of terms – Markievicz's 'ruinous personal relations with her own family, her husband and her only child whom she virtually abandoned as a baby in the cradle to the care of its truly-loving grandmother'. However, O'Faoláin concentrated his attention on Markievicz's distant relationship with her daughter, coyly adding that Casimir 'was more than able to look after himself'.[27] As subsequent biographers have shown, this judgmental assessment of Markievicz's relationship with Maeve does scant justice to the sacrifices that Markievicz consciously made, and minimizes the distress that she is known to have suffered, particularly in her later years, over the lost relationship with her daughter. In addition, it overlooks an obvious double standard, since no such charges are brought against her husband and no mention is made of the fact that other (male) revolutionaries were expected to pay this price in their domestic relationships. Indeed, de Valera is commended for having done something very similar in *The Life Story of Eamon De Valera*, when he is praised for having 'sacrificed all that human side to his country' (*LS* 110). Markievicz's decision to do likewise is read against a different set of criteria, and is considered anything but heroic.

Nor is her husband, Casimir, simply reduced to the role of neglected lover in *Constance Markievicz*. Instead, extended and overly-familiar passages are included throughout the biography which describe the chummily-named 'Cassie's' theatrical interests, his misadventures, his affairs and his heavy drinking. Numerous anecdotes and tall-tales are provided which are wearisome and digressive, and their inclusion frequently interrupts the logic of O'Faoláin's narrative, distracting attention away from, and thereby diminishing the significance of, Markievicz's commitments and dissident activities. It is striking that O'Faoláin felt the need to represent Casimir in this way – neither Sinéad de Valera nor Mary O'Connell are afforded equivalent attention in their husbands' biographies – and it is hard to escape the conclusion that he only did this because he did not consider Markievicz sufficient to command the space of her own biography. In this context, it is almost to be expected that the text does not conclude with an account of her death and funeral, as is conventional, but that it rather ends with a melodramatic report of Casimir's subsequent death, written by one of his lovers. For Markievicz routinely slips out of sight in this biography, and focus is often instead directed towards the men in her life (her husband, Larkin and Connolly, in particular) and the relationships that she shared with them.

Not only is Markievicz repeatedly placed in relation to her male contemporaries in the biography, O'Faoláin's depiction of Markievicz is also filtered through a network of representations by other male writers – in addition to the oral testimonies alluded to in the preface, which are considered 'copious as a legend' (*CM* 9). O'Faoláin's judgments on aspects of her personality are heavily indebted to these published sources. J. Dunsmore Clarkson's lengthy survey *Labour and Nationalism in Ireland* (1925), for instance, is described as 'a touchstone for the history of Constance Markievicz and of her day' in the Acknowledgments page of *Constance Markievicz*, even though Markievicz only features twice in this five-hundred page study (*CM* 10). One of these references is a footnote which simply lists her amongst the officers of the Irish Citizen Army. The other is succinct in its disregard of her as a non-reflective figure. In one short paragraph she is derided for her 'inane' objections to the Treaty and her 'fervent desire' to apply Connolly's theories to a post-Treaty setting; her political activities are also dismissed as 'enthusiastically, but not over-intelligently engaged'.[28] Sean O'Casey's early pamphlet *The Story of the Irish Citizen Army* (1919) likewise provided the fleetest of references while remaining instructive as source material for O'Faoláin's text. O'Casey's depiction of 'the gallant Countess Markievicz [who] tried frequently to be in ten places at the one time', for instance, will be familiar to readers of *Constance Markievicz*, as will his summation of her 'passionate and nervous eloquence' as a public speaker – a description O'Faoláin reproduced, but tellingly misquoted to read 'nervous and impassioned eloquence' (*CM* 199).[29]

The key text, though, is W.B. Yeats's recent elegy 'In Memory of Eva Gore-Booth and Con Markiewicz', dated October 1927, just a few months after Markievicz's death, and first published in *The Winding Stair* (1929) and then *The Winding Stair and Other Poems* (1933). Yeats's poem serves as an epigraph to O'Faoláin's study, where it is reprinted in its entirety; it is also mentioned in his Acknowledgments page and is further alluded to in the main body of the text, where its evocation of lost gentility is applauded, along with its exploration of the workings of memory, its technique and 'lovely lines' (*CM* 75). In Yeats's poem an earlier Anglo-Irish aesthetic, embodied in the memory of Markievicz and her sister as beautiful young girls, is juxtaposed with contemporary visions of debasement and disorder, characterized by descriptions of the two sisters who have prematurely aged. As these two images are counterpointed it is inferred that the sisters' ageing is a direct consequence of their political activities, and that these activities were inadequately thought through. Thus, Markievicz is accused of 'Conspiring among the ignorant', for instance, through her involvement in nationalist and socialist circles, while Eva Gore-Booth's achievements as a social campaigner and suffragette are summarily dismissed as the desire for 'Some vague Utopia'. The description of Markievicz, in particular, draws strength from other Yeats texts, including 'Easter 1916', where she is remembered for her 'ignorant good will', and 'On a Political Prisoner', where her mind is described as 'a bitter, an abstract thing'.[30] In each of these poems the sisters' political beliefs are trivialized, and a causal gendered relationship is supposed between premature age and radical politicization which suggests that such forms of activity run counter to the natural order for women. Each of these poems is considered by O'Faoláin, and each is used to reinforce or to frame a particularly chauvinistic interpretation of his subject – something which emphasizes Markievicz's youthful 'loveliness', her intellectual 'superficiality', and her tendency towards 'fanaticism'.

Thirty years after the publication of *Constance Markievicz*, around the time O'Faoláin was revising his biography for republication, Elizabeth Coxhead looked to Markievicz's life and legacy as part of her feminist study *Daughters of Erin* (1965). 'It is not true that Constance Markievicz has been forgotten', Coxhead cautioned her readers, 'her name is too tightly built into Ireland's history, and even England's, for that. But her legend … has been distorted. She is remembered for the wrong reasons, in the wrong way'.[31] In many respects, Coxhead's complaint was directed against the assumptions and interests that had come to dominate the largely male-centred discipline of Irish history in the mid-twentieth century.[32] And the text that she produced was designed to challenge the image of Markievicz that had become commonplace to historians and the public alike – that of the brave but shrill virago who turned her back on a world of refinement, and who defied all that should have been natural to her as a mother and a wife in the pursuit of a poorly-understood politics. In essence, it is the image of Markievicz that was memorialized by Yeats.

For all O'Faoláin's genuine appreciation of his subject's courage and resourcefulness – something which is exemplified through his representation of her commitment to the urban poor, as well as his stress on her fearlessness and desire for autonomy – it is an image that is, for the most part, repeated in *Constance Markievicz*. There are some important differences, not least in O'Faoláin's approval of Markievicz's socialist activities that Yeats found so lamentable. However, O'Faoláin's Markievicz remains largely circumscribed by the conventions of an established gender discourse, and restricted by the influential sources that he identified and inherited. More than that, as the first published biography of Markievicz, O'Faoláin's text contributed to the memory of this subject in a meaningful way, and helped to determine a particular way of writing about this historical figure. Markievicz, of course, personally rebelled against this kind of thinking in her own lifetime, and refused to accept the roles afforded to her by it or by the politics of a patriarchal nationalism. However, the pressures to conform to these same discourses were immensely powerful, and despite her many rebellions, as Lyn Innes has argued, Markievicz remained 'caught within the *terms* of those discourses' in the course of her life, as she repeatedly found herself performing certain roles and responding to received expectations of what a woman of her class could and should do.[33] O'Faoláin's biography provides a striking instance of the danger of her memory also being trapped – 'in the wrong way', 'in her woman's way' – by these same discourses.

O'Faoláin was dismissive of *Constance Markievicz* in his later years, frequently deleting it from his authorized list of publications and deriding its critical value. In the revised edition of his autobiography *Vive Moi!*, for instance, he suggested that his account of 'that lovely revolver-fondling gazelle of Yeats's' was 'quite unnecessary'.[34] He also inferred that it was written purely for the money – to help support his young family at a particularly stressful time (his daughter, Julia, was born in 1932), and to enable him to complete his first novel *A Nest of Simple Folk*. If his comments support Diana Norman's description of the text as 'affectionate but patronizing', they also speak to the importance of the marketplace in any assessment of O'Faoláin's *oeuvre*.[35] His biographer has since noted the care that O'Faoláin took over contracts, contacts and paycheques, as he sought to gain work as a reviewer with many of the newspapers of the day; what is more, O'Faoláin himself often complained about the hackwork he was required to produce to make ends meet.[36] In *An Irish Journey*, for example, he objected to 'the typical English rubbishy novels, the stuff that forms seventy per cent of the novels it is my lot to review every week of the year', while in *The Bell* he lamented the extent to which 'all our labour consists of patient search for the latent professionalism in Irish free-lance journalism'.[37] Such comments are in part attributable to O'Faoláin's lauded professionalism as a 'Man of Letters' and his ability to earn a living by the pen. However, they also hint at energies wasted, and the need to tailor work to fit the needs of specific publishers and target audiences.[38] Such demands were not restricted to 'minor' reviews and occasional pieces. Even though he was uneasy about his biography of Markievicz, for example, O'Faoláin was nonetheless twice willing to reissue the book in the course of his life: firstly in 1967, with the slightest of revisions, to surf the wave of Anne Marreco's biography as well as the recent anniversary of the Easter Rising; and then two decades later, without further changes, bizarrely, as part of the feminist series 'Cresset Women's Voices'.[39] It is hard not to interpret either instance as anything other than money-driven. His abridged edition of *The Autobiography of Theobald Wolfe Tone* (1937) is, ostensibly, a further instance of this.

O'Faoláin's version of Tone's *Autobiography* is a modest-sized book, which offers a concise synthesis of the diaries, letters and political essays of the famed United Irishman, marketed to readers who might have been deterred by the cost or sheer length of previous editions of the life story. Foremost among these editions were the authoritative two-volume *Life of Theobald Wolfe Tone* (1826), edited by Tone's son William, and silently by his widow Matilda, and the abridged but equally voluminous *Autobiography of Tone* (1893), edited by R. Barry O'Brien. O'Faoláin seems to have lost interest in his own book soon after its publication, seldom referencing it in reminiscences and later labelling it a mere 'potboiling' exercise.[40] Nonetheless the reading of Tone which it advanced was important to the evolution of his thinking, as it provided an early articulation of ideas which were subsequently explored at greater length in the biographies of Daniel O'Connell, de Valera and Hugh O'Neill. In his introduction to the Tone text, O'Faoláin highlighted a few points which he deemed of particular interest. These included Tone's legacy for the spirit of Irish republicanism ('without him Republicanism in Ireland would virtually have no tradition' [*TWT* xvii]); the candour and gaiety of the diaries; the lucidity and vigour of Tone as a prose stylist; and the 'pleasantly human qualities and frailties', which made Tone seem more 'real' as an individual (*TWT* xviii, xix). Special attention was paid to the latter point – 'his drinking, his temper, his realism, his flute-playing, his flirtations, his extravagant protestations, his indiscreet tongue, his utter lack of false dignity' were all cited as evidence of this – and this stress on Tone's humanity was set against the more general tendency to sanitize the memory of this legendary figure (*TWT* xix).

Indeed, it was because of the *Autobiography* that O'Faoláin supposed a distinction could be drawn between Tone and his United Irish contemporaries, especially Lord Edward Fitzgerald and Robert Emmet. Since neither Emmet nor Fitzgerald left behind a textual legacy in any way comparable to Tone's, O'Faoláin contended that both men had become the stuff of romance and easy sentiment. Consigned to 'the sentimental dimness into which piety wraps the great', both men were said to have been transformed into 'graceful falsities' and 'plaster martyr[s]' in the popular imagination (*TWT* xvii, xix). Tone, by contrast, was depicted saved from this fate by the existence of his writings. According to O'Faoláin, the letters and diaries which comprise the bulk of the *Autobiography* captured the essence of Tone, 'the essential man', in print, and ensured that his 'reality' could be described and 'remembered with greater clarity' than any of his peers or fellow revolutionaries (TWT xv-i, xvii). Clearly, this argument was grounded in an understanding of autobiography as an unmediated form of self-expression. It was also founded on the belief that such writing reveals the truth of its subject, as it narrates the details of a life in a coherent and straightforward fashion. Such a belief has grown increasingly problematic in recent years, not least for its reliance upon the idea of a unified and intrinsic self, as well as its understanding of autobiography as a simple narrative practice which reflects rather than constructs its central subject.[41] O'Faoláin's argument was of its time, however – even if his frequent discussion of performance and the multiplicity of selves seems to anticipate some of these later concerns – and was motivated by contemporaneous debates concerning the shape of Irish history. In particular, O'Faoláin was keen to engage with the ways in which knowledge of the past is often received and interpreted through processes of mythification, narrative and storytelling.

In each of the biographies which followed this edition of Tone's *Autobiography*, O'Faoláin adopted what has since been considered a classic revisionist stance, interrogating received wisdoms, questioning mythic, linear or teleological narratives, and privileging positivist and supposedly objective interpretations of history. In his introduction to Tone's text, O'Faoláin laid the foundations for such interventions by laying stress to 'facts' and 'truth', and setting this against what he termed 'vague idealism' and 'folk memory'.

He also repeatedly associated his subject with the values and virtues of 'realism': Tone was 'a born realist', he argued; 'a real man' and not 'a vague figure'; and 'his hardy realism' constituted 'the unique quality' of his life story (*TWT* xxiv, xviii, xvii). At no point did O'Faoláin pause to define what he meant by any of these terms – 'realism', 'realist', 'real' – but they were nonetheless central to his figuration of his subject. As O'Faoláin saw it, Tone was 'simply a brave, unassuming man', who freely acknowledged his anxieties and frustrations in the diaries while displaying great skill and resilience as a pamphleteer and patriot (*TWT* xxv). Given this stress on the humanity of Tone, it is telling that O'Faoláin chose to break with conventional practice in his edition of the *Autobiography* by including passages which were previously omitted from standard editions of the text.

As Tom Bartlett has since commented, O'Faoláin's abridged edition was primarily important in its day for alerting readers 'to the problem of excisions made by Tone's son' in the original two-volume edition, excisions which touched on his father's affairs as well as his difficulties with the in-laws and his loathing of all things American.[42] O'Faoláin defended the reinsertion of these passages on the grounds that they 'added precision' to the understanding of Tone's 'character' (*TWT* xxviii). They also added spice to the text, introducing or re-enforcing topics (some mundane, others sensational) which challenged preconceptions of this revered historical figure, making Tone seem all the more accessible or 'real' to a contemporary audience. The challenging of preconceptions was continued by O'Faoláin in his near-contemporaneous biography of O'Connell, *King of the Beggars* (published within the year by the same publishing house), where some of the events that Tone played a leading role in were reinterpreted through the actions of the young O'Connell, and where traditional expectations of a very different type of figure were defied, revised and once again frustrated. This challenging of preconceptions is of particular importance insofar as it helps to explain the importance of Tone as a biographical subject for O'Faoláin. For one thing that many historians are agreed upon is the variety of influences which constituted, and complicated, Tone's vision and legacy. These influences were diverse and often conflicting, and included atheism, anti-clericalism, Ulster Presbyterianism and Catholic relief, as well as inherited prejudices concerning the masses, sympathy for the poor, revolutionary fervour and an appreciation for the values of modernity, all under the umbrella of a secular and united republic. These influences proved difficult to reconcile in the late-eighteenth century and continue to constitute a challenge today.

Given the complexity of this vision, Marianne Elliott has indicated that interpretations of Tone since the early-nineteenth century have been selective in their engagement with his life and legacy, focusing only on those aspects which sustain a particular approach, 'taking the safe elements, whitewashing the rest'.[43] The image of Tone resisting neat categorizations, and defying pre-designed paradigms and political pigeonholes, is something that would have appealed to O'Faoláin. Equally attractive would have been the thought of Tone striving to draw together a range of influences in the name of a syncretic and integrated republic. Such an impulse was a motivating factor behind some of O'Faoláin's most famous work, after all, including his criticism of the 1930s and his subsequent editorship of *The Bell*. Writing in *Motley* in 1933, for instance, O'Faoláin (somewhat perversely) deployed the term 'Anglo-Ireland' to describe the 'hybrid nature' of Irish people, explaining that this is 'what history and time have made of Ireland. It defines the thousand-and-one processes from colonization to our surrender of the language that have made the Irish world of to-day and yesterday'.[44] Similarly, in *Ireland To-Day* in 1936, he characterized 'what we all are' in modern Ireland as 'the descendants, English-speaking, in European dress, affected by European thought, part of the European economy, of the rags and tatters who rose with O'Connell to win [independence] under Mick Collins'.[45] This point was not advanced in the introduction to Tone's *Autobiography*. Nor was any reference made to the curious blood-logic which informs the more detailed representation of Tone in the character study *The Irish*, where the United Irishman is celebrated for having combined 'what one must call a controlled Anglo-Irish intelligence with a passionate sense of injustice among the native Irish – in so far as there was by now any blood unmixed enough to be called "native Irish"'.[46] Instead, all of the attention is given to the image of

Tone as a warm-hearted revolutionary and a fully-rounded figure – 'a hero with slippers', as he is affectionately termed (*TWT* xxv).

Despite this apparent roundedness, however, the reading of Tone which is advanced is only one of the readings that are available. That is to say, recalling Elliott, it is very much O'Faoláin's Tone that is depicted in this edition of the *Autobiography*. The United Irishman that is represented is an attractive, lovable and humane individual; he is a committed and sincere patriot, for whom revolution 'was a serious matter and not a form of self-dramatization or emotional escape' (the reference to theatre is quietly drawn, but is again significant); and he is an archetypal realist, the 'most human and humorous and unromantic of men' (*TWT* xix). Had Tone lived, his revolution would have been very different to the one initiated by 1916, and his republic would have been unrecognizable to the state that evolved out of the conflicts of the early 1920s. 'What Tone would have done had he been the first President of an Irish Republic nobody knows', O'Faoláin conceded a few years later, 'because he has not told us. But from the nature of the man we can see the kind of life that would have pleased him, and the things (for example) in this modern Ireland that he would not have tolerated, such as the least sign of sectarianism, puritanism, middle-class vulgarity, canting pietism, narrow orthodoxies whether of Church or State'.[47] His revolutionary principles were grounded in radical, European-inflected models, and he would have been appalled by the 'cautious and conservative' class that insinuated its way to power in the latter stages of the struggle for independence (*DV* 166). 'The final stage of the Revolution [was] and is to this day – a middle-class *putsch*', O'Faoláin wrote in the essay 'The Stuffed-Shirts' (1943). 'It was not a society that came out of the maelstrom. It was a class', keen to consolidate its position by means of a life-denying credo of piety, introversion and social respectability.[48] In short, Tone is associated with a different kind of social order for O'Faoláin, and an alternative politics that could have been expansive, inclusive and warm-hearted. Most tellingly, he is described as 'the sort of man who must have dreamed as often of the gaiety as of the comfort he could bring to Ireland should his plans succeed' (*TWT* xxv).

NOTES

1. Sean O'Faolain, 'Principles and Propaganda', *The Bell* 10: 3 (June 1945), p.197.
2. Seán O'Faoláin, 'Celts and Irishmen', *New Statesman and Nation* 4: 74 (23 July 1932), p.94.
3. Seán O'Faoláin, 'Mr. De Valera – Rebel or Reformer?', *New Statesman and Nation* 4: 77 (13 August 1932), p.173.
4. Sean O'Faolain, 'The New Irish Revolutionaries', *The Commonweal* 15 (11 November 1931), p.41.
5. David T. Dwane, *Early Life of Eamonn de Valera* (Dublin: Talbot Press, 1922), p.20.
6. Seán O'Faoláin, 'The Gaelic Corpse', *The Leader* 76: 24 (20 August 1938), p.567. This dispute began with a critical review of *King of the Beggars* by Michael Tierney, 'O'Connell and Irish Democracy', *The Leader* 76: 21 (30 July 1938), pp.492–3. This prompted 'Sean O Faolain replies to Prof. M. Tierney', *The Leader* 76: 22 (6 August 1938), pp.521–2, and 'Prof. Tierney replies to Sean O Faolain', *The Leader* 76: 23 (13 August 1938), pp.538–9. O'Faoláin's article on 'The Gaelic Corpse' pressed Tierney to reply again with 'A Corpse that Came Alive', *The Leader* 76: 25 (27 August 1938), pp.595–6. The dispute with Tierney also spilled into a special issue of the Jesuit journal *Studies* in autumn 1938 on *King of the Beggars*.
7. Frank Shovlin, 'The Struggle for Form: Seán O'Faoláin's Autobiographies', *The Yearbook of English Studies* 35 (2005), p.163.
8. Carlyle has been described as a literary 'painter of historical portraits', who believed that the inner character of heroic subjects could be ascertained through a close study of their physical features. Michael K. Goldberg, 'Introduction' to Thomas Carlyle, *On Heroes*, pp.xxxv–ix.
9. Dermot Keogh, 'Eamon de Valera and the Civil War in Ireland, 1922-1923', in Gabriel Doherty and Dermot Keogh (eds), *De Valera's Irelands* (Cork: Mercier Press, 2003), p.56.
10. Diarmaid Ferriter, *Judging Dev: A Reassessment of the Life and Legacy of Eamon de Valera* (Dublin: Royal Irish Academy/RTÉ, 2007), pp.70–1.
11. Cf. Joseph Lee's comment that de Valera 'pursued his own Via Dolorosa between the Treaty and the civil war'. Joseph Lee and Gearóid Ó Tuathaigh, *The Age of de Valera* (Dublin: Ward River Press, in association with RTÉ, 1982), p.118.
12. The Earl of Longford and Thomas P. O'Neill, *Eamon de Valera* (London: Hutchinson, 1970), pp.171–93.
13. Coogan, *De Valera*, pp.248, 696.
14. William O'Brien, *The Irish Revolution and how it came about* (Dublin: Maunsel and Roberts, 1923), pp.361–2.
15. William Shakespeare, *Hamlet* I.i., 106.15-16, in Stephen Greenblatt et al (eds), *The Norton Shakespeare* (New York: W.W. Norton, 1997), p.1671.

16. Poised photographs are included of a young Markievicz and an unnamed friend dressed 'as dairymaids of Drumcliffe Co-operative Creamery', for instance (facing p.40), as well as images of Markievicz in formal dress in 1908 (facing p.88), acting in her husband's play *The Dilettante* (facing p.118), and in the uniform of the Irish Citizen Army (facing p.220).
17. Anne Marreco, *The Rebel Countess: The Life and Times of Constance Markievicz* (London: Weidenfeld & Nicolson, 1967), p.12; Margaret Ward, *Unmanageable Revolutionaries: Women and Irish Nationalism* (London: Pluto Press, 1983), p.78; Jacqueline Van Voris, *Constance de Markievicz: In the Cause of Ireland* (Amherst: University of Massachusetts Press, 1967), p.58; Elizabeth Coxhead, *Daughters of Erin: Five Women of the Irish Renascence* (London: Secker & Warburg, 1965), p.83; Senia Paseta, 'Constance Georgine Markievicz', in James McGuire and James Quinn (eds), *The Royal Irish Academy's Dictionary of Irish Biography*, 9 vols. http://dib.cambridge.org/ (accessed 10 April 2014).
18. Sean O'Casey, *Drums under the Windows* (1945), rprt. in *Autobiographies 1* (London: Macmillan, 1963), pp.595–6.
19. O'Faolain, *Constance Markievicz*, revised edition, p.82.
20. A very different appraisal of Markievicz's life was provided by Ruth Dudley Edwards in 2007. 'She was a self-indulgent, bloodthirsty show-off who brainwashed children into believing they must die for Ireland, [and] who killed without pity ... Craving excitement and the limelight, she adopted causes she barely understood because she was mesmerised by charismatic male leaders'. Ruth Dudley Edwards, 'Mrs Markievicz', in Myles Dungan (ed.), *Speaking ill of the Dead* (Dublin: New Island Books, 2007), p.87.
21. Kevin Whelan, 'The Revisionist Debate in Ireland', *boundary 2* 31: 1 (Spring 2004), p.186.
22. Sean O'Faolain, *The Irish* (London: Penguin, 1947), pp.99, 105.
23. Marreco, *The Rebel Countess*, p.25; Anne Haverty, *Constance Markievicz: An Independent Life* (London: Pandora, 1988), p.67.
24. Judith Butler, *Gender Trouble: Feminism and the Subversion of Identity* (New York: Routledge, 1990).
25. Evelyn Conlon, 'A Flawed Portrayal', *The Cork Review* (1991), p.73.
26. Constance Markievicz, *Women, Ideals and the Nation* (Dublin: Inghinidhe na h-Éireann, 1909), p.4.
27. O'Faolain, 'Foreword' to *Constance Markievicz*, revised edition, pp.7–8.
28. J. Dunsmore Clarkson, *Labour and Nationalism in Ireland* (New York: Columbia University, 1925), p.472.
29. P. O Cathasaigh (Sean O'Casey), *The Story of the Irish Citizen Army* (Dublin: Maunsel & Co., 1919), pp.21, 37. O'Faoláin's error was not corrected in subsequent editions of *Constance Markievicz*.

30. W.B. Yeats, 'In Memory of Eva Gore-Booth and Con Markiewicz', 'Easter 1916', 'On a Political Prisoner', in A. Norman Jeffares (ed.), *Yeats's Poems*, with an appendix by Warwick Gould (Dublin: Gill & Macmillan, 1989), pp.287, 290, 347.
31. Coxhead, *Daughters of Erin*, p.81.
32. Cf. Mary O'Dowd, 'From Morgan to MacCurtain: Women Historians in Ireland from the 1790s to the 1990s', in Maryann Gialanella Valiulis and Mary O'Dowd (eds), *Women and Irish History: Essays in Honour of Margaret MacCurtain* (Dublin: Wolfhound Press, 1997), esp. pp.5–6.
33. C.L. Innes, *Woman and Nation in Irish Literature and Society, 1880–1935* (Hemel Hempstead: Harvester Wheatsheaf, 1993), p.143 [emphasis as original].
34. O'Faoláin, *Vive Moi!*, revised edition, p.295.
35. Diana Norman, *Terrible Beauty: A Life of Constance Markievicz, 1868–1927* (London: Hodder & Stoughton, 1987), p.13.
36. Harmon, *O'Faolain: A Life*, p.101.
37. O'Faolain, *An Irish Journey*, p.39; Sean O'Faolain, 'Speech from the Dock', *The Bell* 10: 2 (May 1945), p.167.
38. Vivian Mercier, 'The Professionalism of Seán O'Faoláin', *Irish University Review* 6: 1 (Spring 1976), pp.45–53; see also Carson, 'The Barbaric Note', pp.399–400.
39. Sean O'Faolain, *Constance Markievicz* (London: Hutchinson/Cresset Library, 1987). The series included reprints of Christabel Pankhurst's posthumous memoir *Unshackled: The Story of How We Won the Vote* (1959) and Edith Sitwell's *Victoria of England* (1936).
40. O'Faoláin, *Vive Moi!*, revised edition, p.295.
41. Paul John Eakin, *How Our Lives Become Stories: Making Selves* (Ithaca: Cornell University Press, 1999); Linda Anderson, *Autobiography*, second edition. (London: Routledge, 2011).
42. Thomas Bartlett, 'Introduction' to *Life of Theobald Wolfe Tone: Compiled and arranged by William Theobald Wolfe Tone* (Dublin: Lilliput Press, 1998), p.xlvii.
43. Marianne Elliott, *Wolfe Tone: Prophet of Irish Independence* (New Haven: Yale University Press, 1989), p.419.
44. O'Faolain, 'Letter from a Novelist to an Idealist', pp.4–5.
45. Seán Ó Faoláin, 'Commentary on the Foregoing', *Ireland To-Day* 1: 5 (October 1936), p.32.
46. O'Faolain, *The Irish*, p.92.
47. Sean O'Faolain, 'Rebel by Vocation', *The Bell* 13: 2 (November 1946), p.109.
48. Sean O'Faolain, 'The Stuffed-Shirts', *The Bell* 6: 3 (June 1943), p.187.

2

'Let Ireland begin': *King of the Beggars*

In the 'Proem' to *King of the Beggars: A Life of Daniel O'Connell* (1938), O'Faoláin penned one of several repudiations of his erstwhile mentor and friend Daniel Corkery. This was set within the context of a critique of eighteenth-century Irish-language poetry, and was directed against ideas which had been espoused by his former teacher, a decade earlier, in the influential study *The Hidden Ireland* (1924). Corkery's *The Hidden Ireland* is first and foremost a work of cultural recovery, which explores the hidden world of eighteenth-century rural Ireland by way of an analysis of Munster Gaelic poetry. Its origins lay in the ambitions of revivalist organizations like the Gaelic League, of which Corkery was a member, and it carries an appropriately proselytizing edge, as it aimed to attract its readers to an appreciation and study of the Irish language and Irish-language literature. Ostensibly an educational primer as well as a work of literary criticism, the book was also conceived as a supplement to more canonical interpretations of the period, and strove to counter imperialist narratives of Irish history by illuminating aspects of a largely forgotten but illustrious Gaelic heritage. To this end, the text consists of several chapters on poetic conventions, dominant themes and related social contexts, with detailed discussions of a few major poets accompanied by a representative sample of English-language translations and bilingual versions of their works. It was – and it remains – a hugely important text. In the words of Seán Ó Tuama, *The Hidden Ireland* helped to establish the validity of a distinct intellectual heritage, and formulated 'the critical viewpoint that the nature of Irish poetry – its conventions, its directions, its values – is quite different to that ... of the central tradition of English poetry'.[1]

A problem for Corkery was that the poetic heritage that he was celebrating was struggling at the time of his enquiry, and was grappling with the consequences of the collapse of the Gaelic order on which it depended and of which it was an integral part. Writing in the late-seventeenth century, the poet Dáibhí Ó Bruadair summed up the situation when he characterized the period as one of '*briseadh an tseanghnáthaimh*' ('the break-up of the old customs'), following the defeat of the Gaelic chieftain Hugh O'Neill in 1601.[2] Corkery acknowledged this in his study, but held firm to the belief that aspects of this heritage had survived the conquests, confiscations and famines that followed, pointing out that traces of it were still to be found as part of a living culture in the early twentieth century. Various reasons were put forward to account for this survival, including the affections of poorer classes in rural Ireland, the adaptability of some poets to the changing order, and the assistance offered by an intermediary class of strong farmers who circumnavigated the punitive Penal Law system and comprised the remnants of the descendants of the native Gaelic aristocracy. (Daniel O'Connell's predecessors were one such family.) For Corkery, though, the principal reason was the proximity of the poets to the people.

The poets of the period might have pined for the days when they comprised a privileged caste patronized by the Gaelic order, but much of this infrastructure was gone and their position had degraded accordingly. 'Wherever they lived,' Corkery reasoned, 'the Gaelic poets of the time were peasants. They dressed like peasants, spoke like them, lived among the other peasants; they shared their people's life and, indeed, their thoughts', and the subject matter of much of their verse ('the loss of a sheep or old horse, the need of a new handle in a spade') spoke to the daily needs of their neighbours' lives. However, although the poets were 'of the people', Corkery remarked that they continued to perceive themselves otherwise.

'This is what we must remember, they never thought of themselves as peasants. They thought of themselves as poets, as literary men. They were sons of learning'. The artistry and sophistication of their verse hinted at the lost world of their classical antecedents, and this distinguished them from their neighbours as well as from contemporary 'wayside singers' and 'folk poets'. This inheritance also safe-guarded something of their traditional status in the communities that they inhabited, and gave them the confidence and the technical ability to establish innovative new forms like the *aisling* or 'dream vision' poem. For Corkery, the eighteenth-century poets were 'the *literati* of a people'; they were highly skilled 'popular poets', with a broad appeal and a wide audience, whose work enhanced and gave expression to a shared cultural consciousness, and 'touched every active, every unclouded mind in the community'.[3] This was why their poetry had survived, and why it continued to be spoken by people throughout the country.

In the summer of 1926, O'Faoláin provided an early response to this argument. This response was contained within a series of articles on the future of the Irish language for the short-lived weekly nationalist newspaper *The Irish Tribune*.[4] The articles were opinionated and assertive, and were published under the name 'Sean O Faolain' (no *fadas*, but also no apostrophe), with the solid imprimatur 'M.A.' attached in each instance to the young author's name. O'Faoláin's central thesis was that Irish was only worth reviving if sufficient resources were made available to facilitate this project, and a serious commitment was given to realize the language's worth in a truly bilingual context. 'Ireland will speak Irish in proportion to its value,' he insisted, 'and unless Irish is given the intellectual value it actually possesses, unless it is given some other significance than a mere sentimental significance, it will not be spoken at all'.[5] The second of these four articles focused on the Irish education system and its 'slap-dash' teaching of the language. In particular, it attacked those who had devised a curriculum which privileged the rote-learning of 'the decadent drivel of the eighteenth century' over an informed engagement with Irish poetry from different periods. It was in this context that O'Faoláin chose to lock horns with Corkery, claiming, with little sense of justification or substantiation, that although *The Hidden Ireland* 'is a piquant reflection that was intended to do good [it] has actually succeeded in doing more to retard Irish education than three centuries of foreign rule'. This glib accusation was directed against members of the Gaelic League and the Irish Ireland movement, for whom Corkery's text was allegedly 'a bible and the eighteenth century a holy land'. Tucked into a passing aside, it implied that Corkery's study had exaggerated the merits of a particular branch of Irish poetry, and had thereby encouraged the enthusiasts and propagandists of the language revival 'in their ignorance' of a particularly depressed period in Irish history.[6]

Not surprisingly, this claim sparked a thread of activity in the letters page of *The Irish Tribune*. The prominent nationalist critic Aodh de Blacam promptly wrote to the paper in defence of Corkery, stating that *The Hidden Ireland* was a seminal achievement which had illuminated aspects of a lost tradition and provided a template for future discussions of Irish writing.[7] The young Frank O'Connor replied that de Blacam was only supportive of Corkery because he was 'incapable of distinguishing good from bad' verse; he also argued that *The Hidden Ireland* was 'valuable not for its principles but for its enthusiasm'.[8] Corkery, in turn, objected to O'Connor's choice of words, lamenting the 'absurdity' of the younger writer's intervention and bemoaning his 'immaturity of mind'.[9] Each of these responses fed into a larger dispute which was being played out in the same paper concerning the residual significance of the Gaelic heritage and the idea of a national tradition. This dispute was stoked by personal animosities as well as growing ideological differences, and was to prove a significant turning point in the relationship between Corkery and his former protégés. 'Neither Mr. Corkery nor anyone else is the custodian of the national tradition,' O'Faoláin wrote to the paper in support of O'Connor, 'and I have sufficient faith in my own generation, which is not Mr. Corkery's generation, to believe that we shall and in our time make a better tradition for the Ireland of our day and future days than has ever entered into the type of mind that Frank O'Connor has attacked'.[10] This bad-tempered disagreement ran its course without any sense of compromise or understanding, and ended inconclusively, with Corkery insistent that national traditions are, by definition, inherited and prescriptive, and O'Connor and O'Faoláin adamant that they needed to be considered as products of history or as expansive models which are always changing and in process.

Aspects of this dispute were also played out in *The Irish Statesman*, and were revisited a few years later when O'Faoláin reviewed Corkery's *Synge and Anglo-Irish Literature* (1931) for *The Criterion*: 'There is so much that is very good and very bad in this book,' he began, 'that the critic finds it extremely difficult to do justice to it'. The 'good' identified was traced to the 'exuberance and sensibility' of some of the readings of Synge's plays; however, the 'bad', which quickly dominated the discussion, arose out of the critical methodology which informed Corkery's thesis. In short, this thesis was considered crude and propagandist, and was said to have 'over-simplified and over-idealized' the historical experiences of Irish life. 'This criticism is of the type that inevitably follows a revolution,' O'Faoláin estimated, 'with political, even religious bias, thwarting the clear thought of the literary man'.[11] O'Faoláin's sentiments were further developed in a lengthy essay entitled 'Daniel Corkery' for Seumas O'Sullivan's *The Dublin Magazine* (1936). This essay provided a prelude of sorts to the 'Proem' to *King of the Beggars,* and in many respects was an additional response to Corkery's study of Synge, with O'Faoláin concerned to make sense of his former mentor's increasingly doctrinaire approach to the Irish literary heritage. As O'Faoláin saw it, Corkery's approach had narrowed over the years, particularly as a result of the revolutionary period and the Civil War, to the point where he had become a representative instance of 'talent thwarted to theorizing'.[12] This was evident in the older writer's dismissal of the entire tradition of Anglo-Irish literature as 'not national, not normal, not natural', as well as his proposal that unless writers are absorbed by the forces of Nationalism, Religion (by which he meant Catholicism) and the Land, their work should not be considered Irish.[13] O'Faoláin responded to each of these claims with horror, declaring that they were expressive of a belief in favour of 'the nationalization of culture' and akin to the thoughts of 'all Nazis, Fascists, Communists, and every other type of exclusivist for whom the essential test of literature is a political, racial, or religious test'.[14]

As part of this critique, O'Faoláin traced the logic of Corkery's argument back to *The Hidden Ireland*, where an image of traditional Gaelic culture was presented which was deemed to be tendentious, and where many of the more awkward aspects of Irish history were either airbrushed or falsified to fit preconceived notions and 'a priori ideas about life and literature'. Corkery's exploration of this period was dismissed as 'light-hearted … rubbish', with O'Faoláin taking particular offence at his attempts to imaginatively recreate a world which was so different to the world that both writers were a part of.[15] Ironically, Corkery had attested to these same dangers in *The Hidden Ireland*, when he categorized the world of eighteenth-century Gaelic Ireland as 'a dim-descried country, ill-known and far-away to us, their descendants'.[16] However, his attempts to simultaneously illuminate this country incensed O'Faoláin, with the younger writer especially vexed by Corkery's decision to explain it according to a predetermined set of expectations about Anglo-Irish culture and the Irish-language heritage. Such explanations depended upon an 'illusion of veracity', according to O'Faoláin, and masked the difficulty that so little was known – or, at least, known then – about the daily activities of poor farmers and landless labourers in late seventeenth- and eighteenth-century Ireland. 'We know [rural Ireland's] immediate history,' he argued, 'we can follow it back to Parnell, the Land League, to O'Connell [but beyond a certain point] we cannot go':

> And where we have tried to puzzle out what really happened behind the darkness of the Penal Days we have – many of us – formed, in fact, the belief that the modern Ireland is a new and indigenous growth that began when the Irish folk, in disgust with this non-popular, aristocratic, effete, world … threw it all aside to build up, for themselves, and for the first time, a world of their own in the hovels to which that ancient curse … had by its inefficiency reduced them.[17]

In the 'Proem' to *King of the Beggars* O'Faoláin magnified this very point, and further extended the critique of Corkery, remarking that *The Hidden*

Ireland's central claims were grounded in a spurious romanticization of Irish history and its conclusions were indicative of 'irreality and make believe' (*KB* 27). This irreality was best illustrated by Corkery's attempts to impose an imaginary coherence on a previous order, and to represent that order by means of a lucid prose narrative which papered over the fact that so much of this world remained unknown and hidden from view. According to O'Faoláin, one of the harsh realities of Irish history was that people in recent times had lost the ability to decode this earlier Gaelic order, so they could not look to it as a site for revival or as an origin to which they might hope to return. If 'modern Ireland' was born out of the demise of this world (if it was positioned 'after the break', as it were), then contemporary Ireland had to face the consequences of being separated from its predecessors by a history of colonization, fragmentation and cultural trauma. It had to avoid the temptation to fetishize what had been lost, and resist believing in some kind of hidden essence, or shared 'Irishness', which might be traced back to this world. For a revivalist like Corkery, such an essence comprised a continuous link or an underlying frame of reference which transcended time and interlinked the generations; it was the genetic glue which allowed models of cultural continuity and native endurance to be supposed; and it provided the means for contemporary Ireland to regain access to its lost antecedents. For O'Faoláin, by contrast, discontinuity and change were the conditions of the historical process, and modern Ireland was a product of a syncretic range of associations which were neither innate nor essential. Little could be revived and nothing could be gained by any attempt to resuscitate a long-gone order. This thesis is central to the design of *King of the Beggars*, and was supported by reference to the nascent school of revisionist thought.

It has been suggested that the emergence of revisionism in the 1930s might be best understood as the theoretical exposition of post-revolutionary disillusionment, as a generation of disaffected nationalists turned against a society which they had helped to create.[18] The critical stratagems adopted by O'Faoláin in *King of the Beggars* exemplify this turn, as he sought to challenge ideas of continuity, endurance and essence, and question standard historical narratives which seemed to mystify or sanitize the interpretation of the past. O'Faoláin's efforts were partly a response to previous historical accounts which had helped to create a culture of unity – or at least the impression of a culture of unity – during the revolutionary struggle, and which determined the shape of much debate and educational policy in the years after independence. Writing out of this context, O'Faoláin proposed a radical reinterpretation of Irish history, undermining the values which were celebrated by contemporary revivalists, and scandalizing attempts to read the past through a nostalgic or rose-tinted lens. For O'Faoláin, the collapse of the Gaelic order in the seventeenth and eighteenth centuries was not simply attributable to colonialism and brute violence. It was also, more significantly, a consequence of deficiencies within the Gaelic order itself, which included an inability to adapt to change and respond to the forces of modernization: 'There is but small respect due to the end of the old order of Gaeldom, to that eighteenth-century collection of the *disjecta membra* of an effete traditionalism [promoted in *The Hidden Ireland*]', he reasoned, for it was an order that sought to protect an outdated class system and celebrate 'the death and decay' of a culture that had already been consigned to 'antiquity' (*KB* 20).

O'Faoláin's argument was founded upon the contentious belief that inherent failings within Irish culture had led to the demise of traditional Gaelic practices in the seventeenth century. This belief was influenced by the work of Frank O'Connor, to whom *King of the Beggars* is dedicated, and in particular O'Connor's controversial paper 'The Gaelic Tradition in Literature', which was delivered to the Irish Academy of Letters in 1935 and published in two parts the following year in *Ireland To-Day*. In that lengthy essay, O'Connor argued that the Gaelic aristocracy had become so insular and disconnected by the seventeenth century that it was unable to respond to the threat of colonization. 'Behind its attitude,' he claimed, 'there was not only a religious faith, there was also a superb arrogance. Not only the poets, lawgivers, historians and musicians, but their patrons were blinded by scorn, hatred and rage for everything that was not of Gaelic origin'.[19] Extending the terms of this polemic, O'Faoláin suggested that the colonization of Ireland was an historical inevitability brought on by the advent of modernization and the need for Irish society to keep apace in a changing world.[20] That modernization was set to occur within a framework predetermined by the colonizing power – with imperialism often functioning as the harbinger of modernization, in the words of Seamus Deane – was a point downplayed by both writers.[21]

Similarly, O'Faoláin overlooked the fact that the need for modernization was often expressed in terms which justified the colonial project, as certain types of transformation were authorized which suited the claims, and the interests, of the colonizing power. A discourse of evolution was used to underpin such modes of thinking, with seemingly innocuous words like 'modern' and 'contemporary' valorized at the expense of their antonyms 'pre-modern' and 'traditional', with the latter words, in turn, associated with societies (including, in this instance, the Gaelic order) which were deemed to be static or past-fixated. As numerous postcolonial scholars have since shown, such a discourse provided an insidious strand in the rationale for colonialist intervention, and allowed alternative (that is to say, imperialist) practices to be introduced under the guise of altruism and charity. Such practices could be used to assist in the restructuring of so-called 'traditional' societies while claiming to be solely concerned with raising standards, promoting welfare and bringing people into line with the modern (or colonizing) world. In addition, the imposition of this discourse gave credence to the idea that pre-modern or colonized societies were without any sense of internal agency, and that they lacked the capacity to change from within. Incapable of social evolution or cultural development, it could be supposed that colonizing powers were entitled, even obliged, to intervene in such settings.

A specific instance of this kind of thinking was provided in the 'Proem' when O'Faoláin looked to an unattributed source text which had also been used to strategic effect in *The Hidden Ireland*. The text was Samuel Madden's loyalist conduct book *Reflections and Resolutions Proper for the Gentlemen of Ireland* (1738), and in particular one descriptive passage where eighteenth-century Ireland was ghoulishly represented as a paralytic body dragging itself about with one half already dead. For Madden, this grotesque image signified that Ireland was impossibly split along religious lines, and that the future prosperity and peace of the island depended upon a healing of this division under Protestant influence and guidance.[22] In the early pages of *The Hidden Ireland* Corkery referenced this image, but reworked it to signify a split between language traditions rather than religious communities. The division was between the English and Irish-language cultures, he argued, which ultimately was illustrative of the conflict between colonizer and colonized. According to Corkery, 'the dead half of that stricken body' was the world of 'the Gael'. It was a world that had been brutalized since the time of the Tudor plantations and forced underground or pushed to the margins; however, it was also a world that carried the seeds of an historic identity, and was capable of imaginative resuscitation and spiritual resurrection. It might still be revived, Corkery remonstrated, 'as a dead thing is altered when the spirit breathes upon it and speaks'.[23] In the 'Proem' O'Faoláin revisited this image, but did so in order to invest it with an alternative significance which ran counter to his former mentor's thesis. Noting that 'every single historian of [the eighteenth] century has spoken of [Ireland] in terms of some disease', O'Faoláin commented that the 'dead half was her past, alive only in the memory, and slowly rotting even there' (*KB* 12). For the sake of psychological well-being, it was suggested that this past should be exorcised and laid to rest.[24]

O'Faoláin proposed an episodic model of modern Irish history to facilitate this claim, advancing a narrative of the past which was punctuated by rupture, irregularity and loss. The key period in this model was the second half of the seventeenth century, from the Cromwellian conquests through to the turbulent years of Jacobite rebellion, with the Treaty of Limerick in 1691, in particular, marking a central fault-line which signalled 'the end' of the Gaelic order. This end was represented dramatically, and definitively, by the departure of the Irish Jacobite army under the command of Patrick Sarsfield at the end of 1691 (the Flight of the Wild Geese), and it was from this point that Ireland was said to have begun 'draining her jugular into the past' (*KB* 12). The poet Dáibhí Ó Bruadair, one of the last practitioners of the bardic school of Gaelic poetry, was considered uniquely placed to describe the end of this order. '[Ó Bruadair] sums it all up,' O'Faoláin remarked, 'that end of the old Ireland on which O'Connell [would subsequently] turn his back' (*KB* 13). Not only was Ó Bruadair invested with heightened significance because he was writing at this fault-line, he was also considered typical of the world that was to follow, as he was depicted recoiling from the enormity of the pressures that were emerging before him:

> Though he forecast the end of glory, it was an end he never really had the courage to face; and small blame to him. When the end really came, with black poverty, and the death of all patrons after the flight of the Wild Geese, and the iron heel of the last invaders on his people, he lapsed back into a conventional bardism ... The poor wretch shirked the reality when he saw himself threatened by an anonymous grave (*KB* 17).

According to O'Faoláin, this shirking of 'reality' was a characteristic failure of the tradition which succeeded Ó Bruadair, as eighteenth-century poetry elided its moral and social responsibilities, ignoring the plight of the poor and fostering 'a wish-fulfilment concept of reality'. The conventions of the *aisling* or 'dream vision' poem were judged exemplary in this respect, as they concentrated on 'two main ideas', the much-hoped-for, Godot-like return of the Stuart dynasty and the related revival of an anachronistic system of patronage and privilege (*KB* 23). In response to Corkery's description of the poets as 'popular poets' at one with 'the people', O'Faoláin suggested that it was more accurate to speak of them as 'semi-popular poets' who mourned for an earlier idealized age and had little interest in 'a popular audience, however willing they were, equivocally, to be supported by popular sympathy'. The poets should not be celebrated for speaking of the needs of their neighbours, he admonished his readers, since they 'think solely in terms of their own narrow class, have no conception of the hopeless condition of the mass of the people, and have no message for them' (*KB* 23–4). This contentious complaint is at the heart of O'Faoláin's critique of the eighteenth-century Gaelic order and was a reiteration of O'Connor's central charge in the *Ireland To-Day* essays. A consequence, for both writers, was that the vast majority of Irish people were left without representation or advocacy:

> It means either that these semi-popular poets had nothing to say to the people that was related to their real political and social condition; or else it means that the people were themselves living in a conventional attitude of mind, asked for and desired no realistic songs, had no wish for a faithful image of their appalling conditions – were, in one word, sleep-walking. Either conclusion means that four million helots ... were living in a state of political obfuscation, not indeed ripe for a realistic political leader, but badly in need of one (*KB* 24–5).

The image of Ó Bruadair at a crossroads, writing at a moment of momentous change, prompted O'Faoláin to imagine him almost uttering the clarion call that would later be associated with O'Connell: 'Gaeldom is over ... let Ireland begin' (*KB* 19). This call was stifled, however, by the supposedly elitist sensibilities of the Gaelic world. Instead it remained for O'Connell to express the emergent terms of a modern democratic culture over a century later, and to formulate a radical point of departure, or 'a new beginning', for Irish society.

'To us, Ireland is beginning, where to Corkery it is continuing.'[25] The lesson that is drawn from O'Faoláin's *Dublin Magazine* essay provides the burden of the 'Proem' to *King of the Beggars*. In another context, the late Edward Said once remarked that the identification of such beginnings should be considered intentional forms of activity rather than obvious or inevitable points of origin. 'The act of beginning necessarily involves an act of delimitation,' Said noted, as certain incidents or individuals are taken out of context and chosen to represent, 'as well as be', starting points for all that follows. Beginnings '*enable* what follows', he explained, and are often 'problem- or project-directed', as they set out with an anticipated purpose and look forward to a defined outcome, while reflecting the interests of those who have chosen to identify or highlight them.[26] In many ways, Said's comments illuminate a central thread of *King of the Beggars*, where O'Connell is repeatedly credited with enunciating a radical point of departure and anticipating the shape of the nation to come. This sense of new beginnings is written into the text's very (lengthy) subtitle, *A Life of Daniel O'Connell, the Irish Liberator, in a Study of the Rise of the Modern Irish Democracy (1775–1847)*, and underscores O'Faoláin's principal project, which was to depict O'Connell breaking from the past and marking out the path along which subsequent reformers, including O'Faoláin himself, were obliged to tread:

> He is interesting in a hundred ways, but in no way [is he] more interesting than in this – that he was the greatest of all Irish realists, who knew that if he could but once define, he would thereby create. He did define, and he did create. He thought a democracy and it rose. He defined himself, and his people became him. He imagined a future and the road appeared. He left his successors nothing to do but to follow him (*KB* 368).

For O'Faoláin, O'Connell's 'realism' was succinct – hence the short, decisive sentences above – and was grounded in a mode of decolonization that included a refutation of anachronistic forms of self-identification and cultural allegiance. This required a rejection of a culture of servility, as an impoverished people were encouraged to take pride in their origins and emancipate themselves from the 'unwilling loyalties' to which they had been subjected by generations of imperial governance (*KB* 28). O'Connell 'taught simple men to have pride' in themselves, O'Faoláin suggested, and 'was one of the first Irishmen who refused to cower'; his political ideology was 'driven by … a blazing love of place and a fond memory for the lost generations of his tribe, the ineradicable *pietas* of all submerged peoples' (*KB* 367, 83, 145). It was out of this renewal of native pride that modern Ireland was said to have been born, as many people began to question institutional injustices and internalized feelings of inferiority, awakening from 'the torpor of acquiescence' to mobilize for reform under O'Connell's leadership (*KB* 161). If modern Ireland grew out of this mobilization, it was also considered a consequence of people shedding their 'outdated loyalties' to a cultural order that had ceased to speak to their contemporary reality (*KB* 28). Pride in origins and love for lost generations, that is to say, did not stretch to include the rehabilitation of the Gaelic order, since that order was identified with ideas of privilege which, according to O'Faoláin, were anathema to the principles of democracy.

'The horror of the eighteenth century, the hardly less searing horror of the nineteenth century, is the mental horror – the murder of the mind, the spiritual chloroform, the creeping paralysis of the soul that O'Connell checked' (*KB* 153). O'Connell was dramatically depicted putting paid to these horrors in the early nineteenth century, but a similar form of paralysis was said to have emerged in recent times through the activities of revivalist organizations and the Censorship Board – organizations which were quick to cast judgment on 'anybody who shows any unusual shades or variations or complexities in character or thought' (*KB* 93). This later 'mental horror' accounts for the interventionist impulse of *King of the Beggars*, as O'Faoláin used the occasion of the O'Connell biography to engage with many of the prevailing ideologies of his day, outlining the trajectory of an individual life while simultaneously critiquing aspects of the post-Independence state and the historical narratives that were pressed into service to sustain it. This imaginative link between the two ages was recognized by some of O'Faoláin's readers, and was discerned in his representation of various issues, including the proposed veto on ecclesiastical appointments in the early-nineteenth century (which is drawn in such a way that it reflects upon Church-State relations in the Free State), and the attention that was given to 'the task that still goes on in Ireland of finding a *modus vivendi* between opposing interpretations of Irishism and Catholicism' (*KB* 301). In a series of articles devoted to *King of the Beggars*, published in the influential Irish Jesuit journal *Studies* in the autumn of 1938, for example, it was agreed that the interventionist aspects of O'Faoláin's book were amongst the most salient features of this life story. The UCD academic and former Cumann na nGaedheal politician Michael Tierney set the tone for this debate when he remarked in the leading essay: 'At present we seem to be at a resting-point where one perilous stage of our journey is completed, and we are rather uncertain which way to turn next. The great importance of Mr. Ó Faoláin's book is that he offers us, in the guise of a study of O'Connell, very definite advice at the crucial moment of choice'.[27] Tierney disagreed with the advice dispensed, however, and objected – as fellow scholar Daniel Binchy also did – to O'Faoláin's representation of Gaelic Ireland in the 'Proem' and his comments on the future of Irish-language culture. While acknowledging the virtuosity of the text, and its debts to O'Connor's thinking, Tierney cautioned his readers that 'there is a certain danger in our being carried away by the brilliance of [O'Faoláin's] literary power into consenting to a view of Irish history which, if it were to be widely accepted, might be disastrous, especially at the present time':

> The significance of Mr. Ó Faoláin's book is that it once more raises clearly and frankly the dilemma that inexorably faces modern Ireland. Are we bound to rely for all our culture upon an incongruous mixture of etiolated Catholicism, Puritanical individualism, and commercial utility, or is there no hope of our being able to obtain some light from our vanished Gaelic past to brighten our gloom?[28]

This was a central concern in the contemporary reception of *King of the Beggars*, as O'Faoláin was understood to have engaged with present-day predicaments under the guise of historical biography. Alongside its explication of this dilemma, though, as Fiona Dunne has shown, a refreshing case might be made for reading *King of the Beggars* as a book about leadership in Ireland in the 1930s – or as a text about de Valera as well as O'Connell.[29] O'Faoláin's discussion of O'Connell's commitment to constitutional politics, for example, and his assessment of his subject's popularity with 'the people', gains renewed significance when it is read alongside de Valera's attitudes and political affinities. Similarly, O'Connell's tendency towards equivocation and duplicity in thinking is revitalized when it is considered in the context of O'Faoláin's concurrent engagements with de Valera. On some issues the two subjects clearly diverge: O'Connell's utilitarian approach to Gaelic culture, which led him to infamously claim that the English language 'is so great that I can witness without a sigh the gradual disuse of Irish', was poles apart from de Valera's reverence of the Irish language (*KB* 39). What is more, O'Connell's enthusiasm for the British monarchy (notably for the young Victoria following her accession in 1837), which was 'extremely – for some embarrassingly – fulsome', in the words of Gearóid Ó Tuathaigh, was antithetical to de Valera's sympathies.[30] And the stressed internationalism of O'Connell's politics was at odds with the bleak insularity of much post-Independence thinking, although this contrast is blurred by de Valera's achievements on the international stage, most notably with the League of Nations and in the area of foreign policy – achievements O'Faoláin himself identified a year later, in the revised biography *De Valera* (*DV* 174–5).

In other ways, though, the two subjects coalesce. Phrases which carry a lot of weight in the earlier *Life Story of Eamon De Valera* are recycled as chapter headings in *King of the Beggars*, with both men celebrated as 'the Man of the People', and both identified with the inscrutable 'Sphinx'. Both men were devout Catholics, and orthodox religious observance was as much a part of their public persona as it was essential to their private make-up; in O'Connell's case, however, this is possibly complicated by his early radicalism in the 1790s, when he appears to have been sceptical about his inherited faith. Moreover, O'Connell's tussles with the Young Ireland movement in the 1840s are represented as if they were almost prescient of de Valera's struggles with anti-Treaty militants in the early 1920s and the IRA in the late 1930s, while both men's parliamentary careers are traced back to the same origins in Ennis, County Clare – indeed, O'Connell's canvassing for votes in that county in 1828 is explicitly described as if 'all, it would seem, [was] very like a later Sinn Fein election with a De Valera as candidate instead of an O'Connell' (*KB* 254). Both men are also depicted as larger-than-life individuals who were corrupted by the exigencies of parliamentary politics (in particular the need to compromise), and both are invested with a flair for equivocation, semantics and wordplay. The latter point was especially important to O'Faoláin, and was returned to within a year of publication, in his second biography of de Valera. For in that text, O'Faoláin reflected on both men's capacity for sharp practice in political dealings, ascribing de Valera 'precisely the mentality of Dan O'Connell' in the process (*DV* 69–70).

If *King of the Beggars* is about de Valera as well as O'Connell, though, it is also about O'Faoláin and his concerns with the shape and future of an independent Ireland. The tribute to O'Connell – that 'he, at least, had no doubts that Ireland was beginning all over again' – can be read as a virtual palimpsest which underpins O'Faoláin's own writing, and the image of O'Connell as the initiator of modern Irish history is in many ways synonymous with O'Faoláin's preferred self-image as the creator of a post-revolutionary aesthetic (*KB* 39). O'Faoláin admitted as much in a sudden aside in *King of the Beggars*, when he commented, for no apparent reason, that 'all we can ever hope to create is an image of ourselves' (*KB* 240). O'Connell's supposed spirit of 'inclusive and tolerant liberality', his pragmatism and reforming instincts, his hatred of sectarianism, and his concerns over the relationship between the Church and the State – each of these qualities were things O'Faoláin liked to see in himself (*KB* 167). They were principles which set O'Connell apart from his peers and made him a figure 'beyond his time', but they were also qualities which carried a contemporary edge, as O'Faoláin used them to press the need for an O'Connell-type leader 'in our time' (*KB* 239, 95). This need for leadership in a new age is written into O'Faoláin's declaration in the 'Proem', that 'Ireland was beginning all over again', and it is a point that O'Faoláin returned to in other writings of the period.

In this respect, *King of the Beggars* exemplifies those schools of criticism which argue in favour of the self-reflexive nature of biography as a literary form. 'A biography is always apt to be more than an exploration of one's subject,' Robert Gittings stated in *The Nature of Biography*, since 'it becomes, at every step, an exploration of one's self'.[31] It is a simple point to which Paula Backscheider has concurred, remarking that 'the most invisible person in a biography is the most powerful – the author'.[32] There is certainly scope to read O'Faoláin's O'Connell as, at least in part, an historicized projection of the author himself, as O'Faoláin stressed certain aspects of his subject's personality and focused on particular commitments which spoke to a contemporary liberal audience, including O'Connell's battling against a culture of intellectual servility and his urging the necessity for a non-sectarian, modernizing agenda. Donal McCartney gestured towards this some years ago in a discussion of O'Connell's divisive legacy, when he commented on the contextual importance of *King of the Beggars* and the fact that O'Faoláin wrote this text in an attempt at historical reconciliation, 'with the experience of the Civil War behind him'. For McCartney, this perhaps accounted for O'Faoláin's choice of O'Connell as a biographical subject – a champion of non-violence, who was affected by his own experiences of a recent revolution (in France and subsequently in Ireland), and by his involvement in the death of another man.[33] The consistent identification of O'Connell with 'new beginnings' is crucial in this respect, and bears out Said's observation that the identification of such beginnings invariably reflects the interests of those who lay claim to them. It also expresses Said's belief that the concern with new beginnings is proof of a pressing situation, since 'one rarely searches for beginnings unless the present' can be said to matter 'a great deal'.[34]

King of the Beggars is structured in six parts and appears to offer a standard account of O'Connell's life and times. The first chapter (the 'Proem') provides the context for the biography, sketching an image of Irish society quite unlike that popularized in *The Hidden Ireland*, and covering the period between the Flight of the Wild Geese in 1691 and O'Connell's birth in 1775. The second chapter (untitled) traces O'Connell's childhood in Derrynane, County Kerry, as heir to a wealthy Catholic family, his early studies in revolutionary France, and his legal education in London and Dublin, where he immersed himself in the radical literature of the age. If his subsequent flirtation with revolutionary politics is remarked, so is his seemingly contrary decision to enlist in a volunteer corps in Ireland in the later 1790s, dedicated to defending the order on which his family's social position depended. Chapter Three, 'The Bar and Politics', the longest in the book, opens with the aftermath of the failed United Irish Rebellion and the subsequent Act of Union, and spans the period until 1813. The chapter records O'Connell's early career as a practising barrister on the Munster circuit and the popular fame he acquired as 'Counsellor O'Connell' at the Irish Bar. It also documents his emergence as the country's 'popular leader' through the adoption of a policy of agitation, his endless capacity for self-promotion and flair, and his reformation of the hitherto quietest policies of the Catholic Committee (*KB* 148).

Chapter Four, 'The Man of the People', explores the next fifteen years up to Catholic Emancipation in 1829, when O'Connell was granted the title of 'the Liberator' and seemed at the height of his powers, having been elected to Westminster the previous year as MP for County Clare. His dramatic participation in a fatal duel with a Dublin merchant, John D'Esterre, is described, which enhanced his stature in the popular imagination but was also the occasion of great personal remorse. Particular attention is shown to O'Connell's founding of the Catholic Association in 1823, which transformed the fight for Emancipation into a mass crusade, incorporating people from all classes through the so-called 'Catholic rent'. 'Down to the last impoverished beggar in the streets the people were to enrol themselves in a vast army of the poor and downtrodden', O'Faoláin eulogizes, and it was as head of this army that O'Connell was afforded the title 'King of the Beggars' by his adversaries (*KB* 241). Chapter Five, "The Sphinx', covers the following decade at parliament, with O'Connell negotiating with the Whigs, exercising some influence in the area of reform, and battling with the Tories. The repeal of the Act of Union was O'Connell's primary political aim, but his failure to achieve any headway on this issue is reckoned one of his great failures: 'What toil, what little fruit!' the text dramatically remarks of this period in his life, 'ten years of what one must call (in terms of material results) barren labour' (*KB* 307, 315). Narrative focus is also directed towards an image of O'Connell ageing, bereft – his wife, Mary O'Connell, died in 1836 – and gradually losing popularity in Ireland.

The final chapter, 'The "Come-Back"', tells the story of O'Connell's final political resurrection, with the establishment of the Repeal Association in 1840. His election as Lord Mayor of Dublin in 1841 is read as a further instance of this 'come-back', as is his involvement in a series of 'monster' or massive public meetings at historic sites around the country in 1843. These meetings provided a huge boost to O'Connell's ego, allowing him to indulge to the full his sense of spectacle and the flamboyant. The proscription of the last of these meetings in Clontarf, in

October 1843, and O'Connell's acceptance of this ban, is interpreted as the beginning of the end, particularly as it is described alongside O'Connell's increasingly frail condition and his fractious relationship with a younger generation of romantic nationalists, collectively called Young Ireland. This loss of power is further amplified by the larger context of the early stages of the Famine, with O'Connell's demise – aptly, since he is deemed the physical embodiment or 'Man of the People' – explicitly linked to the onset of this catastrophe. As R.V. Comerford has noted in a more recent study of O'Connell, his last trip to Derrynane in 1846 saw him witness, at first hand, the terrible conditions facing the rural poor: 'It was grimly appropriate, if entirely coincidental, that the same vacation witnessed the sudden collapse of his own physical strength'; O'Connell died shortly later, on pilgrimage, in 1847.[35] This is the trajectory that O'Faoláin follows in *King of the Beggars*, and in many respects it is a standard pattern, with a clearly demarcated path carefully advanced. The organization of the narrative in this way, though, also gives the text a slightly theatrical quality, as the 'Proem' and five chapters approximate the prologue and five acts of a classic Renaissance play. Indeed, O'Faoláin's decision to enumerate separate sections within each chapter might be interpreted as individual scenes within a larger prose act. O'Connell, from such an angle, appears as the hero of a Shakespearean tragedy, destined for greatness but betrayed by his own machinations, and brought down by forces beyond his control.

As *King of the Beggars* traces the arc of O'Connell's life, it engages with issues and concerns which were of critical significance to O'Faoláin personally and post-revolutionary Ireland more generally. Most often it engages with these issues in order to undermine popular preconceptions and intervene in established debates on such subjects as censorship, Church-State relations, modernity and the significance of Irish-language culture. However, it also sometimes does the reverse, reinforcing conventional wisdoms and working to maintain aspects of the *status quo*. An example, which is all the more evocative for being only occasionally apparent, is provided by the text's infrequent engagement with the discourse of gender. It will be recalled that gender expectations defined the parameters of the earlier biography *Constance Markievicz*, and repeatedly prescribed limits to the achievements and the narrative of the rebel Countess. A similar discourse is allowed to leak into the representation of O'Connell in *King of the Beggars*, as he is sporadically assigned macho attributes and manly characteristics which sit awkwardly alongside the more obvious concerns of the biography. Discussing O'Connell's work as an agitator with the Catholic Committee, for example, O'Faoláin interrupted a detailed disquisition on the subtleties of early nineteenth-century politics to include the briefest of comments concerning his subject's 'masculine mind' (*KB* 134). This observation is offered without explanation or commentary, and its relevance to the subject is difficult to appreciate or comprehend. What is certain, though, is that the underlying intention is to invest O'Connell with a sense of power and authority, and the inference is that O'Faoláin was working from within an established discourse which considered the meaning of the adjective 'masculine' to be obvious and its application to O'Connell self-evident.

Curiously, this sense of manliness is a topic which O'Faoláin returned to on a few other occasions in the text, as he was drawn to comment on his subject's muscular presence, his physical prowess and his indomitable energy. 'His bulk, his massive body, the magnificent head, handsome face, flash of eye, the roar and vigour of the lungs', these are qualities which seem to have impressed the author and which he took time to detail and enumerate (*KB* 151). 'His massive frame … in turn suggests this energy of a bull,' O'Faoláin gasps at one stage, 'the pedestal of the neck, the brawny shoulders, the chest capacious and protruding, and the curls on the forehead butting like the curls on a giant Hermes' (*KB* 233). It is tempting to inflate the importance of such descriptions and read them as evidence of an uneasy homoerotism which skims the surface of the biography. If this might seem something of an exaggeration, it nonetheless needs to be noted that such descriptions are irregularly employed by O'Faoláin, and that they sit oddly with the rest of the narrative. (What, for instance, is gained by writing O'Connell as if he were a Grecian statue in the above quotation, other than drawing readers back to the possible influence of Thomas Carlyle's idea of the hero?) Such descriptions are not confined to the figure of O'Connell alone, and are occasionally offset by the representation of other historical personages in the text. The Young Ireland leader Thomas Davis, for instance, is abruptly depicted as 'that youth with the soul of a hero and the softness of a woman' at a late point in the life story, while the colourful Chartist leader Feargus O'Connor is praised, but concomitantly lampooned, for his excessively masculine qualities (*KB* 359, 293). Each of these descriptions is left unglossed and their relevance to the respective subjects remain unexplained.

O'Faoláin's use of this discourse accounts for the focus that is given to men, and relationships between men (O'Connell, his associates and his nemeses), in *King of the Beggars*. It also explains why women barely feature in this biography. Very little attention is given to O'Connell's alleged associations with Ellen Courtenay, for instance, with whom he is reputed to have fathered a son, Henry Simpson, and the narrative baulks when it is brought to consider O'Connell's folk reputation as a serial philanderer.[36] This may be a matter of context, for as Barbara Caine has recently argued, biographical studies of public figures generally eschewed the subject of sexuality and sexual identity until after the Second World War.[37] Even so, O'Faoláin's characterization of what he terms 'the traditional light-hearted picture of a whore-mongering Dan' will come as a surprise to many contemporary readers, as will his po-faced suggestion that any discussion of O'Connell's 'possible lapses or emotional disturbances' would be 'an impertinence' undeserving of a serious biographer since these transgressions 'concern nobody but himself and his Maker' (*KB* 227–9).[38] Such a suggestion appears prudish and oddly self-censored, and, notwithstanding Caine's thesis, runs counter to O'Faoláin's decision to reinsert similarly excised passages into his edition of Tone's *Autobiography* a year earlier. It also sidesteps one of the greatest myths about O'Connell – that, as W.B. Yeats famously remarked in a Seanad speech in 1925, 'it was said of him that you could not fling a stone over any workhouse wall without hitting one of his children'.[39]

More importantly, O'Faoláin's dismissal of the subject overlooks the experiences of the women who played a part in these alleged 'lapses', the so-called 'whores' who are trapped by O'Faoláin's chauvinistic epithet, and who are treated so contemptuously by his implied line of thinking. It also ignores the fact that O'Connell's 'emotional disturbances' would have been of interest to his wife. The latter point, though palpably obvious, nonetheless needs to be made, since Mary O'Connell remains a peripheral presence for the best part of her husband's life story. References to her are few and far between – half-a-dozen or so, in all, which is quite unlike the respective attention that is afforded Markievicz's husband in *Constance Markievicz* – as she is safely secured in the role of silent and dutiful wife for the duration of the text. Even her death is subsumed by reflections on her husband's life, specifically his faith and his relationship with the Catholic Church, as she remains buried within the contours of his biography, with O'Faoláin incorrectly recording the year of her passing. 'However much anyone may have hesitated to take his religiosity at its face-value, there seems to be no room for doubt that after his wife's death in 1837 [she died at the end of October, 1836] he surrendered to his God' (*KB* 311). That is all O'Faoláin has to say on the subject, even though O'Connell is known to have grieved deeply for her loss, and a casual reader might miss the implication and overlook the full significance of what has been left unsaid.

If the discourse of gender expectations is written into the text of *King of the Beggars*, so also is the language of role-play and performance. References to the theatre were previously employed in the biographies of de Valera and Markievicz, and similar tropes are utilized (albeit to a diminished degree) in *King of the Beggars* to engage with the many sides of O'Connell, and to tell the story of a man who was famous for creating, projecting, internalizing and promoting carefully constructed images of himself. For the most part, O'Faoláin depicts O'Connell in the role familiar to history, as the high-minded liberal agitator who championed the rights of an oppressed people and tirelessly campaigned in favour of constitutional reform and repeal of the Act of Union. In short, he is 'the Liberator' of the text's subtitle. However, O'Connell also appears as his own foil in the course of this life story, as he is simultaneously presented in the guise of a ruthless demagogue who manipulated popular bigotries and, for all his talk of democracy, accepted certain social hierarchies, including his own quasi-feudal position as a landlord in Derrynane. In a similar vein, O'Connell is celebrated as the driving force and Carlylean 'great man' of modern history, while simultaneously being figured as a stereotypical Kerryman who shamelessly played to the galleries, 'with his tall hat cocked on the side of his curly head, his cloak caught up in his fist, a twinkle in his eye' (*KB* 236, 20). This confusion of roles is never quite reconciled in *King of the Beggars*, and O'Faoláin's admiration of O'Connell remains qualified by a sense of unease and 'a curl of distaste' (*KB* 204). 'Here, as so often, one realizes that there is nothing whatsoever of the romantic hero about O'Connell – little to admire, or idealize' (*KB* 256). O'Connell might be scripted as the classic tragic hero who holds within himself the potential for greatness and self-destruction (he is audaciously contrasted to Lear at a late stage of the study), but this does not preclude him from also appearing as a venal and corrupting politician, or as someone who broke inherited codes of conduct, and who was ultimately responsible for the vitiation of Irish society. 'For O'Connell did a great deal to kill gentle manners in Ireland,' it is coolly stated, 'to vulgarize and cheapen us' (*KB* 204).

In *King of the Beggars* O'Faoláin sought to make sense of this calculating figure and negotiate between his competing legacies. This was done in an attempt to retrieve something of the 'reality' of the man behind the roles and self-images – the Daniel O'Connell who was more than a 'consummate performer' or 'ever the showman', in the words of his most recent biographer, Patrick Geoghegan.[40] From the outset, though, O'Faoláin's attempts were frustrated by his subject's reputation for duplicity, inconsistency and deceit. If O'Connell was remembered as the scourge of sectarianism, for instance, he nonetheless also appeared as the man who manipulated Catholic feelings by playing upon inherited prejudices and anxieties. Or if O'Connell was represented as the champion of democracy who ushered in a new age of political representation, he was also the man who sacrificed the voting rights of the forty-shilling freeholders to secure Catholic Emancipation. Such contradictions are repeatedly attributed to O'Connell's machinations and manoeuvrings, as he is depicted wearing different faces and playing alternate parts to win an argument, secure a political goal, and ingratiate himself to a particular audience. However, duplicity is not only explained by O'Connell's disposition as a politician and a performer, since 'a duality of nature, ambiguity, a serpentining evasiveness' is also diagnosed as a core aspect of the man's very self or being (*KB* 278). Attempting to understand the source of this duplicity, O'Faoláin complained – with more than an echo of his commentary on de Valera – that the more he learned about his subject, the more 'the man becomes a maze and it is impossible to track him' (*KB* 282–3).

Proof of this duplicity was said to exist in surviving visual representations of O'Connell, especially a lithograph that was produced in the early 1830s, and which is included in the biography's frontispiece. 'There comes into his face a mask-like quality,' O'Faoláin remarked, as he paused his narrative to direct readers to the perceived significance of this image:

> and the mobility of his mouth (in the pitiless lithograph made at the time) is matched by the cold Fouché-like secrecy of the right eye. For Minotaur and Sphinx lie in ambush in his countenance, where, as in that of most men, there is the differentiation of his double nature in the play of his looks; always that right eye had held its secret calculation; always the left had been a challenge and a doubt. One corner of the lip is likewise turned upward in a half-smile; the other is gripped downward with a horrible suggestion of latent ruthlessness and brutality. If one covers half the face, one side smiles but holds its secret, and the other challenges and offers no pity. There is almost a slaver about the heavy mouth (*KB* 283).

Such comments provoke a particular reading of O'Connell, which sees him as his own double and ascribes to him an almost bipolar personality. The violence of the language is suggestive of this, as is the viciousness of the imagery, and the allusion to that archetypal opportunist of the French Revolution, the so-called 'master of cruelty and intrigue', Joseph Fouché, compounds the intrusive nature of this remarkable interjection. O'Faoláin inferred that this 'double nature' was peculiar to O'Connell – that is the reason for his tragic greatness, after all, and it is also the dilemma that has confronted his many biographers, since 'it is impossible for anybody who makes a serious study of his life to take him at his face-value' (*KB* 75). But O'Faoláin simultaneously suggested that this was also the case for 'most men' in general and the collective Irish psyche in particular: 'Some such technique of living in a state of repressed scepticism under a shell of apparent acquiescence was inevitable to a race that had learned from brutal experience that frankness was best prefaced by a snail's feeler for danger,' he commented, drawing an explicit link between the psychopathology of the 'Irish mind' and the history of colonization (*KB* 83). Such remarks anticipate the work of postcolonial theorists like Homi Bhabha, whose later theories of 'sly civility' in the colonial context find comparable analysis in the below quotation:

> Crude as it was, it took a hundred years to perfect that technique, and it will take a hundred years more before it disappears entirely; indeed, even yet, frankness is in most Irishmen no more than that wavering tentacle, swiftly retractile beneath the defensive hide of conformity. It is part of the greatness of O'Connell that he discarded that method, not wholly, but to an astonishing degree … If it was inevitable that the duality should persist, in him it at least persisted shamelessly and openly – in the *double entendre*, the mental reservation, the limiting clause, the disingenuous qualification and proviso (*KB* 83).[41]

This is the principal significance of O'Connell for O'Faoláin. That is to say, O'Connell's importance might be partly attributed to his work as a utilitarian Benthamite, counselling against what was perceived to be a moribund culture and promoting in its stead a modern, internationalist agenda. It might also be traced to his abilities as a leader, as he activated a fresh kind of politics and established new modes of representation which were democratic, inclusive and non-sectarian. His continued relevance might be linked to his role as Ireland's 'greatest realist', or as someone who accepted 'the people', ironically, because rather romantically, 'for what they were', and 'who loved them for the simple humanity he found in them' (*KB* 117). He is consequently remembered as a demystifying figure who chose not to look to a world of antiquity and ancient heroes for inspiration, and is celebrated in the 'Proem' for having broken with the Gaelic past, even if some doubts remain to haunt the larger text concerning the shape and consequences of that break – 'there is no doubt that O'Connell overdid the surgery', it is suddenly conceded in a moment of worry (*KB* 117). In addition, he is praised for recognizing that Irish culture had already changed by his own time into a more hybrid or confused practice, as it included aspects of 'the mingled strain of Anglo-Ireland' as a consequence of the colonial process (*KB* 116).

Each of these points occupies an important strand in the fabric of *King of the Beggars*, and each bears witness to the self-reflexive design of the biography as it intervenes in issues and debates which were of critical significance to O'Faoláin personally and his post-revolutionary context more generally. The particular significance of O'Connell, though, for O'Faoláin, rests in his role as a putative decolonizing agent, or as someone 'who exposed the lie of Empire' and 'who taught ['his people'] how to depend on themselves alone, in their own times, in their own conditions, in their own self-respect' (*KB* 367, 117). To achieve this, O'Connell is said to have attempted a revolution of the mind, as he strove to alter the ways in which a people perceived themselves and their relationship to the world that they inhabited, advancing new forms of self-identification, cultural allegiance and native pride. He is consequently depicted challenging not only the supposed pathologies of an inherited Gaelic tradition but also the gravest injustices of colonial rule in Ireland. O'Faoláin's excoriation of Anglo-Irish prejudice, particularly in the third and fourth chapters of *King of the Beggars*, with his lengthy discussion of the sectarian-infested law courts ('one of the filthiest cock-pits known to man' [*KB* 98]), betrays his own republican sympathies while manifestly illustrating O'Connell's hatred of servitude and institutional abuse. Similarly, his exposition of the subtle dynamics of colonialism – including its 'quiet absorption and denationalization' of an entire class of native intellectuals or 'Castle Catholics', and the willed ignorance of the imperial centre ('the English Rome') for the needs of its subjects – carries a multi-layered resonance, speaking to O'Faoláin's postcolonial impetus as well as O'Connell's attempts to change the way a people were seen and saw themselves (*KB* 219, 143).

O'Connell's revolution was, at best, only partly effective, however, as 'his people' succumbed to the horrors of the Famine – pointedly described as 'slow mass-murder', with more than an echo of the Fenian John Mitchel – and were haunted by the so-called 'slave mentality' that they had absorbed and inherited (*KB* 361).[42] The insidious consequences of colonialism were judged too great for the type of emancipation that O'Connell is said to have advanced. What is more, the memory of the Gaelic world was considered too seductive, and necessary, to simply relinquish. O'Connell, therefore, remains an essentially duplicitous figure in *King of the Beggars*, and 'his people' are represented continuing to equivocate and double-speak, as they strived (but failed) to reconcile the conflicting stances of apparent conformity and repressed scepticism, or outward acceptance and inner rebellion. O'Connell 'left an ineffaceable mark on the character of the Irish mind', O'Faoláin concluded, 'so that no man after him but has had to accept its duality as a basic fact' (*KB* 367). It is an uncertain legacy, to say the least. It is for this reason, though, that he is pictured as 'the great prototype of the Irish mind' in the near-contemporaneous study *De Valera*; it is also for this reason that he is boldly attributed the role of 'creator and first exemplar' of a collective way of thinking (*DV* 121).

NOTES

1. Seán Ó Tuama, 'Daniel Corkery, Cultural Philosopher, Literary Critic: A Memoir', in *Repossessions: Selected Essays on the Irish Literary Heritage* (Cork: Cork University Press, 1995), p.246.
2. Margo Griffin-Wilson, 'Dáibhidh (Dáibhí) Ó Bruadair', in McGuire and Quinn (eds), *The Royal Irish Academy's Dictionary of Irish Biography*, http://dib.cambridge.org/ (accessed 14 April 2014).
3. Daniel Corkery, *The Hidden Ireland: A Study of Gaelic Munster in the Eighteenth Century* (Dublin: M.H. Gill & Son, 1924), pp.89, 147–8, 151–2.
4. Sean O Faolain, 'The Language Problem 1: Is Irish Worth Reviving?', *The Irish Tribune* (9 July 1926), pp.20–1; Sean O Faolain, 'The Language Problem 2: Irish – An Empty Barrel?', *The Irish Tribune* (16 July 1926), pp.8–9; Sean O Faolain, 'What Does an Irish Speaking Ireland Imply?', *The Irish Tribune* (23 July 1926),

pp.9–10; Sean O Faolain, 'The Language Problem 4: Constructive', *The Irish Tribune* (30 July 1926), pp.13–5.

5. O Faolain, 'What Does an Irish Speaking Ireland Imply?', p.10.
6. O Faolain, 'Irish – An Empty Barrel?', pp.8–9. O'Faoláin continued to remain dismissive of eighteenth-century Munster Gaelic poetry, deriding the work of such poets as Aogán Ó Rathaille and Piaras Mac Gearailt as 'drivel by the yard' in his introduction to *The Silver Branch: A Collection of the Best Old Irish Lyrics, variously translated and chosen by Seán O'Faoláin* (London: Jonathan Cape, 1938), p.10.
7. Aodh de Blacam, 'Have we a literature?', *The Irish Tribune* (30 July 1926), pp.17–8.
8. Frank O'Connor, correspondence, *The Irish Tribune* (13 August 1926), p.23.
9. Daniel Corkery, 'Mediaeval Irish Poetry', *The Irish Tribune* (27 August 1926), p.22.
10. Sean O Faolain, 'The Spirit of the Nation', *The Irish Tribune* (23 July 1926), p.23.
11. Sean O'Faolain, review of *Synge and Anglo-Irish Literature* by Daniel Corkery, *The Criterion* 11: 42 (October 1931), pp.140–2.
12. O'Faolain, 'Daniel Corkery', p.58.
13. Daniel Corkery, *Synge and Anglo-Irish Literature* (Cork: Cork University Press, 1931), pp.16, 19–22.
14. O'Faolain, 'Daniel Corkery', pp.54–5.
15. Ibid., pp.53, 59.
16. Corkery, *The Hidden Ireland*, p.110.
17. O'Faolain, 'Daniel Corkery', pp.53, 59, 60.
18. Luke Gibbons, 'Challenging the Canon: Revisionism and Cultural Criticism', in Seamus Deane, Andrew Carpenter and Jonathan Williams (eds), *The Field Day Anthology of Irish Writing*, 3 vols. (Derry: Field Day, 1991), iii, p.562.
19. Frank O'Connor, 'The Gaelic Tradition in Literature: Part II', *Ireland To-Day* 1: 2 (July 1936), pp.31–2.
20. It is a point to which O'Faoláin would return. In the American edition of *The Irish*, for instance, a section is included with the suggestive title 'Invasion Inevitable'. This section was not included in the original Penguin edition; nor was it included in the revised and expanded Penguin edition, published in 1969, and reprinted several times thereafter. Sean O'Faolain, *The Irish: A Character Study* (New York: Devin-Adair, 1949), pp.74–8.
21. Seamus Deane, *Strange Country: Modernity and Nationhood in Irish Writing since 1790* (Oxford: Clarendon Press, 1997), p.192.
22. Samuel Madden, *Reflections and Resolutions Proper for the Gentlemen of Ireland, as to their Conduct for the Service of their Country, as Landlords, as Masters of their Families, as Protestants, as descended from British Ancestors, etc.* (Dublin, 1738), pp.67–8.
23. Corkery, *The Hidden Ireland*, pp.4–5.

24. 'It is as if man's adoration of the miraculous is attracted by the idea of a resurrection', O'Faoláin wrote a couple of years later. 'Or it may be that nothing is so safe to play with as something that is half-dead but not quite'. O'Faolain, *An Irish Journey*, p.145.
25. O'Faolain, 'Daniel Corkery', p.60.
26. Edward W. Said, *Orientalism* (London: Routledge & Kegan Paul, 1978), p.16 [emphasis as original]; Edward W. Said, *Beginnings: Intention and Method* (New York: Basic Books, 1975), p.50.
27. Michael Tierney, 'Politics and Culture: Daniel O'Connell and the Gaelic Past', *Studies: An Irish Quarterly Review* 27: 107 (September 1938), p.362.
28. Ibid., pp.363, 367; D.A. Binchy, 'Comments on the foregoing article', *Studies: An Irish Quarterly Review* 27: 107 (September 1938), pp.368–72; cf. Brown, *Ireland: A Social and Cultural History*, pp.157–8. For further analysis of the reception of *King of the Beggars*, see O'Leary, *Gaelic Prose in the Irish Free State*, pp.443–5.
29. Dunne, '*King of the Beggars*', p.30.
30. Gearóid Ó Tuathaigh, 'Daniel O'Connell', in McGuire and Quinn (eds), *The Royal Irish Academy's Dictionary of Irish Biography*, http://dib.cambridge.org/ (accessed 14 April 2014).
31. Robert Gittings, *The Nature of Biography* (London: Heinemann, 1978), p.85.
32. Backscheider, *Reflections on Biography*, p.3.
33. Donal McCartney, 'The Changing Image of O'Connell', in Kevin B. Nowlan and Maurice R. O'Connell (eds), *Daniel O'Connell: Portrait of a Radical* (Belfast: Appletree Press, in association with RTÉ, 1984), p.28.
34. Said, *Beginnings*, p.42.
35. R.V. Comerford, 'Daniel O'Connell', in *The Oxford Dictionary of National Biography*, http://www.oxforddnb.com/ (accessed 14 April 2014).
36. Patrick M. Geoghegan, '"An Unprincipled Libertine": The Private Life of Daniel O'Connell', in *King Dan: The Rise of Daniel O'Connell, 1775–1829* (Dublin: Gill & Macmillan, 2008), pp.179–86.
37. Barbara Caine, *Biography and History* (London: Palgrave Macmillan, 2010), pp.42–3.
38. O'Faoláin's restraint with respect to this subject is repeated elsewhere in *King of the Beggars*. In an earlier chapter, for instance, he remarks: 'As to [O'Connell's] private morals it would be unfair to drag them in here, and however saintly or however lecherous he may have been, they can hardly be of first relevance to the opinions of a man who held that they were matters of secondary importance. But here, I recognize, we are treading on very delicate ground' (*KB* 75–6). Delicate ground indeed, given that O'Faoláin was enjoying his own 'matters of importance' with Elizabeth Bowen around the time *King of the Beggars* was published.

39. W.B. Yeats, Seanad speech on Divorce, 11 June 1925, in Richard J. Finneran and George Mills Harper (gen. eds), *The Collected Works of W.B. Yeats*, 14 vols., Colton Johnson (ed.), *Vol. X: Later Articles and Reviews: Uncollected Articles, Reviews and Radio Broadcasts* (New York: Scribner, 2000), p.190.
40. Geoghegan, *King Dan*, p.57, the phrase is repeated on page 90; Patrick M. Geoghegan, *Liberator: The Life and Death of Daniel O'Connell, 1830–1847* (Dublin: Gill & Macmillan, 2010), p.52.
41. Homi K. Bhabha, *The Location of Culture* (London: Routledge, 1994), pp.93–101.
42. In the widely-read texts *Jail Journal* (1854) and *The Last Conquest of Ireland (Perhaps)* (1861), John Mitchel expressed the opinion that Britain was complicit in the Famine and that the British government deliberately used the Famine as an instrument of genocide. Mitchel's comments were influential for subsequent generations of nationalists and the Irish diaspora in North America especially. Traces can be detected in the thoughts of O'Faoláin's friend, Frank O'Connor, who similarly commented that '"Famine" is a useful word when you do not want to use words like 'genocide' or 'extermination''. Frank O'Connor, *The Backward Look: A Survey of Irish Literature* (London: Macmillan, 1967), p.133.

3

Iterations and Revisions: *De Valera*

Although only six years separate the publication of the two texts, O'Faoláin's *De Valera* (1939) provides neither a simple response to nor a straightforward reprisal of *The Life Story of Eamon De Valera*. The treatment of the central subject or 'hero' in both books is different, and the style employed contrasts significantly, as the melodrama of the first biography gives way to the clipped, measured prose of the second. Curiously, *De Valera* includes no allusion to the *Life Story*, and the title of the earlier study is erased from the later book's liner notes, with only two biographies included in the list of other texts 'by the same author', *Constance Markievicz* and *King of the Beggars*. This omission can be linked to O'Faoláin's unease with the first biography more generally. This unease seems to have begun almost before the first book was completed, with the closing chapter of the *Life Story* gesturing towards reservations and possible criticisms which had barely surfaced in the preceding pages of the biography, in particular de Valera's 'tendency to being "doctrinaire"' and his passion for 'very abstract formula' (*LS* 108). Within a few months, O'Faoláin was further considering these reservations and revising his opinion of his subject's 'vision of the Ireland he would create', a vision that might have seemed 'real and vital to Ireland' in the early 1930s but which appeared increasingly divorced from reality following de Valera's accession to power (*LS* 106, 107) What is more, within a year of publication O'Faoláin was distancing himself from the earlier biography, as any reference to the book was cut from his authorized back catalogue – no mention is made of it in the list of other publications by O'Faoláin in either *Constance Markievicz* or *A Nest of Simple Folk*, or in any text published thereafter. This process of dissociation culminated a decade later, in an editorial for *The Bell*, when O'Faoláin dismissed the entire content of the *Life Story* as 'arrant tripe' and 'utterly rubbishy'.[1]

Of course, O'Faoláin's decision not to mention the earlier biography might have been motivated by a desire to stress the originality of the later text. It is easy to imagine O'Faoláin regretting authorship of the first de Valera biography, not only because of its propensity for hyperbole and hagiography, but also, quite simply, because of the fact of the book's existence. By omitting reference to the *Life Story*, it is as if the author sought to disremember the earlier book and avoid the embarrassment of hero-worship. It is also as if he hoped to sidestep the need to distinguish between the two texts – the first published by the Irish-based Talbot Press, the second commissioned by the new, urbane publishing house Penguin Books, as part of a major series on 'Biography and Memoirs'. (Penguin was founded only a few years earlier, by Allen Lane, in 1935.) Avoiding reference to the *Life Story* also meant that O'Faoláin could escape the charge of having rehashed previously published material, and eschew the need to explain why the second book was being produced so soon after the first. The physical design of *De Valera* reinforces this sense of newness and originality, as the modish front cover, with its smart Penguin blue and white horizontal bands, its off-centred profile shot of de Valera, and its startling juxtaposition of modern typefaces, bears little comparison to the antiquated design of the earlier *Life Story*. Moreover, originality is promised in the publisher's message, which is emblazoned across the front cover in partial upper case and in an arresting mixture of black and blue sans serif type, that *De Valera* is 'A New Biography, Written specially for this series'.[2] Conversely, though, it could be argued that the very need to stress this biography's newness implicitly leads the reader back to the earlier text (why else mention it?), especially since other biographies in the series did not carry an equivalent caption.

The appearance of the author's name on the Penguin book further distinguishes *De Valera* from its excised antecedent. The author of the *Life Story*, it will be recalled, was ascribed an identifiably Gaelic name, 'Seán Ó Faoláin', on the spine and title page. This name is quasi-anglicized on the cover and spine of the second biography to read as an apostrophized and *fada*-less 'Sean O'Faolain'. This version of O'Faoláin's name also appears inside the dust jacket, in the publisher's blurb, and in the brief biography that is given of the author, as well as amongst the 'Latest Additions' to the Penguin catalogue listed on the book's back cover. It is not the only name *De Valera* bears, though, as the author's name is additionally presented in the preferred syncretic form, as a fusion of Irish and English-language elements (containing *fadas* and an apostrophe), on the flyleaf and title page, 'Seán O'Faoláin'. A further name is added to both pages, with the anglicized 'John Whelan' also included in round brackets and in smaller font size beneath 'Seán O'Faoláin'.

As Frank Shovlin has noted more generally, such confusion was to remain a persistent feature of O'Faoláin's publishing career, as editors, typesetters, reviewers and publishers struggled with the spelling of his name.[3] Many of O'Faoláin's British publishers, including Penguin, Constable and Rupert Hart-Davis, favoured the *fada*-less 'Sean O'Faolain', as did most British, Irish and American journals. Jonathan Cape, who published the majority of O'Faoláin's books during the 1930s, was the exception, and published under the author's favoured name 'Seán O'Faoláin', although Edward Garnett temporarily slipped between 'Seán O'Faoláin' and 'Sean O'Faoláin' in his acerbic introduction to *Midsummer Night Madness*. In America, the Viking Press was also attentive to the use of the *fada*, but occasionally added the birth name 'John Whelan' in parentheses on its title page (the American version of *Come Back to Erin* does this, for instance). Amidst this confusion of spelling, *De Valera* is uniquely complicated for including three different names – Sean O'Faolain, Seán O'Faoláin and John Whelan – in its prelims. This profusion of names might simply be attributed to poor proofreading on the part of the publishers. However, it can also be read to bear witness to O'Faoláin's own interests in the possibilities of self-fashioning, as it provides a strikingly graphic example of the author's cultivation of roles, and his tendency to take on different personas and masks – something Julia O'Faolain would later describe as her father's 'several selves'.[4]

The inclusion of the birth name on the flyleaf and title page anticipates a remark that is made in the main body of *De Valera*, where O'Faoláin alludes to the mystique that was sometimes created through the adoption of an Irish-language version of a name, and identifies a correlation between the gaeliciziaton of some names and the mythification of certain historical figures. Describing the bitter relationship which existed between the leading IRA men Cathal Brugha and Michael Collins, for instance, O'Faoláin interrupted his characterization of Brugha to comment in a caustic aside 'or to call him as all his friends did, Charlie Burgess, which helps to replace the "hero" by the man' (*DV* 54). This nominal deflation of Brugha supplies a key with which readers might retrospectively comprehend the slippage between names in *De Valera*'s prelims, as the equally euphonious 'Seán O'Faoláin' is translated into the more mundane, lower font-sized 'John Whelan'. It also provides a subtle reflection on the marketability of names, as multiple versions of O'Faoláin's name were used by the author and his publishers to sell the de Valera books to very different audiences – one discernibly nationalist, the other primarily British-based but with an international reach.

The brief synopsis of O'Faoláin's life, which is included in the dust jacket of *De Valera*, also pitches the book towards the latter type of audience. O'Faoláin's university education in Ireland and at Harvard is marked out for special mention, as is his four years' teaching in England, at Strawberry Hill, and both of these details are used to add weight to the image that O'Faoláin constructed for himself as an educated, cosmopolitan figure. The author's decision to return home to 'his native Ireland' is also noted, along with the prolific and varied shape of his writing career to date ('two books of stories, two novels, two biographies, a play'). That the book is directed towards a 'high-brow' readership is signalled by the casual reference to O'Faoláin's associations with 'all the well-known periodicals' (well-known, presumably, to a certain 'class' of reader), as well as the inclusion of a photograph of an earnest-looking young author at the back of the dust jacket. Brief attention is additionally drawn to O'Faoláin's involvement in the revolutionary period and his falling foul of the Censorship Board. Concerning the former point, the publishers pithily note that O'Faoláin abandoned his career as a commercial traveller 'to fight on the side of De Valera in 1921', and that he was a 'member of the Irish Republican Army for six years'. The chronology is slightly confusing here (O'Faoláin's six-year involvement in physical force nationalism began in late 1918 not 1921), and the claim is somewhat misleading (he first joined the Irish Volunteers not the IRA, and the 'six years' mentioned includes membership of both organizations). The point, though, is made to speak to O'Faoláin's republican credentials and thereby confirm his suitability as a biographer of de Valera.

Interestingly, it is a point O'Faoláin also felt the need to stress in the course of the biography, as he twice took pains to identify himself as 'a Republican then and now' and 'as a Republican anxious for a united Ireland' (*DV* 102, 158). O'Faoláin's self-identification with republicanism, with a capital 'R', is underlined by the occasional references in the text to his experiences of the revolutionary period, particularly the War of Independence: 'The brutalities and the secret murders for which the [British] Government was responsible' are mentioned without equivocation or hedging, for example, and imagined readers are taken to task if they seem to entertain 'any doubts about the existence of such a secret yet official "murder-gang"' sanctioned by British intelligence (*DV* 77). O'Faoláin's choice of words in such passages is unambiguous, and his descriptions of life during the period are pointed and direct. The unbearable suspense of living in a city under curfew is carefully reconstructed, as it is also imagined in several of the stories in *Midsummer Night Madness*, and the atrocities inflicted upon combatants and civilians are recorded in considerable detail. What is more, O'Faoláin's republican associations are advanced through his allusions to two recently-published texts, Dorothy Macardle's historical study *The Irish Republic* (1937) and Ernie O'Malley's IRA memoir *On Another Man's Wound* (1936). Macardle's text is especially significant in this respect, as it was conceived (in its own words) as 'an attempt to supply what has been too long lacking: an account of the Irish Republican struggle from the viewpoint of an Irish Republican', and reinforced O'Faoláin's preferred representation of the politics of the period.[5] Twice-described as an 'invaluable' guide in the second biography, Macardle's study has nonetheless also been read as a thinly-veiled apologia for de Valera, which did much to bolster a carefully cultivated image that de Valera himself liked to advance (*DV* 34, 60). Piaras Béaslaí, for instance, who had his own axes to grind, interpreted *The Irish Republic* as largely de Valera's own creation in the second edition of his authorized biography of Michael Collins (also published in 1937), warning future readers that they would only find 'just such an account of past controversial events' in the book 'as has met with the approval of Mr. de Valera'.[6] O'Faoláin avoids any such suggestion in *De Valera*.

Instead, a sustained attempt is made to stress the value of O'Faoláin's republican credentials and, more to the point, his associations with a certain strand of Irish republicanism which is closely linked to the figure of de Valera. However, the publisher's synopsis also highlights the importance of a competing self-image of O'Faoláin, as a nonconformist figure, pointing out that 'two of his books are banned in Eire' – *Midsummer Night Madness* and *Bird Alone*. This is reiterated in the blurb, which is included on the inside leaf of the book's dust jacket, where O'Faoláin's dissident capital provides a subtext to the marketing description of the biography: 'This frank, candid biography, written for this series by De Valera's famous countryman, reviews the whole eventful course of the great Irish leader's life. In a simple straight-forward account, more critical than romantic, he draws a tremendous picture of the drama of the Irish rebellion, its background and De Valera's part in it' (*DV* np). Alongside the publisher's stress on candour and critique, though, the blurb identifies tensions within the text which bring *De Valera* back to its original source. For if the argument of the book is judged 'more critical than romantic', this nonetheless implies that a residual romanticism disrupts the surface of the text; it also does not preclude an occasional idealization of de Valera ('the great Irish leader') from breaking through in a manner which is reminiscent of the mythopoeic style of the first biography. It is quite apt, therefore, that de Valera is suddenly described as 'the Fiery Cross of Irish Nationalism' in the publisher's blurb, even though this metaphor is at odds with the more conventional prosaic idiom that is otherwise deployed in the book's marketing pages. Crucially, this image is lifted from the prologue to the *Life Story*, where de Valera is eulogized by O'Faoláin in almost precisely the same terms as 'this stormy petrel, this Fiery Cross of Irish politics' (*LS* 11). The image is not recycled in the main body of *De Valera*.

Other images and passages are reprised, though, particularly regarding de Valera's physical appearance and his part in the Easter Rising. In some instances, these passages are reprinted almost verbatim and testify to the latent intertextual significance of the otherwise unmentioned *Life Story*. The alignment of de Valera with the shape of the nation's history is repeated, for instance, as is his physiognomical identification with 'his people's' suffering, with O'Faoláin again commenting that 'his face to-day is a palimpsest of his country's history for the last quarter of a century, every crisis has left more lines on his face' (*DV* 33). Previous references to *La Divina Commedia* are repeated, as it is said of de Valera, with respect to the Civil War, that he 'lived in those days through his Inferno. Like Dante he descended into Hell, and his face began to show the marks of his journey' (*DV* 105). Subtle and more obvious differences also indicate the evolution in O'Faoláin's thinking in the period between the publication of the two texts. A case in point is provided when one compares O'Faoláin's assessment of the Rising in the two biographies. 'It is now over sixteen years since that glorious Week,' the *Life Story* proclaims in an adjectivally rich and inflated register, 'and no disparager of the Irish cause has yet been able to besmirch the history of that gallant adventure, or detract from the bravery of those who took part in it. But if it was magnificent, it was terrible' (*LS* 39). The basic point is reiterated in *De Valera*, but the syntactical changes are revealing: 'It is now nearly twenty-five years since that Easter Week,' it is remarked in more muted tones, 'and nobody has yet been able to besmirch the history of a gallant adventure. It had its terrible side which has gone into literature with such masterpieces as the plays of Sean O'Casey' (*DV* 38).

Nowhere are the changes and iterations more marked than in O'Faoláin's account of de Valera's involvement in the Easter Rising. In the

Life Story, in a short section entitled 'Boland's Mills', a spectacular account is offered which depicts de Valera as one of the truly heroic figures of 1916, which is worth quoting in full:

> In action he proved himself a born organizer and soldier, cool and brave in every unexpected crisis or desperate situation. I have heard one of his men say that De Valera, hurrying to and fro among the barricades, or directing the firing from the tall windows of the mill, indifferent to the bullets thudding into the flourbags they used for defence, or ricocheting off the window-ledges, reminded him of Napoleon on the bridge at Lodi. His lieutenants had great difficulty in keeping him from performing every dangerous task himself. 'Be careful, Dev.,' one of them said. 'We can't afford to lose you.' 'There are better men that I being killed,' cried De Valera. And another time: 'Dev., remember we can't do without you! It's for you we're fighting!' 'It's for Ireland!' he replied angrily, and once more thrust his rifle into a loop-hole and fired, emptying and re-emptying his magazine until, when he did rest, they said there was powder on his lips, and the man who took his gun found the barrel almost red-hot. That is typical of De Valera – a man of little talk, he burns himself out in action (*LS* 27–8).

The use of clauses and sub-clauses, the dramatic deployment of active verbs and multiple commas, and the juxtaposition of longer descriptive sentences with short, snappy pieces of reported dialogue, addressed to the popularly familiar 'Dev.', cut short by the curtness of an exclamation mark or full stop – all of this combines to create a scene which is extraordinarily energetic and vivid. And the dramatic qualities of this passage are augmented by de Valera's supposed reference to the abstraction that is 'Ireland' as well as the strategically placed allusion to Napoleon at the 1796 Battle of Lodi. (The choice of battle is itself revealing, since Lodi played a decisive part in the cultivation of the myth of Napoleon as the chosen leader destined for great things. At Lodi, Napoleon secured a dramatic victory against great odds, and was nicknamed 'the Little Corporal' by his men in recognition of his leadership and courage.) Aspects of this scene are revisited in *De Valera*, but the earlier descriptions are refined, as the narrative is brought into line with O'Faoláin's more guarded ambitions for the later text:

> Legend inevitably gathers in later years, about such a man and such an incident as his defence of the Dublin road. One record says that his men had difficulty in keeping him from performing every dangerous task himself. Seeing him hurry to and fro between the barricades, directing the firing from the tall windows of the mill, indifferent to the bullets thudding into the flourbags used for defence, or ricocheting off the ledges, one of his men warned him that he was more important than anybody else in the place. 'There are better men than myself being killed,' cried De Valera, and took his place at a loop-hole, emptying and re-emptying the magazine until, when he did rest, the record says that the barrel was 'red-hot'. Apocryphal or an actual fact, it is at least symbolic – the man burns himself out in action (*DV* 32–3).

O'Faoláin notably distances himself from his source in his second account of the fighting at Boland's Mills. In the *Life Story* the source is identified as an unnamed member of de Valera's 3rd Dublin Battalion who personally participated in the incident and passed the information on to the author. In *De Valera* the material is attributed to an impersonal 'record' which, although quoted, is treated with a measure of circumspection and denied the authoritative status of the earlier eyewitness account: the text tellingly suggests, for instance, that the source is both 'one record' and 'the record'. Details in the second account are substantially condensed, with reported conversations pruned and references to the heroic (Napoleon) and the familiar (Dev.) cut. At the same time, de Valera is unexpectedly brought closer to his comrades in the latter account, as the subaltern 'lieutenants' with whom he interacts are replaced by an unranked body of 'men' who remain devoted. What is more, although some of the descriptions of the fighting are repeated virtually verbatim in the second account (hurrying between barricades, bullets thudding and ricocheting, the emptying and re-emptying of magazines), the context of these descriptions is subtly altered, with the climactic image of de Valera's 'red-hot' gun tellingly placed in inverted commas. Obvious clues are also supplied to assist the reader in the intended interpretation of the second passage, as the entire scene is framed by two words – 'legend' and 'apocryphal' – which cast doubt on the episode's basis in 'actual fact'.

It is important, then, that O'Faoláin chose the word 'symbolic' to describe the lasting importance of the story in the latter account. For the word 'symbol', along with its variants 'symbolic', 'symbolism', 'symbolically', 'symbolized', is the keyword in *De Valera,* and is used at least three dozen times to allude to the source of de Valera's power as well as to indicate a critical preoccupation of modern republican thinking. (The symbolic value of the Rising is considered in the text, for instance, as is the symbolic importance attached to the revolutionary Dáil, the Oath of Allegiance, and the idea of the Republic.) Because de Valera was the only commandant to survive 1916, he was afforded unmatched levels of veneration and respect in the years after the Rising, and was often represented – and chose to represent himself – as an embodiment of the national struggle in the period that followed. According to O'Faoláin, this 'was to prove his greatest asset as a national leader' and 'is the true secret of his power today' (*DV* 63, 60). As Ronan Fanning has since argued, this symbolic credit meant that what de Valera actually 'did in the Rising mattered little when set against the iconic stature he acquired in its aftermath'.[7] His political reputation soared, for instance, because of his associations with the so-called 'Irish Thermopylae' that was the battle at Mount Street Bridge. That de Valera took no part in this celebrated, brutal episode of the Rising was less important than that it happened under his command.

For all de Valera's subsequent divisiveness as a political figure, this symbolic credit largely survived the fall-out over the Treaty negotiations and the bitterness of the Civil War. Indeed, as Charles Townshend has remarked in his comprehensive account of the Rising, although the nature of de Valera's career in the 1920s 'made it likely that his performance [during Easter Week] would be controversial. In fact, criticism was surprisingly muted until the 1960s'.[8] When that criticism eventually came – initially in eyewitness accounts included in Max Caulfield's detailed recreation *The Easter Rebellion* (1964), and in the conflicting memories of some of the surviving members of de Valera's battalion, notably two volunteers Sam Irwin and Simon Donnelly – much was made of the claim that de Valera behaved erratically throughout the week, and that many of his orders were indecisive and his behaviour showed signs of extreme agitation and hyperactivity.[9] Although this claim did not become generally public until the mid-1960s, it is possible to read aspects of its central charge in O'Faoláin's frenetic representations of the fighting at Boland's Mills in both of the de Valera biographies. For in both accounts de Valera seems to be everywhere, in the thick of everything, as his men are twice reported to have had 'difficulty' ('great difficulty' in the first account) 'in keeping him from performing every dangerous task himself', and he is twice said to have 'burn[ed] himself out in action'.

That is to say, de Valera's recorded bravery in both texts might as easily be read as the actions of a man under extreme strain – someone 'on, or over, the threshold of nervous breakdown' as has been memorably remarked – and the energy that characterizes both passages might be considered evidence of this.[10] It is surely significant in this respect that one of the excisions made in O'Faoláin's second, more critical account is the seemingly objective, unattributed statement that precedes the eyewitness report in the *Life Story*, that throughout Easter Week de Valera 'proved himself a born organizer and soldier, cool and brave in every unexpected crisis or desperate situation'. For this comment explicitly rebuffs the subsequent charges of nervousness, indecision and hyperactivity. However, it is also revealing that in neither instance did O'Faoláin choose to relate the signs of de Valera's stress to the simple fact that he was an ordinary man who suddenly found himself caught in an appalling situation. Little mention is made of de Valera's military inexperience in either account, for example, or the pressures that must have resulted from this, and no mention is made of the fact that this inexperience was shared by almost all of the leaders of the Rising.[11] In addition, little attention is given to other, more personal forms of bravery that de Valera did demonstrate throughout Easter Week and its aftermath, as he took part in the rebellion fully aware of the dangers involved and is known to have been fearful of the consequences for his wife and young family. (A loving letter to Sinéad de Valera, written in Lewes Jail in Easter 1917, and included in Tim Pat Coogan's otherwise critical biography, provides poignant testimony to de Valera's 'high and rare form of courage' in this regard.[12]) The latter omission is especially notable in O'Faoláin's two biographies, given that the expressed aim of both texts was to demystify de Valera and reveal something of 'the man' behind the myth.

Much is made of de Valera's involvement in the Easter Rising, his subsequent terms of imprisonment, and his eighteen months in America from mid-1919 to late 1920 in the second biography. By contrast, de Valera's part in, or rather, his self-imposed abstention from the Anglo-Irish Treaty negotiations at the end of the War of Independence receives the scantest of attention: 'First it must be noted that De Valera did not go as a Delegate, and that Arthur Griffith took his place as head of the Delegation', it is brusquely stated. 'Subsequently much discussion took place with regard to the powers of these delegates, and De Valera was much blamed for not leading them himself. To that discussion there is no end' (*DV* 85). More to the point, there is little start in *De Valera*, as O'Faoláin avoided any serious engagement with what was has often been considered the most controversial decision of his subject's life. De Valera's decision not to go to London as head of the Irish plenipotentiaries, to give the delegates their correct title, has frequently led to claims that he knowingly shirked the responsibilities of leadership. It has also led to accusations that, at the very least, he grossly miscalculated the pressures that the Irish plenipotentiaries faced in London, and, at worst, he deliberately manipulated members of the Irish negotiating team, most notably Griffith and Collins, to play the part of fallguys in the acceptance of an inevitable compromise. As Patrick Murray has demonstrated, the many explanations de Valera subsequently gave to retrospectively account for his absence from the Treaty negotiations suggests that he himself 'felt that he had a serious case to answer' on the subject.[13] O'Faoláin largely evaded discussion of this topic in *De Valera*, and also sought to minimize de Valera's part in determining the dimensions and the scale of the ensuing Civil War.

Reflecting on de Valera's manoeuvrings over the taking of the Oath of Allegiance in the mid-1920s, for instance, O'Faoláin rejected outright the idea that had de Valera accepted the oath in 1922 the Civil War would have been avoided: '(The only comment necessary there is that though he may have thereby made it more easy for the IRA to start the war, they would, it is safe to believe, have started it without him)' (*DV* 119). This thesis is consistent with the earlier argument of the *Life Story*, which also claimed that de Valera was largely ignored by the more militant opponents of the Treaty, and that he was reduced to a position of powerlessness and increasing irrelevance for the duration of the Civil War. 'Not until the soldiers began to realize that the game was up,' O'Faoláin maintained, 'did they think about him, or turn to him, and then they turned to him only to give the task of announcing defeat' (*DV* 105–6). It is an argument that was re-articulated by the Earl of Longford (Francis Pakenham) and Thomas P. O'Neill many years later, in their authorized biography of de Valera.[14]

If other historians have since concurred with the general outline of this thesis, however, some have questioned its finer details, including its downgrading of the political weight afforded to anti-Treaty republicans by de Valera's denunciation of the oath and opposition to the Treaty. (The equivocal modal verb in the clause 'he *may* have thereby made it more easy', hints at de Valera's influence over republicans in the period prior to the outbreak of the Civil War.) This is all the more striking given O'Faoláin's stress on de Valera's symbolic value throughout the text, along with his frequent representation of de Valera as the self-fashioned conscience of the nation, where it is remarked that 'the great secret of this man's power in his own country is his power to represent Ireland symbolically to his people' (*DV* 147). Of equal concern is the high-handed manner in which O'Faoláin's judgement is exerted in the above passage, for it seems reductive to claim that only one comment can ever be sufficient, or 'necessary', to make sense of a conflict like the Civil War, and it seems equally odd to place such a comment in brackets, as if it should be treated parenthetically, as a digression or mere afterthought.

Within months of the end of the fighting, P.S. O'Hegarty clearly suggested otherwise, arguing in his polemic *The Victory of Sinn Féin* (1924) that had it not been for de Valera's 'encouragement to the wreckers' (by which he meant anti-Treaty militants), opposition to the Treaty would have been nominal:

> For all the bloodshed and suffering which followed, he must be held responsible. That there would be growls and objections against any Treaty which did not give Ireland complete independence was certain; but it was also certain that it was the moral support and prestige which he gave to it which created the Anti-Treaty movement, and which was responsible for a large number of people who went Anti-Treaty.[15]

O'Faoláin clearly did not subscribe to such a thesis in *De Valera*. However, he did refine the adulation of the earlier *Life Story* to the extent that references to de Valera as a natural 'Mediator', or relentless peace-maker, are quietly removed. O'Faoláin's subject instead appears a far more complicated, calculating figure in the second biography. Much attention is given to his 'non-committal, semi-theological, discriminating mind,' for instance, as well as 'his capacity of discrimination (what his enemies have called hair-splitting)', and double-edged compliments are paid to de Valera's 'earnest assertion of his own honesty', with questions asked as to whether he has done enough to justify the 'trust' of the electorate since his election to office (*DV* 49, 50, 129). In addition, care is taken to explain what is meant by the description of de Valera's remarkable 'power of self-dissociation – i.e. of dissociating one's self from all responsibility for mental reservations; or, indeed, a power of dissociating one's self by means of mental reservations from the responsibility of what one is actually doing' (*DV* 68–9). Each of these attributes feeds into the general characterization of de Valera as a wily politician, or someone who is difficult to identify with, like, or understand. They find collective focus when O'Faoláin represents the choreography surrounding the taking, or not taking, of the Oath of Allegiance in 1927. According to O'Faoláin, this was the critical decision in his subject's political life and it was 'from this on one's admiration for the man increases', as he transformed Fianna Fáil from being a peripheral abstentionist party to a participant in mainstream constitutional politics (*DV* 118).

'Here he stops being the lecturer and becomes the leader in the best sense – the first in the gap whom others will imitate' (*DV* 118). *De Valera* is largely supportive of its subject's decision to take the oath and enter the Dáil, reading it as an example of his unique political 'courage'; in the *Life Story*, this praise was amplified, as it is taken to indicate his 'immense moral courage' (*LS* 104). However, this support is qualified by criticism of the manner in which de Valera took, or claimed not to take, the oath that he had long objected to. His attempts to sugar this pill and argue that it was merely 'an empty formula' are dismissed as 'righteous self-belief' such as to 'make one squirm', for instance, with O'Faoláin angered by the pretence that allowed his subject to claim that there had been no change in position despite the volte-face in policy (*DV* 123). 'The fiddling business of pretending that he was an angel out of heaven who never did, and could never do, wrong. One may imagine how Daniel O'Connell or Michael Collins would have faced such a situation, and come out of it, if not as angels, certainly as men' (*DV* 124). The casual gendered inflection here is as unexpected as it is telling (for when O'Faoláin says 'men' he means *men*); and the references to O'Connell and Collins are illustrative of a recurring comparison which is a structural feature of the second de Valera biography. Of particular interest to O'Faoláin, though, is the accusation that de Valera obscured the reality that he faced by talking around the subject of the oath, spinning the issue through strategies of discrimination (or 'hair-splitting') to mask the compromise that was being made. O'Faoláin is critical of this fudge in *De Valera*, but stops short of suggesting that his subject acted untruthfully as a result.

Intriguingly, this very claim had been made a few years earlier, in O'Faoláin's biography of Constance Markievicz, when he characterized de Valera's actions over the taking of the oath as 'a highly ingenious tergiversation', only to add the proviso 'that its authors will ever be able to clear themselves of the charge of common dishonesty is very doubtful' (*CM* 304).[16] At no point is de Valera's integrity questioned in this way in *De Valera*. Instead, the ability to 'tergiversate' is treated in two interrelated ways, as it is associated with de Valera specifically while also being considered more generally as an aspect of the so-called 'national genius' or collective 'Irish mind'. On the one hand, this tendency to prevaricate is considered a consequence of de Valera's peculiarly 'metaphysical brain' or 'theological turn of mind', and is explained biographically through references to his chosen profession as a mathematics teacher as well as his passion for small details and abstract formulas (*DV* 117, 68). This pedantic nature is said to set de Valera apart from his contemporaries and 'keep him so very lonely – so cut off from all that is casual, and idle, and of the common, warm run of life' (*DV* 55). Conversely, though, this tendency is also used to link de Valera to the rest of the populace, and more specifically to that vaguely defined entity that he and his fellow citizens share, and supposedly embody, 'the Irish mind'.

This term – 'the Irish mind' – is used freely throughout *De Valera*, as it was also deployed, albeit less regularly, in *King of the Beggars*, but O'Faoláin notably avoids any explanation of what it might signify, half-jocularly remarking that this would be impossible given that 'the Irish mind is as labyrinthine as the caverns of Minos' (*DV* 121). The one thing that is clear is that it is associated with a facility for equivocation and shiftiness, for when O'Faoláin is not discussing 'the scholastic turn of the Irish mind,' with its 'magnificent indifference to every single fact', he is alluding to the 'ingenious subtlety of the Irish mind' which is supposedly able to negotiate life's complexities with 'the greatest finesse' (*DV* 116, 123). 'I do not think any Irishman can afford to blame De Valera', it is alleged. 'It is precisely the mentality of Dan O'Connell, the first native Irish leader. It is rooted in the national genius, which adores reservations, loop-holes, wordy discrimination, postulation, conjecture, surmise, hypothesis, academic supposition – anything on earth and under heaven except a clear statement of simple fact or intent' (*DV* 69-70). It is hard to overlook the patronizing basis of such claims, as they breathe life into the tired image of the loquacious, fact-defying, stage Irishman, and carry traces of an associated litany of well-worn clichés and types. This resuscitation of jaded stereotypes was not O'Faoláin's aim, though, as he was more concerned with deflecting responsibility for equivocation over the oath away from de Valera specifically, and considering it more generally as an example of a national trait or collective characteristic. For O'Faoláin, this trait was rooted in a history of colonization and subservience, and was a defining aspect of the mentality of those disfranchised 'helots' that O'Connell had come to represent – and that O'Faoláin had explored at length – in *King of the Beggars*.

A further instance of de Valera's capacity to postulate is included late in the Penguin biography, when O'Faoláin was drawn to comment on the recently-enacted Irish Constitution, *Bunreacht na hÉireann* (1937). It is well known that de Valera kept a tight rein over the drafting of the text of the constitution, personally writing some of the articles that were deemed especially sensitive. De Valera also oversaw the framing of the rest of the document by a small committee of hand-picked senior civil servants who reported directly to him, with additional input from a few senior figures of the Church. The resulting text provided a blueprint for the state, enshrining the rights of the individual citizen while curtailing some of those rights in significant ways, as well as stabilizing changes that had occurred across Irish society over the preceding fifteen years of independence. It is a remarkable achievement, especially given the volatility of the international context in which it was drafted and passed into law. 'Every biographer of the man must pause before it,' O'Faoláin reflected less than eighteen months later, and applaud it for having defined the principles of Irish sovereignty, thereby 'put[ting] a seal upon the prolonged struggle of De Valera for the independence of Ireland' (*DV* 146). Applause was at best half-hearted, however, as O'Faoláin simultaneously noted that the constitution was not met with great enthusiasm by the Irish electorate when they voted on it, and many against it, in the summer of 1937.[17] Nor was O'Faoláin especially excited by the text, as he criticized its unimaginative and overly conservative ethos, and in particular its tendency to endlessly qualify statements and interject attenuating clauses and unnecessary interpretations. 'It is pedantic and circumscribed,' he complained. 'It states no fine general truth that it does not immediately qualify with so much care that the force of the original statement is lost and made to seem puny' (*DV* 147). This was linked to de Valera's earlier vocation in the classroom, and used to reinforce the description of him as a man 'fated to "educate"', or 'less a leader than a teacher' (*DV* 53, 54). According to O'Faoláin, this accounted for his subject's 'fatal tendency' to always proceed with the greatest caution – a habit which exasperated his contemporaries, and meant that the radical potential of the constitution was reduced to 'a series of pious aspirations', or 'a theologian's distinction rather than a statesman's assertion' (*DV* 150, 148).

O'Faoláin's criticism of the constitution was not just a response to its meticulous syntactical discriminations, however. More importantly, it was directed against some of the restrictive clauses contained within the text, and in particular those articles that infringed upon basic rights, most notably the provisions 'which endeavoured to protect, or interfere with (according to one's reading of the intention) the rights of women' (*DV* 150). Combined with recent changes in the Conditions of Employment Act (1936), these articles were designed to confine women to the domestic sphere or to limited types of work in the public place. As Yvonne Scannell has observed, such restrictions were 'rooted in a patronising and stereotyped view of womanhood' that was shared by, but not exclusive to, de Valera, and was representative of the opinions of a chauvinistic society that was extremely hostile to the employment prospects of women, particularly married women outside the home.[18] De Valera's provisions gave constitutional support to this prejudice, O'Faoláin noted, and spoke of an inability, or an unwillingness, to appreciate the contributions that women made across many different sectors of Irish life. O'Faoláin also indicated that the inclusion of these provisions should be attributed in no small part to 'De Valera's well-known, rather old-fashioned, ideas about the place of women in society' (*DV* 150).

In the *Life Story,* an incidental comment was included to the effect that de Valera 'is nothing of a feminist'; this comment was left hanging in that text, and no attempt was made to substantiate the charge or relate it to the larger narrative (*LS* 107). In *De Valera* the charge resurfaced but was given greater prominence, as it provided O'Faoláin with the opportunity to reflect upon patriarchal relations and the restriction of rights more generally in de Valera's Ireland. O'Faoláin's comments chime with the concerns of many contemporary feminists who protested against the provisions in the constitution and the legislation of gendered inequality. As Margaret Ward has shown, feminists of different shades were 'unanimous in denouncing the omission of any statement regarding women's equal rights and opportunities' in the constitution, and interpreted this omission as 'sinister and retrogressive'.[19] The popular right-wing columnist Gertrude Gaffney remarked in the *Irish Independent*, for instance (a newspaper with little sympathy for Fianna Fáil or de Valera), that de Valera 'has always been a reactionary where women were concerned. He dislikes and distrusts us as a sex, and his aim ever since he came into office has been to put us in what he considers is our place, and keep us there'.[20] At the far end of the political spectrum, Maud Gonne commented that 'if, when Ireland is free,' following a future reunification of the island, 'a more detailed Constitution were needed, the Articles concerning women … would damn [de Valera's text] in my eyes'.[21] Criticism also came from closer to home, with Dorothy Macardle privately censuring de Valera for a perceived betrayal of republican ideals. 'As the Constitution stands.' she wrote, 'I do not see how anyone holding advanced views on the rights of women can support it, and that is a tragic dilemma for those who have been loyal and ardent workers in the national cause'.[22]

O'Faoláin's objections ran along similar lines, as he noted the inconsistencies with republican thinking and the constitution's ignorance of the many reasons why so many women in Ireland worked, wanted to work, or needed to work, outside the home. His comments, though brief, were progressive, and were in accordance with his liberalist agenda. They were also aligned with his representation of various female figures in the short-story collection *A Purse of Coppers*, including the former revolutionary Sally Dunn, the ostracized Kitty Canavan, and the bewildered Helen Black, in 'A Meeting', 'Kitty the Wren' and 'There's a Birdie in the Cage', respectively. Any claim for O'Faoláin's progressive gender politics is complicated, however. In the only feminist appraisal of O'Faoláin's work to date, Evelyn Conlon commented that although 'some of O Faoláin's concerns were exactly those of the Irish Feminist Movement,' he nonetheless 'stop[ped] short of holding up the mirror to the domineering paternalism of Ireland'. 'He was certainly the most enlightened of his generation,' Conlon conceded, 'an encourager' of contemporary feminists and a spokesperson for civil liberties, 'but who, in that role, could not have been aware of the chasmic silence of Irish Women?'[23] From such a perspective, the modifying adverb in the above quotation – concerning de Valera's '*rather* old-fashioned ideas about the place of women' – softens the edge of O'Faoláin's complaint, and suggests a degree of complicity in the discourse that is under scrutiny.

In a number of ways *De Valera* is presented as critical of its subject, and writes back to the tailored eulogies which characterized the earlier *The Life Story of Eamon De Valera*. This criticism is qualified, however, and is never as simple as O'Faoláin pretended or as is often supposed. It is noteworthy, for instance, that the later text frequently repeats arguments that were first articulated in the *Life Story*, implying that O'Faoláin's opinion of de Valera, at least as far as the late 1930s, was complex and not always unfavourable. At the same time, his criticism of de Valera intensified as the years passed, as policies pursued by successive Fianna Fáil governments proved increasingly anathema to O'Faoláin and those closely associated with *The Bell*. 'We are in many respects a despotism disguised as a democracy,' he wrote a few years later, in an extended article on the long-serving politician he had once celebrated as a natural leader and born 'Mediator' (*LS* 56).[24] By this time, the mid-1940s, de Valera had been reconceived as 'the Great Splitter' in Irish society, 'the man who split Sinn Féin, split the IRA, split Cumann na mBan, split Clan na Gael, double-split Sinn Féin, double-split the IRA, split the whole country, and spends the rest of his time splitting words'.[25] In addition, though, O'Faoláin's equivocal attitude to de Valera points to the quizzical nature of the life stories more generally, and to the fact that they seldom present a straightforward, 'factual' prose narrative for all their claims to the contrary. Over and again, these texts express frustration with their intended subjects, implying that something always remains unknown or hidden from view – the Sphinx-like descriptions of O'Connell and de Valera are illustrative of this. O'Faoláin's contemporaneous comment in *The Criterion*, that biographies respond to the need for a 'fundamental reality', should be treated with a measure of circumspection, therefore.

Indeed, his observation in the same essay that they are expressive of 'one kind of search for truth' seems closer to the point, since 'one kind' implies that other narratives – or 'truths' – might also be required.[26]

NOTES

1. O'Faolain, 'Principles and Propaganda', pp.190, 197.
2. The cover follows the standard Penguin design for biographies in this respect; its inclusion of a photograph, though, is slightly unusual for the late 1930s. Phil Baines, *Penguin by Design: A Cover Story, 1935–2005* (London: Allen Lane, 2005), p.13.
3. Shovlin, 'The Struggle for Form', p.162.
4. Julia O'Faolain, 'Afterword' to O'Faoláin, *Vive Moi!*, revised edition, p.vii.
5. Dorothy Macardle, *The Irish Republic: A documented chronicle of the Anglo-Irish conflict and the partition of Ireland, with a detailed account of the period 1916–1923, with a preface by Éamon de Valéra* (London: Victor Gollancz, 1937), p.23. O'Faoláin had produced a favourable but quibbling review of O'Malley's memoir a few years earlier. See 'Guerilla', review of *On Another Man's Wound* by Ernie O'Malley, *Ireland To-Day* 1: 5 (October 1936), pp.67–8.
6. Piaras Béaslaí, *Michael Collins: Soldier and Statesman* (Dublin: Talbot Press, 1937), p.ix. Béaslaí was a close supporter of Michael Collins and wrote a family-approved biography of the revolutionary leader in 1926, *Michael Collins and the Making of a New Ireland*; this was revised and expanded as a second edition in 1937. As the late Peter Hart recently commented, Béaslaí 'appointed himself guardian of [Collins's] memory' in the early decades of the Free State, and both biographies provide 'a sort of origin myth and apologia for the new Irish regime'. Peter Hart, *Mick: The Real Michael Collins* (London: Macmillan, 2005), pp.xv–i.
7. Ronan Fanning, 'Éamon de Valera ("Dev")', in McGuire and Quinn (eds), *The Royal Irish Academy's Dictionary of Irish Biography*, http://dib.cambridge.org/ (accessed 15 April 2014).
8. Charles Townshend, *Easter 1916: The Irish Rebellion* (London: Allen Lane, 2005), p.199.
9. Max Caulfield, *The Easter Rebellion* (London: Muller, 1964).
10. Coogan, *De Valera*, p.69.
11. Townshend, *Easter 1916*, p.201; Ferriter, *Judging Dev*, pp.26–7.
12. Coogan, *De Valera*, p.72.
13. Patrick Murray, 'Obsessive Historian: Eamon de Valera and the Policing of His Reputation', *Proceedings of the Royal Irish Academy* 101C: 2 (2001), p.50.

14. Longford and O'Neill, *Eamon de Valera*, pp.195–223.
15. P.S. O'Hegarty, *The Victory of Sinn Féin: How it won it, and how it used it* (Dublin: Talbot Press, 1924), p.72.
16. This charge was further qualified in the mid-1960s, when O'Faoláin produced a revised edition of *Constance Markievicz* and deleted 'very' from the text so that the passage was instead left to read 'the charge of common dishonesty is doubtful'. O'Faolain, *Constance Markievicz*, revised edition, p.207.
17. 686,042 people voted in favour of the Constitution; 528,296 voted against.
18. Yvonne Scannell, 'The Constitution and the Role of Women', in Brian Farrell (ed.), *De Valera's Constitution and Ours* (Dublin: Gill & Macmillan, in association with RTÉ, 1988), p.134; see also Mary E. Daly, *Women and Work in Ireland* (Dundalk: Dundalgan Press/The Economic and Social History Society of Ireland, 1997), p.49. For a detailed exploration of the different types of work carried out by Irish women during this period, see Caitriona Clear, 'Women in de Valera's Ireland, 1932–48: a reappraisal', in Doherty and Keogh (eds), *De Valera's Irelands*, p.114.
19. Ward, *Unmanageable Revolutionaries*, p.239. Many historians have concurred with this assessment; however, Joseph Lee has added a notion of caution, commenting that 'De Valera's image of woman was widely cherished in Ireland, not least by women themselves'. If Lee's argument is impossibly homogenous (which 'women'?), his point is supported by comments from some contemporary feminists, including Helena Moloney. J.J. Lee, *Ireland 1912-1985: Politics and Society* (Cambridge: Cambridge University Press, 1989), pp.206–8.
20. Gertrude Gaffney, 'A Woman's View of the Constitution', *Irish Independent* (7 May 1937); qtd. in Pauric Travers, *Eamon de Valera* (Dundalk: Dundalgan Press/ Historical Association of Ireland, 1994), pp.40–1.
21. Maud Gonne, *Prison Bars* (July 1937); qtd. in Ward, *Unmanageable Revolutionaries*, p.243.
22. Dorothy Macardle, letter to Éamon de Valera (21 May 1937); qtd. in Nadia Clare Smith, *Dorothy Macardle: A Life* (Dublin: The Woodfield Press, 2007), p.84.
23. Conlon, 'A Flawed Portrayal', p.74. Conlon's criticism focuses on the representation of female characters in some of O'Faoláin's short stories; however, her argument also holds good for his non-fiction.
24. O'Faolain, 'Eamon De Valera', p.18.
25. Ibid., p.2.
26. O'Faolain, 'It No Longer Matters', pp.51–2.

PART II

FICTION

Literature Revivified?

'Irish prose literature has hardly yet as much as begun,' but 'in what has been accomplished we may observe two main divisions,' that which was written 'pre-1916 and post-1916'.[1] O'Faoláin's confidence in 'The Emancipation of Irish Writers' (1934) might seem misplaced to a reader in the twenty-first century, given what is now known about the history of prose fiction in Ireland. Recent scholars such as Rolf and Magda Loeber, for instance, and those associated with the 'Early Irish Fiction' research network, have unearthed a wealth of prose narratives stretching back as far as the mid-seventeenth century, constituting a tradition that is vibrant, varied and extensive.[2] Writing in the 1930s O'Faoláin thought otherwise, and in many respects his comments are representative of a critical commonplace of that time – with the novel considered a relatively recent practice in Ireland, particularly when set against the more established forms of poetry and non-fiction. It is not only that prose fiction was seen as a recent literary development, with the Irish Revival of the late-nineteenth and early-twentieth centuries principally associated with poetry and drama in the popular imagination. As John Wilson Foster has shown, such thinking was only possible by neglecting the many fictional texts that were produced, in different genres, to different audiences – 'popular' and 'highbrow'; traditional and avant-garde; romantic, sensationalist and politically-minded – during this period.[3] O'Faoláin was careful to qualify the above statement, acknowledging that his categorization of Irish fiction 'may be completely altered by the light subsequent developments throw on what we are doing'. He also partly anticipated Foster, alluding to some novelists of the Revival in his enumeration of pre-1916 fiction: Canon Sheehan, Katherine Tynan, Edith Somerville, George Moore, Gerald O'Donovan, Seumas O'Kelly, James Joyce, James Stephens and Daniel Corkery were the writers mentioned.[4]

O'Faoláin's choice of writers is remarkable for many reasons, not least its grouping together of dissimilar artists and its concentration on a recent period in Irish cultural history. This was not simply attributable to ignorance on O'Faoláin's part, since he was obviously aware of the differences between the writers listed while also being familiar with canonical figures of the eighteenth and, in particular, the nineteenth centuries. It is more likely that earlier figures were omitted because of a belief that they did not comprise a coherent tradition, as O'Faoláin elsewhere recorded that 'there has never been any literary doctrine for Irish prose, as there was for Irish verse'.[5] More immediately, his choice was founded upon a desire to stress a specific generational divide in Irish writing, and to suppose a distinction between writers (and not only novelists) who came to prominence in the pre- and the post-revolutionary years, with the former group associated with a degree of enthusiasm and purpose and the latter generation characterized by disillusionment and uncertainty. Talking up the merits of his peers at the expense of his predecessors (with Joyce obviously problematizing such attempts at neat periodization), O'Faoláin argued that 'it is patent that this modern dissatisfaction is roused by the work of such writers as [Sean] O'Casey, [Liam] O'Flaherty, [Brinsley] MacNamara, [Peadar] O'Donnell, [Austin] Clarke, [Eimar] O'Duffy, Frank O'Connor, and myself, who have touched the national consciousness on the raw'. Post-revolutionary writers were accordingly credited with producing a 'full and sincere' body of work, and 'fac[ing] certain sides of Irish life which the public declined to face'. This was deemed an affront to the policies of censors and exclusivist critics (Corkery was cited as a typical example) who thought that literature should be dictated by politics, sentiment or acts of obeisance. 'We are at the beginnings of a prose literature,' he concluded, 'and we must establish moulds of our own'.[6]

A series of essays published in magazines and journals, in Britain and the United States throughout the 1930s and early 1940s, provided an attempt to establish such moulds. Some of these essays focused specifically upon the terrain of Irish writing; others were broader in scope and engaged with the practice of prose fiction in an international context. A recurring concern was the legacy of naturalism and its representation of the wholly determined individual. 'Those of us who are dissatisfied with the heritage of Naturalism,' O'Faoláin wrote in *The London Mercury*, 'with its inherent pessimism, its destructivism, its distaste for what it handles, its bitterness, its aimless objectivity, its accurate descriptions of insignificant detail, have but few alternatives'.[7] Like many other commentators, O'Faoláin's thinking on naturalism was indebted to the work of Émile Zola, and the idea of the writer as an objective, detached scientist, whose responsibility was to present accurate portrayals of contemporary life, cutting through codes of politeness and respectability to reveal the 'inner realities' of human behaviour and the social order. Those realities were fundamentally determinist, and aligned with naturalism's Darwinian interest in the laws of heredity, evolution and the forces that curtail, or shape, human action and the social environment. By understanding these forces, Zola believed, conditions might be improved, particularly for the destitute and the working class, and this fed into the political impulse which animated many French, Scandinavian and Russian naturalists in the mid to late nineteenth century. As Joe Cleary has noted, however, such beliefs also constituted a 'fundamental problematic' for naturalists, as they tried to reconcile 'deterministic and reformist sensibilities', and attempted 'to conceive of meaningful human agency in a world where action and understanding, comprehension of the forces that shape society and meaningful intervention into society, are always perceived to thwart and compromise each other'.[8] This problematic provided part of O'Faoláin's dissatisfaction with the naturalist legacy in the 1930s.

Naturalism originated in 'a reaction against romanticism', O'Faoláin wrote in 'The Modern Novel: A Catholic Point of View' (1935), and advanced images of a diseased and brutalizing society, indifferent to the needs of its subjects. Its aesthetic was grounded in an 'approach to human behaviour [that] was almost wholly materialist and sceptical', and imagined the individual as a passive victim of larger forces, suggesting that the potential for agency and change was constrained despite the overt commitment for reform. Naturalism's debt to and influence on realism (to which it is closely and complexly related) was considered so pervasive that its legacy was said to 'still rule' the practice of fiction in English.[9] Similar observations were made the same year in *The Criterion*, but with the caveat that despite its enduring significance, naturalism 'did not offer an adequate seed of growth'. 'It offered nothing in its place', O'Faoláin claimed, as he stressed its fatalistic qualities and its 'refus[al] to agree that all human actions tend to a significant end'.[10] Traces of this legacy are played out in O'Faoláin's own fiction of this period. In the novel *Bird Alone*, for example, the protagonist, Corney Crone, struggles with the belief that 'life stamps us all out like tin cans, and we can't help much what we do'; Corney also fears that he and his beloved, Elsie, have been 'played on by some secret wind we never heard', and that they have been 'caught by an immovable hand' that pre-determined the choices they thought that they had made (*BA* 221, 129, 235). Tellingly, in each of O'Faoláin's two novels of the 1930s, and in both of his collections of short fiction, tropes of circularity and containment are in evidence, as are issues of inheritance, despair and the experience of being controlled or conditioned by external forces; what is more, in each of these texts the idea of the writer as observer and social anatomist is advanced. It is fitting, therefore, that, O'Faoláin finally found himself conceding a couple of years later that 'intensely as [the Irish novelist] may dislike naturalism, he has to use it'.[11]

The type of naturalism deployed, but also criticized, by O'Faoláin was fluidly defined. On the one hand, it was described in negative terms, as an 'acidulation of the realistic school' and the prerogative of writers who 'loved facts, human documents, the exact anatomy of life'. Such writers 'talked of fiction as if it were a kind of experimental science', O'Faoláin complained, and endorsed an entirely 'pessimistic' view of society.[12] At the same time, though, it was understood to have evolved out of unease with a previous generation's ideals. In its 'post-1916' manifestation, especially, it was considered anti-romantic and counter Revivalist, providing a note of 'corrective deconstruction' to approved configurations of identity as well as to poeticized literary styles and established political ideologies.[13] In this depressed environment, writers were obliged to reflect upon the cost of heroism in the aftermath of a violent revolutionary struggle; they were also drawn to consider the plight of the imaginative individual in a stultifying society, and to engage with a newly-independent order that was often intransigent and increasingly inward-looking.

O'Faoláin's fiction of the 1930s is, at least in part, an attempt to make sense of this order by constructing a narrative of the history of modern Ireland. The genre favoured in many instances is that of historical fiction, as O'Faoláin proposed to sketch the contours of a society that appeared, to him, fractured and shapeless. Initially this shapelessness was explained by the history of colonialism, with the collapse of an integrated Gaelic order, the experience of centuries of penury and social division, and the eventual emergence of an as-of-yet undefined people through the reforming principles of Daniel O'Connell. In later years this explanation was modified, and extended, to incorporate reflections on the supposed 'flattening' of Irish society (even though it is structurated, gender-divided and class-ridden), and the virtual disappearance of the Anglo-Irish gentry as a result of the struggle for national independence. Historical fiction allowed O'Faoláin space to tease out these processes and to interrogate the act of writing history, engaging with the ways in which narratives of the past are authorized, and exploring the interleaving of public records and private memories. *A Nest of Simple Folk* accordingly covers the period from the aftermath of the mid-nineteenth century Famine to the outbreak of the Easter Rising; the context of *Bird Alone* is the Parnellite split of the early 1890s; and the stories in *Midsummer Night Madness* deal with the critical years of the Troubles, from 1919 to 1923.

In addition, though, each of these fictions is grounded in the moment of its production and explores, either directly or by implication, aspects of the post-Independence society that it is a part of. This is clearest in *A Purse of Coppers*, where images of life in the Irish Free State are carefully distilled. However, it is also the case in *Midsummer Night Madness*, where stories of the recent revolutionary period are presented from some vaguely defined, but historically posterior, vantage point. *Bird Alone* might be set against the fall of Charles Stewart Parnell, but it is nonetheless told in retrospect, during the mid-1930s, while Denis Hussey's critique of the bourgeois ambitions of his lower middle-class parents, in *A Nest of Simple Folk*, carries a distinctly contemporary edge, as does his attraction (through theatre) to the forbidden world of sex and the exotic. Such allusions give added significance to each of these texts, running counter to the received wisdom that O'Faoláin was either incapable of or unwilling to represent post-revolutionary society in his fiction. It has been argued, for instance, that O'Faoláin's early novels and short fiction reveal an 'indulgence in the past as an escape from the conditions in contemporary Ireland', and that they should be interpreted 'as a symptom of [a] kind of emotional caution'.[14] Instead, it might be suggested that O'Faoláin looked to the past in some, but not all, of his fiction, and that he did this to articulate and displace, but also to contextualize and thereby enrich, issues of pressing concern.

There may have been practical reasons for this coded or metonymic narrative strategy, since O'Faoláin was writing at a time of deep censorship and was all-too-aware of the power of those who twice banned his work. In addition, though, this strategy was linked to his mordant belief in the choices available to the prose writer in 1930s Ireland. For O'Faoláin, those choices were few, and in 'The Gamut of Irish Fiction' (1936) he outlined some of the reasons for this. 'For many Irish writers life exists on a small number of planes and their stories are lighted only from a few angles.' This is because the different strata of Irish society are only known to those who inhabit specific cultural, religious and political ecologies. Without any hope of a unifying synthesis, he contended that novelists 'in this divided country', with the rarest of exceptions, are fated to produce works of provincial merit, dealing with local problems and 'life with a small *l*'. At the heart of O'Faoláin's argument was an understanding of the classic nineteenth-century realist novel, with its exploration of the workings of an interwoven, stratified society, and its emphasis on the need for an all-encompassing vision – an understanding which is deeply revelatory, since it speaks to O'Faoláin's own assumptions concerning the nature of the novel, and the legitimate forms fiction should properly take. 'The *consciousness* of the existence of many modes of life, and some intimacy with them, heightens the treatment of any one mode of life,' he wrote, 'gives the sense of echo, reverberations wider than the scene displayed', and the absence of such a consciousness explains the paucity of the prose tradition in Ireland.[15] It is a point which was repeated, and revised, on numerous occasions in the years to follow, and which gained most significant expression a decade later in 'The Dilemma of Irish Letters' (1949).

In that later polemic, O'Faoláin quoted extensively from Henry James's famous depiction of the 'social dreariness' of early-nineteenth century New England in his critical study *Hawthorne* (1879). Recalling James's central argument, that 'it needs a complex social machinery to set a writer in motion' – something absent from or not yet formed in the society that his subject, Nathaniel Hawthorne, inhabited – O'Faoláin suggested that this was also the case a century later in Ireland:

> We see this very clearly in Ireland to-day where the stratified, and fairly complex social life which a writer of 1915, say, could have known in Dublin has given way to a far more simple and uncomplex, a much 'thinner' social life. The life now known, or knowable, to any modern Irish writer is either the traditional, entirely simple life of the farm (simple, intellectually speaking); or the groping, ambiguous, rather artless urban life of these same farmers' sons and daughters who have, this last twenty-five years, been taking over the towns and cities from the Anglo-Irish. They have done it, so to speak, by rule of thumb, empirically, with little skill. Their conventions are embryonic; their social patterns are indistinct.[16]

The important difference, as Joe Cleary has observed, was that Ireland and the United States were moving in opposite directions: 'In the US at least the general curve of historical development had been from the simple and uncultured republic, of the kind Hawthorne had had to survive, to a complex and advanced industrial society where a high national literature could finally prosper'; however, 'in the case of Ireland the curve of historical development had apparently been the reverse of this', with decline rather than progression the operating principle.[17] (Decline, it should be said, for critics like O'Faoláin; for contemporaries like Corkery, Ireland was slowly moving in the other direction, towards cultural restoration and an increased measure of political independence.) Such circumstances presented 'an almost insurmountable aesthetic problem' for the writer of prose fiction, Terence Brown has noted, and so, in a characteristically candid assessment of his own attempts at novel-writing, O'Faoláin was left to despair that:

> The 'whole of life' does *not* remain when social conventions and social institutions are simple, few, or in flux. In such an unshaped society there are many subjects for little pieces, that is for the short-story writer; the novelist or the dramatist loses himself in the general amorphism, unthinkingness, brainlessness, egalitarianism, and general unsophistication.[18]

For O'Faoláin in the late 1940s, this 'thinness' helped explain the shortcomings of his three novels, *A Nest of Simple Folk*, *Bird Alone* and *Come Back to Erin*. However, it also accounted for his success as a short-story writer, since the post-revolutionary context was considered well-suited to a form that was insistently fragmented or partial, and that privileged Chekhovian-style 'slices of life' over omniscient views of an integrated society. As he argued in his contemporaneous study *The Short Story* (1948), the short story is attuned to capture the experience of marginality and isolation, especially in places that have experienced recent social upheaval, and encourages the art of compression and implication.[19]

O'Faoláin's diagnosis of the 'thinness' of Irish society, and the supposed failure of the novel form in Ireland, served a particular purpose, of course, and it has been convincingly argued that his thesis is significant less for its discussion of a national literary problem and more for its revelation of the narrowness of his critical programme.[20] One of the most notable things about O'Faoláin's criticism is his near-evasion of the subject of modernism, and his distrust of the experiments of several of his contemporaries. There are no references in any of his essays to Samuel Beckett's *More Pricks than Kicks* (1934) or *Murphy* (1938), for instance, while Elizabeth Bowen's fiction is often squeezed into an ill-fitting conventional paradigm.[21] His assessment of Flann O'Brien's comic masterpiece, *At Swim-Two-Birds* (1939), was less than flattering – it has 'a general odour of spilt Joyce all over it' he caustically remarked in a review – while his response to Yeats's later work was marked by bafflement and preference for the elder poet's 'purer' lyrics.[22] However, it would be misleading to conclude as a result that O'Faoláin's own novels of the period were entirely bound to old-fashioned modes of representation. His most traditional text, *A Nest of Simple Folk*, might take the form of a standard nineteenth-century saga, and carry references to the work of Walter Scott and Ivan Turgenev, amongst others, but it also fuses the form of historical fiction with other genres, interspersing its narrative with less traditional techniques, such as indirection, perspectivalism and focalization. *Bird Alone* employs a tighter frame of reference but is more inventive in design and achievement, employing a tortured, Faust-like first-person narrative, and self-reflexively engaging with the practice of storytelling and the process of memory. Whatever the problems in each of these novels, and there are problems aplenty (the narratives can be tiresome, plotlines digress, certain characters are especially wooden), both texts merit careful consideration and are more complex, and accomplished, than is often assumed. Ironically, though, both novels also provide ample evidence of O'Faoláin's talent at writing compressed scenes (the struggle over the terms of a will at the start of *A Nest of Simple Folk*, for instance, or Elsie's anguished suicide attempt in *Bird Alone*), and both bear witness to the fact that his true *métier* as a creative artist was the short story.

O'Faoláin's essays of the 1930s and 1940s are noteworthy not only for their critique of the naturalist legacy, and their wariness of the subject of modernism, but also for their attempt to establish a working model, or 'literary doctrine', for contemporary prose writing in Ireland. As O'Faoláin contended in 'Plea for a New Type of Novel' (1934), this model should press the need for 'a greater sense of the poetry of life', incorporating realist modes that would include elements of romance (rather than simply setting 'realism' and 'romance' in a crude binary), and eschew naturalist methods while not being afraid to engage with 'the undefined, the unreliable, the dark'.[23] It should look to, without being bound by, the example of non-

Irish writers for guidance – in particular a writer like Anton Chekhov, who is frequently cited as someone who successfully fused 'poetry and realism', and who criticized a society that he also described with sympathy and sensitivity, preaching a 'gospel of "normality"' that focused on the individual and the mundane.[24] This notion of 'poetic realism' was repeated in other essays and amplified in an extended discussion of Chekhov in *The Short Story*, where O'Faoláin asserted that the Russian writer 'was a realist of his own special sort and not of anybody else's sort. He held on to poetry, to mood, to poetic feeling'. Chekhov's 'ironic sympathy' was judged one of his greatest characteristics, as was his ability to universalize the local (a trait that is often, incidentally, ascribed to O'Faoláin): 'there is one thing about him that will specially interest Irish writers. He was Russian in his work, but he was never regionalist in his thought'. In addition, like the great French realist, Honoré de Balzac, his work was defined as 'a constructive criticism of life. The foundations of that criticism, its standards of reference, were with him, as with Balzac, Christian foundations', grounded in an established moral system and an ethical code of conduct.[25]

For O'Faoláin, the deterioration of that code in contemporary fiction was a process that needed to be arrested, and it is for this reason that he argued in favour of a restoration of a general ethic to the novel and 'the revivification of literature by a spiritual view'.[26] This was not presented as an apologia for a reactionary or puritanical approach to literature; instead, it was seen as a way out of the enervated legacy of naturalism, with its 'mechanistic approach to human action', and its stress on collective groups and deterministic forces.[27] Breaking the naturalist bind would allow for a resuscitation of the importance of the individual, according to O'Faoláin (a crucial strand in his liberal politics), and an exploration of issues pertaining to choice, character, circumstances and inner struggle; it would also present opportunities for reform and expressions of autonomy. 'The novelist is always on the side of personality,' he argued in 'The Proletarian Novel' (1937), and in favour of that which 'defines and illustrates *its own* conceptions of the moral and philosophical implications of the drama of life'.[28] It is significant, therefore, that O'Faoláin's fictions of the 1930s repeatedly stage conflicts within thoughtful, imaginative or disillusioned individuals as well as between these characters and the societies that they inherit or inhabit – whether it is the Parnellite society of late-nineteenth century Cork, or the recent period of revolutionary activity and enthusiasm, or the trauma of the Civil War, or the 'dreary Eden' that was consolidated in post-Independence Ireland (*DV* 180). However, it is equally significant that those conflicts are seldom, if ever, resolved in his 'post-1916' novels and short stories.

NOTES

1. O'Faolain, 'The Emancipation of Irish Writers', p.488.
2. Rolf Loeber and Magda Loeber, with Anne Mullin Burnham, *A Guide to Irish Fiction, 1650–1900* (Dublin: Four Courts Press, 2006); Aileen Douglas, Moyra Haslett and Ian Campbell Ross (eds), *Irish Fiction, 1660–1830*, special issue, *Irish University Review* 41: 1 (Spring/Summer 2011). Accompanying critical editions of texts from the seventeenth and eighteenth centuries have been annotated and published as part of an 'Early Irish Fiction' series by Four Courts Press.
3. John Wilson Foster, *Fictions of the Irish Literary Revival: A Changeling Art* (Dublin: Gill & Macmillan, 1987); John Wilson Foster, *Irish Novels 1890–1940: New Bearings in Culture and Fiction* (Oxford: Oxford University Press, 2008).
4. O'Faolain, 'The Emancipation of Irish Writers', p.488.
5. Sean O'Faolain, 'Ah, Wisha! The Irish Novel', *The Virginia Quarterly Review* 17 (Spring 1941), p.265.
6. O'Faolain, 'The Emancipation of Irish Writers', pp.490, 491, 496, 502. O'Faoláin's stress on exposing 'the raw' is repeated in other texts of this period. In the 'Proem' to *King of the Beggars*, for instance, it is boldly asserted that 'literature must inform life, reveal its bones, or else become a mere distraction or amusement' (*KB* 37).
7. Seán O'Faoláin, 'The Proletarian Novel', *The London Mercury* 35: 210 (April 1937), p.584.
8. Cleary, 'This Thing of Darkness', pp.114, 123.
9. O'Faolain, 'The Modern Novel', pp.340, 349.
10. O'Faolain, 'It No Longer Matters', p.52.
11. O'Faolain, 'Ah, Wisha! The Irish Novel', p.273.
12. Seán O'Faoláin, 'Don Quixote O'Flaherty', *The London Mercury* 37:217 (November 1937), p.173.
13. Corcoran, *After Yeats and Joyce*, p.71.
14. Marie Arndt, 'Building a Nest for a Bird Alone', *The Irish Review* 26 (Autumn

2000), p.14; Derek Hand, *A History of the Irish Novel* (Cambridge: Cambridge University Press, 2011), p.170. O'Faoláin's third novel, *Come Back to Erin* (1940), further problematizes such claims, as it unfolds against the backdrop of de Valera's crackdown on the IRA in the mid-1930s.

15. Sean O'Faolain, 'The Gamut of Irish Fiction', *Saturday Review of Literature* 14 (1 August 1936), p.19 [emphasis as original].
16. Seán O'Faoláin, 'The Dilemma of Irish Letters', *The Month* 2: 6 (December 1949), pp.369, 373.
17. Cleary, 'Distress Signals', p.63.
18. Terence Brown, 'Sean O'Faolain and the Irish Short Story', in Badin, et al (eds), *O'Faolain: A Centenary Celebration*, p.63; see also Brown, 'After the Revival: Seán O Faoláin and Patrick Kavanagh', in *Ireland's Literature: Selected Essays* (Gigginstown: Lilliput Press, 1988), pp.98–100; O'Faoláin, 'The Dilemma of Irish Letters', pp.375–6 [emphasis as original].
19. Sean O'Faolain, *The Short Story* (London: Collins, 1948), p.138. A series of five essays on 'The Craft of the Short Story' was published by O'Faoláin in *The Bell* in the period between January and July 1944. These essays were based on lectures broadcast on Radio Éireann in the spring of 1942 and provided the germ of the book-length critical study.
20. Cleary, 'This Thing of Darkness', pp.148–9.
21. In O'Faoláin's study of the novel, *The Vanishing Hero*, for example, Bowen is ultimately described as 'a romantic up against the despotism of reality'; this Arnoldian frame of reference scarcely does justice to the subtleties of her work or her lasting significance. Sean O'Faolain, *The Vanishing Hero: Studies in Novelists of the 1920s* (London: Eyre and Spottiswoode, 1956), p.166.
22. Sean O'Faolain, 'Irish Gasconade', *John O'London's Weekly* (24 March 1939), p.970. In a long review essay, O'Faoláin described Yeats's verse as 'the glittering, glimmering, pale music of the purely lyric poet'. 'His quality is precision of word and phrase, and whenever he is obscure one may be certain that he has betrayed himself'. Sean O'Faolain, review of *Selected Poems, Lyrical and Narrative* by W.B. Yeats, *The Criterion* 9: 36 (April 1930), pp.527–8.
23. Sean O'Faolain, 'Plea for a New Type of Novel', *The Virginia Quarterly Review* 10 (April 1934), p.199; see also Cleary, 'Distress Signals', pp.53–4.
24. O'Faolain, 'Ah, Wisha! The Irish Novel', pp.268, 272; see also O'Faolain, 'The Emancipation of Irish Writers', p.500.
25. O'Faolain, *The Short Story*, pp.80, 96, 97, 99.
26. O'Faolain, 'It No Longer Matters', p.53.
27. O'Faolain, 'The Modern Novel', p.349.
28. O'Faoláin, 'The Proletarian Novel', p.588 [emphasis as original].

4

MODULATED PERSPECTIVES: *MIDSUMMER NIGHT MADNESS*

O'Faoláin's debut collection of short stories, *Midsummer Night Madness and other stories*, was published in 1932, and promptly banned under the recently-enacted Censorship of Publications Act (1929) on the grounds of being 'in general tendency indecent'.[1] The volume consists of seven stories which draw upon O'Faoláin's experiences as an IRA volunteer and republican propagandist during the charged period of the Troubles, from 1919 to 1923. All of the stories are set in Cork city or its hinterland, and six are narrated against the backdrop of the War of Independence; the final tale, 'The Patriot', takes place slightly later, in the closing days and aftermath of the Civil War. In many respects, the collection can be read as a short-story cycle, or the nearest thing to a cycle which O'Faoláin would ever write, as individual stories overlap and are enriched by cross-references to one another. These links are sometimes obvious, with several characters stepping across the pages to join in conversations and activities that are elsewhere reported. The republican insurgent Stevey Long, for instance, appears in the opening story 'Midsummer Night Madness' and again in the penultimate 'The Death of Stevey Long', where he stumbles into the vacated scene of the preceding tale 'The Bombshop'. Similarly, Rory, an IRA volunteer, is killed in the third story 'Fugue', only to return to life in the closing moments of the fourth story 'The Small Lady'. Such cases are few, however, and interconnections are more generally achieved through the use of overarching themes and motifs, and recurring situations and narrative strategies. Many of the characters who are embedded in separate stories also bear a close resemblance to their fictional peers – most of the insurgents are indistinguishable, as are the youthful lovers and the murderous Black and Tans – and this further impresses a sense of continuity and cycle.

If the stories are amplified and interlinked in this way, this is not to suggest that *Midsummer Night Madness* is univocal or repetitive. Rather, the collection engages with shared anxieties and concerns, but does so in an uncertain and occasionally conflicting way. A significant leitmotif in the text is movement, as the principal characters are represented in transit (many of them are gunmen on the run) and the stories trace their journeys from one place to the next. This is often expressed through an idiom of vagrancy as the characters, and the narrators, draw upon phrases and keywords which are appropriate to their travels. Early in 'Fugue', for instance, the speaker longs 'for an end to this vagabond life', and his wishes are echoed in other parts of the collection – in 'The Small Lady', where Denis is 'fully a year tramping around the mountains with the rebels', and again in 'The Patriot', where Bernie has grown weary 'going from place to place in search of food and rest' (*MNM* 94, 136, 259). Movement is enforced structurally in the volume through the form of the cycle, as ideas and characters circulate between stories, and is compounded intertextually, as references are made to other works of literature which are also constructed around the idea of travel. The slender sketch 'Lilliput' is a ready example, with its ironic invocation of Swift's *Gulliver's Travels*. 'Fugue' likewise contains the clearest of references to Yeats's 'ancient, ceaseless gyre', while Shakespeare's romantic journey *A Midsummer Night's Dream* provides an interpretative paradigm for reading the titular story as well as the larger collection (*MNM* 114). Movement is signalled through the tropes and motifs which punctuate the text – the passage from city to countryside, and countryside back to city, which effectively maps the collection, as well as the images of hunting and entrapment which recur across the volume.

It is also conveyed through the use of certain character-types, including guerrilla gunmen, pursuing Tans, wayward romantics, local guides, vagrants, migrants, and conventionally-drawn 'tinkers' or Travellers.

Just as the collection interrogates the leitmotif of movement, so it refuses to settle into any easily defined position with respect to its central anxieties. Instead, many of O'Faoláin's characters appear restless and uneasy, as they find themselves at odds with their peers and their surroundings. In a number of instances, the characters are brought to question received wisdoms and political ideologies in the course of the stories; in some cases, they move from exuberance in the idea of the rebellion to cynicism regarding politics and the cost of military action. Disenchantment is clearly registered through the characterization of Stevey Long, for example (he is presented as a volatile, cruel individual in the two stories 'Midsummer Night Madness' and 'The Death of Stevey Long'), and dominates 'The Bombshop', where a story is told of boredom and waste. It also provides the context for 'The Small Lady', which opens with a sideswipe at the self-proclaimed heroism of republican fighters who commemorate in mock-heroic ballad the execution of a vulnerable woman.[2] Such concerns are repeated in other stories in the collection, and reach a climax in 'The Patriot', where the informing ideals of the revolution are presented in the most pessimistic of lights and are transformed into the stuff of drunken clichés and bigoted propagandists. Not only are earlier ideals scandalized in this, the final story, heroic deeds also seem to be a thing of the past as Bernie is forced to consider whether the rebels' 'humiliation of poverty and hunger was not, as he had long since begun to feel, a useless and wasted offering' (*MNM* 262). Bernie's comments are amongst the most depressed recorded in *Midsummer Night Madness* and it is significant that they are included in the one story which deals with the Civil War. Even still, they give voice to an underlying fear which runs through the larger volume – that the initial hopes and dreams which were invested in the rebellion might not have been all that they seemed – and this provides O'Faoláin with the basis for his collection's unifying title.

The title, *Midsummer Night Madness and other stories*, carries an obvious allusion to *A Midsummer Night's Dream*, and calls to mind the spirit of romance and disorientation which characterizes Shakespeare's play. It also suggests the latter's world of transformative potential, where identities become fluid and interchangeable, and the focus is given to things transitional, unexpected and young. In *A Midsummer Night's Dream* attention is often centred on the symbol of the moon, as it presides over sleep and is associated with love, lunacy and change; this is matched in *Midsummer Night Madness* by the stress on the dawn, with its connotations of romance, uncertainty of light and perception, and the possibilities of another day. In both texts youthful lovers escape the confines of the city, and in both works unlikely relationships are supposed – Shakespeare's iconic image of an ass-headed Bottom being cradled by an ethereal Titania finds a correlation of sorts in Gypsy Gammle's embrace of Old Henn in O'Faoláin's title story. What is more, in both instances daring journeys are undertaken into spaces which are at once liberating, confusing and self-revelatory.

If O'Faoláin looks to Shakespeare's popular comedy, however, it is in a spirit of unrest. For if in Shakespeare's play chaos threatens to reign but is finally brought into line through the restoration of order and the promise of marriage, in O'Faoláin's world the characters do not wake to find that all has been resolved, or that peace and harmony have been restored, by the start of the new day. A number of the stories begin with a symbolic injunction against romance and movement, as they open with the declaration of curfew – a recurring image which discreetly binds the collection together is that of young lovers being torn apart as the Tans invade Cork's streets – but few stories offer anything like resolution. Indeed, most of the stories avoid the simplicity of a neat conclusion and remain fragmented or open-ended; many also include identities and character-types which proved difficult to accommodate after the conflict. 'Tinkers' feature prominently, and perhaps unexpectedly, in several of the stories ('Lilliput', 'Midsummer Night Madness', and on the margins of 'The Small Lady'), and other 'remaindered communities', to use Seamus Deane's suggestive phrase, are also represented, including political loyalists, 'die-hard' republicans and remnants of the Anglo-Irish Ascendancy.[3] Some stories also portray characters who transgress the most carefully patrolled of boundaries. 'The Small Lady', for instance, includes several people who act in the despised role of the informer, including the title character Bella Browne; Denis's RIC father who is unknowingly tracking down his own son; and a stock alcoholic who is looking for a cure. Stories also give voice to expressions of animosity and bitterness which are not easy to resolve or forgive, and which survived to shape political life in the decades after independence. A late scene in 'The Patriot' makes this clear, as it records differences at a Sinn Féin rally several years after the end of the Civil War, with the State still struggling to emerge from the trauma of conflict and the realities of partition and social division.

At times there is a disquieting eroticization of military activity in the volume, as sexual energies are projected onto violent acts and brutal episodes. Sometimes this is explicitly critiqued, as violence is shown to pervert the potential for love and companionship. This is linked to a more general unease which is a defining feature of the volume, and which finds compelling focus through the inclusion of various victims of violence in the collection. Throughout *Midsummer Night Madness,* O'Faoláin sketches characters – combatants and civilians, British soldiers and IRA volunteers – who are killed in the course of the fighting. What is striking is the way in which each of these deaths is represented, as the text shies away from depicting the actual moments when the characters are killed and instead chooses to portray death in a distant, oblique or deliberately underdeveloped manner. In 'Fugue', for example, the garrulous figure of Rory is carefully introduced in the early pages of the story, tramping through West Cork with the narrator and singing lusty ballads 'of passionate life' (*MNM* 100). This gradual delineation of the country-bred Rory is loving and detailed, as is the juxtaposition of him with the more sensitive and reserved, city-born, middle-class narrator. However, this slow portrayal is at odds with the abrupt way in which Rory's death is subsequently dealt with, for when he is ambushed and killed by British soldiers, the event is neither represented on the page nor witnessed by the narrator. Instead, news of Rory's death is relayed second-hand and presented as a sudden burst of information which disrupts an erotically-charged encounter between the narrator and a mysterious young woman. 'A rush of feet came to the door,' it is recalled, 'and the little girl from the roadside house flung it wide with a cry to me to run, to run; Rory was shot dead: they were coming West for me!' (*MNM* 110). On hearing this the narrator takes to the road, 'full of terror for such a death as I knew Rory's was I filled every house with armed men, fierce men to whom killing was a little thing and torture but little more' (*MNM* 111). 'Fugue' thereafter mutates into a lyrical meditation on the vagaries of life and the cycles of nature, complete with an extended reference to an eleventh-century Gaelic poem which sits cryptically in relation to all that has preceded it. No further details are provided about Rory, and his death provides a textual fissure which retrospectively haunts the heart of the story.

Significantly, this strategy of representing death is repeated in other stories. In 'The Bombshop', the nationalist sympathizer Mother Dale dies unheard and alone, downstairs and also off the page, as she is accidentally shot by the very men she is providing with a safe-house. In 'The Small Lady', Bella Browne is killed by a drunken band of insurgents, but the text barely registers the moment of her execution as she is moved to an unidentified location, somewhere beyond the margins of the text – 'far up the coom', the narrative simply states, 'there reverberated through the echoing hills a volley of rifle-fire' (*MNM* 170). 'The Death of Stevey Long' ends before the announced death of the eponymous insurgent, and in the same story an anonymous Tan deserter is presented to the reader bound and helpless at his executioners' feet, before the narrative pointedly looks away and he is discharged without further detail by 'a horrible double sound of a revolver' (*MNM* 233). The inclusion of such incidents gives the lie to any easy claim for dispassionate heroism in the collection. However, the simultaneous excision of these deaths is not without significance and suggests either a kind of squeamishness on the part of O'Faoláin and his narrators, or a reluctance to perpetuate cycles of violence by imaginatively portraying murder scenes. Such a stance distinguishes *Midsummer Night Madness* from many contemporaneous texts which also grappled with this formative period in modern Irish history. Frank O'Connor's affecting title story in *Guests of the Nation* (1931) is an obvious point of comparison, as it bears stark witness to the ugliness of murder in the name of a seemingly just cause. O'Connor's equally harrowing essay 'A Boy in Prison' (1934) also invites contrast, as do Liam O'Flaherty's short stories of the Troubles – 'The Sniper' (1924), 'Civil War' (1926) and 'The Mountain Tavern' (1929) – and the third of Sean O'Casey's Dublin plays, *The Plough and the Stars* (1926), where the death-throes of Lieutenant Langon and Bessie Burgess are painfully realized on stage.

To some extent, this revulsion is indicative of the spirit of romanticism which informs *Midsummer Night Madness*, and which distinguishes the collection, or rather most of the stories in the collection, from much of O'Faoláin's subsequent work as a prose writer. Pierce Butler suggested as much when he argued that a romantic aesthetic provided O'Faoláin with 'a means of glossing over the sort of shattering experience' which is recorded in more graphic representations of the Troubles, as the young writer 'suppress[ed] his anger and disillusionment in favour of a celebration of youth and the rugged beauties of the countryside'.[4] Butler's comments are aligned with O'Faoláin's later unease with the collection. Looking back in 1957, in the 'Foreword' to his selected volume *The Finest Stories of Sean O'Faolain*, O'Faoláin labelled the stories 'very romantic' in their engagement with his experience of the rebellion, an experience which was 'too filled with dreams and ideals and a sense of dedication to be an experience in the meaning of things perceived, understood and remembered'.[5]

Many of the stories in *Midsummer Night Madness* are clearly informed by a romantic impulse. This is especially true of the stories which were first published separately, with minor variations, sometimes under slightly different titles, in the mid-to-late 1920s: 'In Lilliput', which appeared in *The Irish Statesman* in 1926; or 'The Bomb Shop', which was included the following year in the modernist magazine *The Dial*; or 'Fugue', which was published in 1928 in the American journal *Hound and Horn*.[6] There is a pronounced lyrical quality to each of these stories, as well as a stress on reflective acts and intense feelings, and love stories feature prominently in the larger collection's struggle for personal and political independence. Characters often appear alone in the text, either literally or metaphorically, and are often depicted on the run, as they flee from enemy soldiers and a law which is alien and unjust, but also from a part of themselves that has been sacrificed or put to one side. In keeping with this impulse, many of the stories are overwritten with youthful fervour, and are lavish in their references to colour, scents, tastes and the body. Music, the weather, light and the landscape are also drawn upon and transfigured in the volume, and are used to indicate the psychological wellbeing or emotional outlook of a particular character or narrator. 'Fugue', for instance, is narrated by a sensitive young man who describes his feelings for a young woman in language which is unashamedly emotive, while the title story opens with an intentionally overblown scene in which the narrator, John, travels out of the city and into a world that seems to reflect his own romantic sensibility, as references to 'fallen hawthorn blossoms', 'wisps of hay', and 'the chuckle of a waking hen' suggest (*MNM* 20). Such descriptions are not restricted to rural or pastoral settings, with the cityscape of Cork similarly re-imagined as a space 'on whose purples and greens and blues the summer night was falling as gently as dust' (*MNM* 19).

Edward Garnett, the writer and influential publisher's reader, noted this point in his introduction to the first edition of *Midsummer Night Madness*. Describing O'Faoláin as 'a poet at heart', he enthused: 'Here indeed is the Irish sensitiveness to place and emotional mood, in a style free and flowing ... Atmosphere he renders most delicately. The feeling of the mournful Irish mountains, of their brooding, sad austerity, and their tenderness is beautifully caught'. In the same breath, however, Garnett discerned a counter-commitment, to realism and objective scrutiny, when he remarked that the stories should also be praised for their 'social value as well as [their] aesthetic force', with O'Faoláin's flowing style said to be 'punctuated by passages of that brutal frankness which is the conscience of the younger generation'.[7] Observing both styles at play in the text, Garnett identified a tension which lies at the heart of O'Faoláin's collection. This tension can be crudely characterized as a pull between the competing modes of romanticism and realism, as the poeticism of an earlier generation was drawn against the disappointed prose or 'brutal frankness' of post-independence youth. Critics have since considered this pull a defining feature of O'Faoláin's *oeuvre* more generally, with Joe Cleary recently describing it as the 'basic agon' that provides 'an absolute constant' in his writing.[8] This is especially evident in the dichotomies that repeatedly mark O'Faoláin's work – romance and realism, idealism and poverty, poetry and the prosaic, the Revival and its aftermath – as well as his attempted fusion of and movement between these dichotomies.

O'Faoláin's residual romanticism, or his 'inverted romanticism', to use the phrase he once ascribed to Liam O'Flaherty, is not the only reason he avoids representing violence in *Midsummer Night Madness*, however.[9] Violence is also eschewed because O'Faoláin's focus in the collection is less on the representation of such acts, and more on the narrativization of these incidents and the way that they are filtered through the perspective – and sometimes the memory – of certain characters or narrators. As Heather Ingman has noted, a story like 'Midsummer Night Madness' is 'shaped not by external forces but by the narrator's partial consciousness', as the experimental techniques of suggestion, indirection, irony and perspectivalism are deployed 'to probe the inner consciousness' of the characters and the narrator.[10] Thus, the narrator declines to represent the most significant act of violence in the story – the burning down of a Big House, Henn Hall – because he does not witness this incident firsthand. This explains why so much of the story is either inferred or left unsaid. It also accounts for the uncertain or conflicted nature of the narrative, as the narrator, a young IRA officer, feels his way through the story. The decrepit landlord, Alexander Henn of Henn Hall, turns out not to be the 'strange mad owner whom as children we thought more terrifying than any of the ogres in the fairy-books', nor is he quite the jaded cliché who inhabits much thinking about the Big House in Ireland (*MNM* 21). 'You may pity him as I tell you of him,' the narrator cautions the reader early in the story, 'but I … had nothing in my heart for him but hate. He was one of the class that had battened for too long on our poor people' (*MNM* 25).

As this long story unfolds, Henn's relationship with 'our poor people' (the possessive pronoun and the adjective are both revealing) proves to be more complex than is initially supposed. What is more, the narrator's representation of the ageing aristocrat, which is initially defined by an inherited hatred, is transformed into an uneasy mixture of admiration, pity, envy, fear, ridicule and distaste. As the narrator is drawn into a more nuanced understanding of this figure (Henn's cultural sophistication sets him apart from other characters in the story, and he is presented as a spokesperson for local co-operative schemes), so the narrator is brought to question preconceptions and ideas that he inherited as a child. Such 'superstructural complications ... disturb the familiar romantic-nationalist base on which the story at first appears to rest', Adrian Hunter has observed.[11] Stevey Long, a long-standing comrade of the narrator, similarly bucks the stereotype of Troubles literature as he operates as an uncouth, cowardly villain in the story. It is Stevey who exploits the vulnerable people around him, as he uses the local battalion of the IRA to settle personal scores rather than engage in guerrilla warfare. (In this respect, O'Faoláin anticipates the late Peter Hart's observations regarding the experience of guerrilla activity in some parts of Munster during the War of Independence.)[12] It is also Stevey who refuses to take responsibility for his actions, as he compels the marriage of Henn and Gypsy Gammle, a Traveller girl whom he has almost certainly made pregnant.

Together, Gypsy and Henn are said to comprise 'a strange pair', and much of the supposed comedy of this story derives from the impending marriage of these two characters (*MNM* 75). Their unlikely marriage is presented as a carnivalesque 'resolution of extremes', with its wedding of age to youth and Big House to tent, and critics have often viewed the union as 'an ironical suggestion of cultural fusion'.[13] O'Faoláin's conclusion is certainly intended to sound a comical note, with Henn's assertion that the marriage will keep his family name alive evoking the disbelief of the narrator: 'As if he were a Hapsburg or a Bourbon!' (*MNM* 74). It is important to remember, however, that the final scenes in the story are forced, and that the wedding violates a basic rule of Shakespearean romance, for the intended couple in this instance are not true lovers. Rather, the pregnant Gypsy has been abandoned by her lover (Stevey) who has in turn threatened to burn down Henn Hall if the old aristocrat refuses to marry the young Traveller. Such a marriage is deemed unthinkable at the outset, when the narrator refuses to believe that 'even such a house [as Henn Hall] would fall so low', and is subsequently depicted as the final disgrace of a once-powerful ruling elite (*MNM* 26). Gypsy and Henn's subsequent remove to Paris, in a postscript to the story, is used to hint at both characters' – and, by implication, both classes' – marginalization from life in the fledgling Free State.

Significantly, their marriage is forced upon them by someone who comes from within that community – indeed, someone who is valorized by that community as a freedom-fighter – and is brought about through the transference of his desires onto the 'old libertine' Henn (*MNM* 56). However, although O'Faoláin – or rather, O'Faoláin's narrator – comes to question inherited stereotypes in this story, some preconceptions remain unchallenged. The narrator resists making Henn a particularly likeable character, for instance, with the old man instead represented as a drunken, snobbish degenerate who lives his days in fallen splendour, weeping tragic-comically and somewhat self-reflexively to Mozart's *Don Giovanni* (*MNM* 38). As Ronald Tamplin has inferred, Henn is a recognizably generic figure in this respect, 'embod[ying] all the eccentricity, crabbiness, and decay that the literary tradition so frequently proposes for the Big House owner', as he is consigned to ponder former glories in depressed circumstances, in squalid rooms 'battered and unkempt like a tramp' (*MNM* 38).[14] The reference to 'tramp' lingers and creates an implied link between Henn and Gypsy Gammle in the mind of the narrator, so it is apt that they should be brought together in the closing pages. It is also appropriate that the Traveller should remain bound by narratorial preconceptions in this story. Gypsy, that is to say, continues to be presented as a stereotypical 'tinker' by the narrator, and is depicted in a style which is simultaneously scandalous, sexualized, brutish, unknowable and utterly Other to those around her.[15] O'Faoláin's use of certain narrative strategies allows for the reconsideration of some stereotypes – his stress on acts of narration and the technique of perspectivalism, for instance, facilitates this. However, over and again, the contours of these stereotypes are tested only to be reaffirmed.

These techniques also enable O'Faoláin's narrator to hint at unexpected associations which draw the various characters together. For all their differences, each of the characters in the title story has strained relations with the local community: the narrator is a displaced 'city-fellow'; Henn is the classically alienated Anglo-Irishman; Gypsy's surname aligns her with 'a tinker tribe' from North Cork and Limerick; and Stevey appears deracinated and without origins. Each of the figures also appears introspective and lonely, and each is described through an index of animal-like images and metaphors: the growling Gypsy; the sheepish Stevey; the birdlike Henn; the foxy narrator. The significance of these associations is not fully explicated, even if the choice of animals seems obvious for what it implies about the characters named, and the inference might be that the associations are particularly telling insofar as they reveal something of the narrator's consciousness – rather than aspects of the characters or, indeed, preconceptions of the writer. The associations are also revealing as they hint at some of the ways that the narrator chooses to perceive other characters in his story.

It is inferred that the narrator of 'Midsummer Night Madness', like other narrators and characters in the collection, has lost faith in military activity by the time he tells his story – 'Midsummer Night Madness' is in part a memory narrative, and is told from an unidentified point, sometime after the events narrated. This loss is not absolute, however, and it would be wrong to conclude, as some critics have, that 'criticism of nationalist romanticism' and 'the irrationality of fighting' is a consistent focus of either this story or the larger volume.[16] It would be equally simplistic to argue that 'IRA characters are louts, not fighting heroes' in all of the stories in the collection.[17] Rather, if disillusionment with nationalist ideology and guerrilla activity is expressed on numerous occasions in *Midsummer Night Madness* ('vomit on Ireland' an exasperated character cries in 'The Bombshop' [*MNM* 210]), it is repeatedly offset by incidents and perspectives which sound a more equivocal note. Although the narrators of 'Fugue' and 'Midsummer Night Madness' are unhappy with their lot, and although the narrator of the former story longs for a home and a settled life, they nonetheless both appear committed to the cause of the insurrection. The narrator of the latter story seems to have remained involved in the insurgency long after the events articulated – looking back to the summer of 1920, which provides the setting for the story, he recalls a time when 'there was enough romance left in the revolution' (*MNM* 20). Had the story unfolded 'six months later', he adds, by which time guerrilla fighting had intensified and much of the southern province of Munster was under martial law, Stevey could have done anything he wished: 'and we should not have dared, nor cared, nor had the time, nor even wished in the heat of passion – for things grew very hot by then – to question any such act of his' (*MNM* 64).

Things committed 'in the heat of passion' are described in subsequent stories, and if they sometimes give rise to expressions of regret or unease, they are also recalled with an occasional sense of relish. In 'The Small Lady', for instance, the narrative gathers pace once the kidnapped informer Bella Browne is executed and Denis realizes that his comrades are in danger of being tracked down by the British soldiers. This happens at a pivotal point in the text, when Denis is seeking to extricate himself from further involvement in Bella's abduction. Rather than being a participant in her execution, Denis attends mass and seeks absolution – not for what he priggishly terms 'the whole hateful business', but rather for another 'dark secret', that Bella and he made love the previous night (*MNM* 169, 154). Denis's actions appear cowardly and evasive, as he avoids admitting the full extent of his involvement in her captivity and murder. At the same time, his actions – or rather, his lack of action – speak to an interpellated fear of sexuality and the body which was a defining feature of post-Famine Catholic teaching in Ireland.

The young Catholic Denis genuinely believes that he has committed the most grievous of sins by sleeping with Bella, and this is clear to Bella, and the narrator, on the very night the couple make love. Bella was 'never so moved', it is said, 'as when she felt his body tremble at the meeting (terrible to him as she knew) of their limbs' (*MNM* 143). O'Faoláin's parenthetical interjection stresses the point, however awkwardly, and a conventional third-person narrator describes Denis subsequently at confession, and then at mass, begging for forgiveness and trying to find solace in prayer. Denis's hopes are abandoned once he hears the executioners firing in the distance, and the dispassionate third-person narrator gives way to an unidentified internal voice which is close to Denis's. 'Not so easily, not so quietly was life to be left behind,' it is suddenly stated, in a passage which draws on the intimate, modernist technique of stream of consciousness (*MNM* 170).

Not only does the text invade Denis's innermost thoughts and fears at this point, it also registers the degree of his interpellation as a Catholic subject, as his response to the gunshot is presented in the form of a densely ritualized litany: 'O Immense Passion, O profound wounds, O sweetness above all sweetness, grant her eternal rest' (*MNM* 170). When Denis realizes that the sound of gunshot has disclosed the position of his comrades to the pursuing Tans, the narrative changes tack once again:

> Then the boy to whom he had given his rifle was pulling at his shoulder and all the little congregation were looking with frightened eyes up along the dark-green slopes where a scattered line of troops was moving slowly down out of the shaggy fog. In a second he had his rifle in his hand and was out of the chapel and was racing under the shelter of the graveyard below the mountain out towards his comrades in the coom. It was a long way and there were innumerable turf-cuttings and dikes hewn out of the bog and he splashed in and out of brown bog-water and sank to his knees many times in the spongy mould as he ran his way ... His voice as he shouted made but little noise in the wide, ravine-high place, for his throat and palate were dry and his heart beating madly against his side and his gasping breath robbed it of all energy. But soon they saw him stumbling toward them and he waved his hand behind him and made for the nearest stream to clamber up its course out of the trap of the coom. They understood at once and scattered up the slopes and for a long while he saw nobody, climbing up hand over hand, resting as long as he dared like a hunted stag in the trickling water, drinking it up as he lay (*MNM* 170–1).

The speed of the narrative at this point seeks to capture something of the fear and exhilaration of Denis, as he flies across the page and through the countryside in a style which is reminiscent of other narratives of the War of Independence. Bella's death and Denis's guilty 'dark secret' are forgotten here, as the story assumes the form of a high-speed chase, with active verbs used in abundance, and clauses and sub-clauses interlinked through the stressed repetition of the conjunctions 'and' and 'but'. Despite obvious ideological differences, there are many similarities to the representation of guerrilla activity in more conventional nationalist texts. Although O'Faoláin was highly critical of Corkery's propagandist short-story collection *The Hounds of Banba* (1920), for instance, dismissing what he considered its 'lyric, romantic, idea of revolution and revolutionaries', there is nonetheless an echo of his former mentor's work here.[18] There is also a foretaste of the many acts of daring and bravery which are described time and again in Ernie O'Malley's *On Another Man's Wound*, as well as in other memoirs of the period, including Tom Barry's *Guerilla Days in Ireland* (1949) and Dan Breen's *My Fight for Irish Freedom* (1924). Fittingly, in the ensuing gunfight, Denis savours the moment when he shoots an English officer, and his sudden burst of machismo is recorded in staccato-like fashion, without any gloss or counter-commentary:

> 'I plugged the Tan that led them,' said Denis.
> 'Are you sure?'
> 'I saw him drop.'
> 'The son of a bitch.'
> 'He nearly finished us. He'll talk no more.' (*MNM* 175)

'Fugue' unfolds in a similar if more lyrical vein, and focuses on the nervous excitement of a young gunman as he careers through the remote landscape of West Cork. Unlike Denis, however, the nameless narrator of 'Fugue' seems to have lost his nerve along the way. 'Earlier in the evening,' he confides to the reader, 'I had heard a noise before us in the lag, and had clicked a bullet in my rifle-breech and fallen flat, but Rory swore at me and asked me in amazement if I meant to fight them? After that I had no guts for anything but to get away from the danger of an encounter' (*MNM* 90). This sudden deflation is registered in suitably phallic terms, and implies a ready association between the discourses of militancy and masculinity which is repeated in other stories. In 'The Death of Stevey Long', for instance, the 'cruel, and ... cunning, and (it must be admitted) fearless' insurgent is awkwardly set against an overweight, cowardly schoolteacher, while in 'The Small Lady', Bella fantasizes about 'my boys', the Black and Tans, 'these fine, black-bonneted, tight-breeched, khaki-coated, pipe-smoking, six-shooter men' (*MNM* 222, 151). In 'Fugue', however, despite his weariness with life on the road, at no point does the narrator express doubts about the cause he is serving as a volunteer. On the contrary, his continued commitment to the cause is implied by his use, as a narrator, of one of the most redolent metaphors in Irish nationalist discourse – the figuration of a young woman as the embodiment of a violated nation.

In the course of his adventures the narrator of 'Fugue' twice crosses paths with a mysterious young woman. As he struggles to describe this woman, the narrator draws on this metaphor to add depth to his portrayal, turning her from a mere character in his story into a locus of symbolic potential. The woman is accordingly made to stand for a host of images including the contours of the natural landscape, the romanticization of rural life, a lost erotic potential, the sacrifices made by the insurgents, and an implied idea of Ireland. Beautiful and passionate, but impoverished and lonely, she recalls the forlorn maiden or *spéirbhean* (sky-woman) of seventeenth and eighteenth-century Gaelic *aisling* (dream vision) poetry. In a typical *aisling*, Ireland is presented as a beautiful young woman who has been wronged by foreign invaders and who pleads for a gallant lover to come to her aid. Many of these motifs are presented by O'Faoláin's narrator: the unnamed woman appears as a representative rather than an individuated figure; she is clearly politicized and supportive of the republican cause (her brother is also on the run); and she is assigned an almost spiritual presence, as she ghosts the narrator's imagination and moves with impossible speed across the countryside. (When the narrator moves from one safe-house to the next, he is left to wonder at 'how she came before me to the hither side of the country twelve long miles from her last night's hostel' [*MNM* 107]). It is most appropriate, therefore, that the narrator imagines himself as her would-be saviour, thinking of her 'smiling at me as a sick woman might smile upon a doctor who brought her her ease from pain' (*MNM* 110).

O'Faoláin is careful not to delimit the young woman in this role, however, and sufficient information is provided to suggest a very different life story. When the narrator offers the woman empty clichés to describe the beauty of the surrounding countryside, her response is both forceful and resonant. Recalling the words of some of J.M. Synge's female protagonists, she insists: 'You would soon tire of these mountains! The city, though, that's where I'd like to live. There's company there, and sport and educated people, and a chance to live whatever life you choose!' (*MNM* 109). The woman rebels against the narrator's expectations, as she longs for a modern, urban, independent existence; and the strength of her response bears witness to her feelings, and the fact that the circumstances of her life have taken their toll on her emotional and psychological health. 'Lonely' and 'desolate' are the keywords which are used several times in their brief exchange, and the clear inference is that there is more to this woman than the way that she is being imagined by the narrator. Significantly, this is also the case for other female characters in *Midsummer Night Madness*.

'Midsummer Night Madness', 'The Bombshop' and 'The Patriot' each feature young women who can be figured, to a greater or lesser degree, as Róisín Dubh-type characters, while 'Lilliput' and 'The Bombshop' include older women who carry a trace of Cathleen Ní Houlihan or the Old Woman of Beare. On each occasion, O'Faoláin's narrators seem tempted to slip these characters into pre-defined discursive paradigms. However, in each instance the paradigms prove insufficient, as the women demonstrate that they cannot be reduced to the metaphor that is being applied. In some cases they turn out to be extra-national subjects, seemingly beyond the concerns or imaginative parameters of the emerging nation – the young 'tinker' Gypsy Gammle and the nameless Traveller matriarch in 'Lilliput' remain liminal characters who are difficult to place. In other instances they are simply the vulnerable poor who are caught in the midst of the crossfire (old Mother Dale in 'The Bombshop'), or they are disappointed youths who turn against the tide of abstract politicization in favour of the privacies of love and desire (Norah in 'The Bombshop' to some extent, and her namesake Norah in 'The Patriot' for certain). Whatever the case, in each of the stories the character's figuration is less simple than is initially supposed, as the attempted application of this metaphor says little about the reality of the women's lives. At the same time, the metaphor reveals much about the thoughts and interests of O'Faoláin's male protagonists and narrators.

The interrelationship between stories is a defining feature of *Midsummer Night Madness* and makes the collection slightly anomalous in O'Faoláin's career. Although O'Faoláin repeated themes, tropes and concerns in subsequent volumes of short stories, it was never again to this heightened pitch; nor did he allow characters to flit between stories in his later works. This sense of interconnection is reinforced by the collection's focus on a particular time and place (Cork during the Troubles), and this carefully-drawn context makes the book additionally unusual in O'Faoláin's *oeuvre*, since all of his subsequent collections are more or less contemporaneous with the world that they describe. Such techniques distinguish *Midsummer Night Madness* and mark it out as an example of the form of the short-story cycle. Short-story cycles are, by definition, carefully patterned, and stories within cycles are typically interrelated through shared motifs, questions, themes, characters, settings, moods and metaphors. The level of interdependence varies from one cycle to another, although it is widely assumed that some degree of continuity is vital for the form, and that this is what distinguishes cycles from more general collections of short fiction. As Susan Garland Mann has indicated, 'there is only one essential characteristic of the short story cycle: the stories are both self-sufficient and interrelated'.[19] However, although cycles suppose a measure of coherence and integrity, critics have argued that discontinuity is also a feature of the form, since individual stories are often told from the perspective of characters or narrators who approach events from conflicting sides. In the words of James Nagel, 'a narrative modulation of perspectives' is an important aspect of the short-story cycle, with overarching acts of omniscience avoided in favour of 'more personalised modes of perceiving', and recurring elements and concerns presented from 'a number of angles'.[20]

This modulation of perspectives contributes to the many uncertainties which course through *Midsummer Night Madness*, as O'Faoláin engages with critical issues relating to politics, violence, ideology and insurrection without seeming to settle on any one single position. This variety of angles adds to the central leitmotif of movement in the book, as ideas and commitments circulate through the volume but are challenged and contested by different characters and narrators. If the collection resists settling into any one stance with respect to these anxieties, this is at least partly a consequence of the form of the cycle which is deployed by O'Faoláin. It is also, though, a consequence of the short-story form more generally, as it has been noted by practitioners and critics that short stories are particularly suited to capturing states of ambiguity, uncertainty and irresolution, offering glimpses of characters, episodes, narratives and ways of thinking which are fragmented, partial or various. As O'Faoláin himself claimed in *The Short Story*, 'telling by means of suggestion or implication is one of the most important of all the modern short story's shorthand conventions. It means that a short story writer does not directly tell us things so much as let us guess or know them by implying them'.[21]

The many uncertainties which underpin *Midsummer Night Madness* are also suggestive of O'Faoláin's thinking at the time that the stories were produced. In this respect, the collection might be considered less a representation of the Troubles *per se* and more a reflection on this period from the vantage point of the mid-to-late 1920s and early 1930s. Writing in *Motley*, in 1933, O'Faoláin expressed the opinion that 'there can be no true criticism in a revolution', since the need for a united front during a military struggle precludes space for dissenting voices; the implication, however, was that this space had opened up in the years since the War of Independence.[22] If *Midsummer Night Madness* is read with this in mind, it is hardly surprising that the collection appears so uneasy, since O'Faoláin was revising his own understanding of the Troubles at this time, questioning earlier beliefs and the influence of former mentors. This process of revision was far from complete by the time the book was published, as is clear from the tone of his near-contemporaneous *The Life Story of Eamon De Valera*, with its idealization of its subject and the revolutionary period. The two framing stories in the collection, 'Midsummer Night Madness' and 'The Patriot', appropriately foreground questions of memory, and suggest that the recent experience of the Troubles has already receded into the past and become entwined with other emotions and recollections, to the extent that it has been transformed into a Proustian '*temps perdu*' (*MNM* 75). The two stories also contain numerous autobiographical references which implicate O'Faoláin: the narrator of the title story is a 'city-fellow' named John whose parents are from the countryside and whose father is a policeman in the RIC; while the young couple in the final story resemble O'Faoláin and his young wife, Eileen, with the propagandist and eponymous 'patriot' bearing traces of O'Faoláin's old teacher, Daniel Corkery.

If *Midsummer Night Madness* is read as a retrospective reflection on the Troubles, Edward Garnett's vituperative introduction gains in significance. For in this essay, Garnett engaged with Irish cultural politics in the early 1930s and upset a considerable number of potential readers in the process. Not only did Garnett pour scorn on the recently-enacted censorship laws, for instance, he sneered at 'the average Irishman's almost Puritanical fear of sex'. Garnett also lamented the trend whereby 'nearly every Irishman of talent' had emigrated in the preceding two decades, ridiculing Corkery's recently-published *Synge and Anglo-Irish Literature*, and pronouncing the Irish 'culturally speaking contemptible' and 'the most backward nation in Europe'.[23] As Maurice Harmon has noted, such remarks did O'Faoláin few favours and probably contributed to the reasons for the banning of the collection.[24] At the same time, Garnett's comments (intentionally or otherwise) granted *Midsummer Night Madness* an additional sense of coherence, as they placed this loosely-defined 'Troubles collection' firmly within a post-independence context, and a world characterized by disappointment, lost enthusiasm, cultural impoverishment and 'brutal frankness'.

This sense of continuity is further impressed through the trajectory of the final story, 'The Patriot', where a dejected view of guerrilla activity is provided and the central character, Bernie, is heard to describe with ruthless candour 'what he knew of the state of the men among those hills, all of them weak and scabby and sore, not a penny in their pockets, not a pipeful to smoke, nothing to do from one week to another but run when danger approached, never together, badly led, beaten all but in name' (*MNM* 269). Bernie's comments relate specifically to the latter stages of the Civil War, when demoralization was rife amongst many republicans, and are aligned with other remarks that O'Faoláin made in the early 1930s concerning his experience of this bitter conflict. However, they can also be read backwards to reflect upon previous depictions of militancy across *Midsummer Night Madness*. 'The Patriot' refuses to re-romanticize these images, as Bernie and his wife, Norah, walk out of a Sinn Féin meeting a few years after the end of the conflict, no longer affected by the 'the terrible passion' and political rhetoric of their former friend Edward Bradley (*MNM* 282). The characters reject Bradley's thesis, and the story ends with Bernie, quite literally, turning his back on previously held beliefs and a once admired comrade. As Patrick Walsh has noted, there can be little doubt that the story's quiet conclusion, where Bernie and Norah silently embrace in the privacy of their bedroom, is intended to provide 'a valedictory gesture, indicating a clear break with the past'.[25] This tender image replays the Shakespearean motif of separated lovers that runs through the volume, but finally injects this image with a sense of promise, as a young couple are re-united and love is shown to prevail over abstractions and empty rhetoric. Norah is manifestly not a metaphor for Ireland in this, the final story, and the union of lovers at the story's end which also provides the closing image for the entire collection – does not signify another Irishman giving himself over to a political ideal.

Bernie and Norah's embrace is clearly intended to provide a retrospective key with which to read the collection, as a moment of hope is registered and a break from inherited paradigms is effected. The Troubles have ended by the time *Midsummer Night Madness* concludes, although Bradley's late speech at a political rally attests to the fact that some things have yet to be resolved. In many respects O'Faoláin's importance as a writer dates from this point, as he sought to make sense of the State that the revolutionary period had brought into existence. If the final image in *Midsummer Night Madness* is definitive or valedictory, however, some problems remain to trouble its place in the larger collection. For one thing, Bernie and Norah are placed in a privileged position, outside and after the conflict, and this allows them to see things from a perspective that is unavailable to any of their fictional peers. In addition, their embrace is (perhaps necessarily) quietly drawn, and seems all the more fragile when it is set against the louder emotions which are registered elsewhere in the volume.[26] What is more, their embrace – or rather, the stress on their embrace – can be interpreted as an act that sidesteps rather than resolves the multiple uncertainties that punctuate *Midsummer Night Madness*. Indeed, one could argue that this concluding image shies away from engaging with these difficulties at all, since it seems to signal a renunciation of politics rather than a considered recoil from abstractions and empty idealizations – a renunciation in the name of nothing more substantial than a weakly-defined plea for privacy and romance. Such resolutions seem a little too neat, and are not in tune with the many competing energies which course through this uncertain volume.

NOTES

1. Harmon, *O'Faolain: A Life*, p.98.
2. Diarmaid Ferriter, *Occasions of Sin: Sex and Society in Modern Ireland* (London: Profile, 2009), p.96. Michael Storey has similarly noted that 'The Small Lady' raises 'serious questions about the morality of the rebels'. Michael Storey, 'Postcolonialism and Stories of the Irish Troubles', *New Hibernia Review* 2: 3 (Autumn 1998), p.65.
3. Deane, *Strange Country*, p.163.
4. Pierce Butler, *Sean O'Faolain: A Study of the Short Fiction* (New York: Twayne, 1993), pp.11, 16.
5. Sean O'Faolain, 'Foreword' to *The Finest Stories of Sean O'Faolain* (Boston: Little, Brown & Co., 1957), pp.vii, viii.
6. 'In Lilliput', *The Irish Statesman* 5: 22 (6 February 1926), pp.680–1; 'The Bomb Shop', *The Dial* 82: 3 (March 1927), pp.197–209; 'Fugue', *Hound and Horn* 2: 1 (September 1928), pp.7–28.
7. Garnett, 'Introduction', pp.15–16.
8. Cleary, 'This Thing of Darkness', p.147.
9. O'Faoláin, 'Don Quixote O'Flaherty', p.173.
10. Heather Ingman, *A History of the Irish Short Story* (Cambridge: Cambridge University Press, 2009), p.136.
11. Adrian Hunter, 'Frank O'Connor and Sean O'Faolain', in *The Cambridge Introduction to the Short Story in English* (Cambridge: Cambridge University Press, 2007), p.102.

12. According to Peter Hart, fighting was not only about politics for many volunteers, it was also about attaining power and 'settling old scores'. Peter Hart, *The IRA and Its Enemies: Violence and Community in Cork, 1916-1923* (Oxford: Clarendon Press, 1998), p.114; cf. Ferriter, *Transformation of Ireland*, pp.227–8.
13. Gary T. Davenport, 'Sean O'Faolain's Troubles: Revolution and Provincialism in Modern Ireland', *South Atlantic Quarterly* 75 (1976), p.315; Richard Bonaccorso, *Sean O'Faolain's Irish Vision* (New York: State University of New York Press, 1987), p.106.
14. Ronald Tamplin, '*Troubles* and the Irish Tradition', in Ralph J. Crane (ed.), *J.G. Farrell: The Critical Grip* (Dublin: Four Courts Press, 1999), p.52; see also Denis Sampson, 'The Big House in Seán O'Faoláin's Fiction', in Jacqueline Genet (ed.), *The Big House in Ireland: Reality and Representation* (Dingle: Brandon Books, 1991), p.182.
15. José Lanters, *The 'Tinkers' in Irish Literature* (Dublin: Irish Academic Press, 2008), pp.60–3; Paul Delaney, '"A Marginal Footnote": O'Faoláin, the subaltern, and the Travellers', *Irish Studies Review* 11: 2 (2003), pp.155–64.
16. Arndt, *Critical Study of O'Faolain*, p.42.
17. Arndt, 'Sean O'Faolain', p.814.
18. O'Faolain, 'Daniel Corkery', p.52.
19. Susan Garland Mann, *The Short Story Cycle: A Genre Companion and Reference Guide* (Westport, CT: Greenwood, 1989), p.15.
20. James Nagel, *The Contemporary American Short-Story Cycle: The Ethnic Resonance of Genre* (Baton Rouge: Louisiana University Press, 2001), p.17.
21. O'Faolain, *The Short Story*, p.138.
22. O'Faolain, 'Letter from a Novelist', p.4.
23. Garnett, 'Introduction', pp.11–13.
24. Harmon, *O'Faolain: A Life*, pp.88–9.
25. Patrick Walsh, 'Sean O'Faolain's *Midsummer Night Madness and Other Stories*: Contexts for Revisionism', in Kathleen Devine (ed.), *Modern Irish Writers and the Wars* (Gerrards Cross: Colin Smythe, 1999), p.138.
26. John Hildebidle, 'Sean O'Faolain: The Cave of Loneliness', in *Five Irish Writers: The Errand of Keeping Alive* (Cambridge, Mass: Harvard University Press, 1989), p.135.

5

'Rising in the World': *A Nest of Simple Folk*

For all its equivocation and uncertainty, *Midsummer Night Madness* ends with a clear statement of intent as young lovers turn away from an older mentor and attempt to shake free from the politics of the Troubles. O'Faoláin's next work of fiction suggests that things are not so easily resolved or achieved. *A Nest of Simple Folk* (1933) looks back over the sixty-year period which preceded the War of Independence, from the impoverished late days of the Famine in 1854 to the outbreak of the Easter Rising in 1916. Working through this period, the novel traces various associations, echoes and memories which interlink the generations and dissolve the neatly defined polarities of past and present. In *A Nest of Simple Folk* this web of interconnections is shown to be complex and confused for all – so confused that the author includes a genealogy at the start of this bulky book – and this has implications for the ways that the past is understood and narrativized in the text. O'Faoláin signalled as much in an early scene in the novel, when he introduced the protagonist's grandfather, Theo Mor O'Donnell, and said of this ancient patriarch that 'his bottomless memory ... reached back so far that in that one decaying brain one might see, though entangled beyond all hope of unravelling, the story (as well as the picture) of his country's decay' (*NSF* 39). It is not only Theo's memories which are ensnarled in this appropriately convoluted passage, as his body also provides a residual link to pivotal moments in previous decades. His back is inscribed with wounds received during the United Irish Rebellion of 1798, and at various points he is heard to speak of his experiences of the latter days of the Gaelic hedge-school system as well as the Act of Union, Catholic Emancipation and the horrors of the Famine.

O'Faoláin's inclusion of such a figure typifies the importance of historical forces and inherited memories throughout *A Nest of Simple Folk*. As the young Conor Cruise O'Brien once observed, the novel is 'situated almost entirely in the shadow of preceding generations: a penumbra of folklore and historical conjecture' in which 'atavism' appears the defining feature.[1] *A Nest of Simple Folk* casts back over these generations, connecting the lives of several unlikely characters, and charting their travels from the countryside to the town and city. This pattern of internal migration is representative of an historical reality, as many country people (O'Faoláin's parents included) opted or were forced to make similar journeys through the course of the nineteenth century. It also motivates an articulation of some of the harsher consequences of migration, as the narrative brushes against the experiences of alienation, deracination, internal exile and cultural loss. The novel is organized into three books – 'Book One 1854–1888, The Country' is set in rural Limerick; 'Book Two 1888–1898, The Town' moves to the small town of Rathkeale; and 'Book Three 1898–1916, The City' takes place in Cork city – and supposes a clear trajectory, advancing a linear account of the politics of the period. While the narrative follows this path, however, it routinely folds back on itself to suggest multiple points of repetition, recurrence and reversion. This is anticipated at the outset of *A Nest of Simple Folk* – before the story even begins, on the Contents page – when each of the three books is shown to consist of four chapters and in each case the fourth chapter is entitled 'A Desperate Character'. The recurrence of chapter titles is repeated in the third chapters of the first and third books, 'Rising in the World', and this formal device supplies an underlying structure as well as a coherent, if at times forced, rhythm to the text.

Such acts of repetition alert the reader to the various interconnections and patternings which play such a large part in the fabric of the narrative.

The most important of these is the interrelationship between the two principal characters Leo Donnel, whose life story gives shape to the novel, and Denis Hussey, who unexpectedly provides the focus of the third book. Ironically, most of *A Nest of Simple Folk* predates the birth of Denis (he is born in Cork in 1898), and the two characters barely meet or communicate in the course of the novel. Despite the infrequency of their interactions, however, their stories interrelate in strategic ways – just as Leo, as a boy, is hugely influenced by the presence of his paternal grandfather Theo and his uncle Nicholas, so Denis is inspired by the legend of his elderly uncle Leo when he reaches adolescence. Both characters draw on this influence to rebel against the world into which they are born, and both are transformed into outlaws of sorts in consequence. The final iteration of 'A Desperate Character' relates to both Leo and Denis, whereas the previous instances in Books One and Two refer solely to Leo. Their rebellions are underscored by a formal symmetry which bookends the text, as *A Nest of Simple Folk* opens and closes with seminal struggles in the O'Donnell and Hussey families. Each of these struggles carries an Oedipal significance, with the novel beginning with the death of Leo's father, Long John O'Donnell, and concluding with the rupture of Denis's father's power as patriarch and embodiment of the law – Denis's father, Johnny Hussey, is a sergeant in the RIC. Their stories are not only patterned at a formal level, however, for there is also a sense that both characters' actions are determined by larger forces over which they have little or no control. The discourse of 'blood' looms large in this novel (Leo's 'mad, black blood', or his Anglo-Irish inheritance, is frequently cited as the reason for his wayward behaviour [*NSF* 218]), and the world that is presented to the reader is a world where people can be identified according to their ancestors and individuals are recognizable to apparent strangers because it is said that their 'seed and breed' is known 'for generations' (*NSF* 114).

The first two books focus on the life of Leo Donnel. Leo is born Leo O'Donnell, before the narrative commences, in 1840, and is the third son in a poor tenant farmer's family from rural Limerick. The novel opens with a dramatic encounter between his mother and his dying father as they struggle over the terms of the O'Donnell inheritance. His mother, Judith

Foxe, proves victorious and condemns the rest of her children to penury by ensuring that the young Leo is willed the family's only valuable piece of land. This alienates Leo from his siblings, and the boy is further estranged when he is sent to live with his mother's unmarried sisters in their ancestral home, Foxehall. Leo's remove to Foxehall is portrayed, at least in part, as an attempt at reconciliation between Judith and her sisters, as Judith cut herself off from her family when she married into the O'Donnells years earlier. By doing so, Judith transgressed the clearest of boundaries, marrying beneath herself socially and committing apostasy (or 'turning Catholic') along the way. Leo is brought to Foxehall in the hope that amends might be made and the young protagonist groomed to inherit the Foxe estate. He is quickly made to realize the complexity of his origins, however, since, as the child of a mixed marriage, his dual inheritance speaks of divided loyalties, conflicting traditions and interconnected tensions. Leo learns that although his grandfather Theo was flogged for his involvement in the 1798 rebellion, it was a maternal great-uncle, Carey Foxe, who led out the local yeomanry to suppress that insurrection; he also hears that an uncle on the Foxe side was responsible for the murder of an O'Donnell uncle during the Famine.

The stresses of this heritage are initially staged through competing cultural and linguistic forms, especially through the conflict at Foxehall between Leo's Hibernicized idiom and his aunts' more conventional use of English. 'Talk proper English,' his aunts snap in a particularly charged scene, in response to his use of 'some Irish word!' (*NSF* 98). These stresses come to a head when the aunts re-name the young protagonist Leo Foxe-Donnel. The aunts' insertion of the metronymic Foxe and inclusion of the double-edged hyphen is presented as a form of ownership of their charge, while their gutting of the illustrious name of O'Donnell and reconfiguration of it as the historically meaningless Donnel is also symbolically rich. Through this act of re-naming, the aunts attempt to fashion a new identity for Leo, intervening in the way he perceives himself and altering his relationship with his native (Catholic, Gaelic) heritage and immediate (O'Donnell) family. Their efforts are belated, at best, since it is clear from the outset of the novel that any power the Foxes might once have wielded has long since been lost. O'Faoláin is careful not to simplify the issue, though, and it is notable that when Leo rebels against the Foxes later in Book One, shedding the identity that has been created for him by his aunts, he nonetheless chooses to hold on to part of this identity by re-naming himself Leo Donnel.

When Leo rebels against his Foxe inheritance, with all its associations of prestige and detachment, he also revolts against the world of respectability which his mother desires for him. This is an additional reason why Judith fosters her favourite son to Foxehall, as she hopes to see him 'rise in the world' and become 'a gentleman'. Leo decides otherwise, and opts for a life of dissipation and ease until he happens upon the Fenian organizer James Stephens in a pub in East Limerick. This chance encounter provides the turning point of the novel, as 'the foolish Leo' is suddenly politicized and his 'heart and mind' sent 'crackling like a fiery furze' towards republicanism and rebellion (*NSF* 165). Reflecting upon this scene, it is as if Stephens's seductive rhetoric provides the means with which Leo can finally formulate various inchoate beliefs and ill-defined prejudices. 'He had always disliked the priests,' it is said, 'now he could hate them. Those pubs of Irishtown had set in him, year after year, a seed of interest in his people and his country; at last it burst through him like a well' (*NSF* 164). Within a couple of pages Leo's new-found politics fall flat, as they result in nothing more than a drunken non-assault on a police-barracks and a lengthy prison sentence in England. In prison, Leo is brought to reflect on his relationship with the people he had sought to represent:

> And yet why should he have any love for that place, or for the people of it – dead, lazy, lifeless wretches, as he called them. But he would chuckle like a madman to himself at that; remember that it was not love for them, but that little burly fury in the pub … that drove him to what he did. Aye! First it was his mother, forcing him to what he had no wish for, then it was his aunts, then came Frankie O'Donnell [Leo's uncle], with his smooth tongue, sending [James] Stephens on his track; and then Stephens himself who, so a warder taunted him one night, had dodged jail like a hare, and was now drinking in the pubs of Paris (*NSF* 169).

As the narrator subtly substitutes the possessive 'his' for the more distant 'that' and 'the' ('his people and his country' is quietly translated into 'that place' and 'the people'), so Leo touches on the principal reason why he was drawn to rebellion. Crucially, this has nothing to do with abstract political beliefs or deeply-held ideological convictions. Rather, it is borne of the pettiest of grudges: Judith's desire for her son's respectability seems to be at the heart of his revolt, as Leo complains that his mother 'forc[ed] him to what he had no wish for'. The full extent of this complaint is not articulated – it does not lead to an interrogation of the inequities of the class system or the moral bankruptcy of ideas of respectability and status – and Leo's continued immaturity is reinforced by the simple fact that he remains blind to the price his siblings have paid for his early privileges. Because of the terms of his father's will, the sombre reality is that his brothers have been indentured to the land and his sisters forced to emigrate or marry young. In future years, it is mentioned in passing, they will be 'merely flung from one slavery into another' (*NSF* 173).

Leo's non-realization is illustrative of a larger thesis which runs through O'Faoláin's *oeuvre*. A couple of years earlier, in an article for the journal *New Statesman and Nation*, O'Faoláin drafted the outlines of this thesis when he identified a distinction between what he termed the 'ineffectual rebel' and the 'effective revolutionary'. The former, he suggested, was simply reactive to the situation in which he or she found themselves, while the latter was thoughtful and imaginative and agitated for 'a fundamental change in the conditions of life'.[2] This distinction was said to account for the absence of change in post-Independence Ireland, as the recent struggle for independence was shorn of its radical or revolutionary impetus, resulting in nothing more than the consolidation of a conservative, patriarchal, Catholic middle-class. It is a point that O'Faoláin returned to in other works. In the novel *Come Back to Erin*, for instance, Frankie Hannafey, an IRA gunman on the run in de Valera's Ireland, is adamant that 'revolutions are very slow processes' which have yet to be realized in an Irish context, and the lack of progress in this slow-burning tale of the mid-1930s seems to stem from this depressed belief.[3] Similarly, in the short story 'A Meeting', in *A Purse of Coppers*, a woman who was once active in the Troubles is robbed of her potential in the independent state. Restricted to a life of domestic servitude in a rural backwater, she finds herself unable to make sense of the betrayal of earlier ideals and never quite manages to say, 'Jesus, I'm fed to the bloody eye-teeth with this bloody hole and all in it!' (*PC* 212). The distinction gains its fullest expression in *The Irish*, where it is supposed that:

> Rebels deprived themselves, and Ireland, of as much as they gave, they choked the critical side of their minds, they were good rebels in proportion as they were bad revolutionaries, so that their passion for change and their vision of change never pierced to organic change, halted dead at the purely modal and circumstantial. It had to be that way since they devoted their lives and all their beings to passion rather than thought, or in Arnold's words describing the French Revolution 'had their source in a great movement of feeling, not in a great movement of mind'.[4]

O'Faoláin's nod to Matthew Arnold – and Arnold's essay 'The Function of Criticism at the Present Time' (1865) – sounds an alarming note here, as it risks recycling an old discourse which was often used to justify imperial governance in Ireland. The separation of thought and passion carries latent echoes of the distinction between the rational Saxon (who is fit to rule) and the excitable Celt (who needs ruling), which gained currency through another of Arnold's influential essays, 'The Celtic Element in Literature' (1867). O'Faoláin's separation of these attributes is explicitly linked to his belief in diverse strains or bloodlines in *The Irish*. Talking about 'The Rebel', for example, he imagined that the ambition of Wolfe Tone in the late-eighteenth century was to unite 'the logic of the Northern Scot to the passions of the Southern Irish', or 'a controlled Anglo-Irish intelligence [with] a passionate sense of injustice among the native Irish'.[5] Such distinctions between logic and passion, or intelligence and energy, appear particularly contrived in the wake of various interventions inspired by the late Edward Said, interventions which have critiqued the dichotomization of such attributes in the process of identity formation. What is more, the association of such characteristics with specific groups of people sounds condescending and uncomfortably essentialist. O'Faoláin's basic point, though (which is itself debatable), is that rebels in Irish history have often been non-conformists who acted rather than reflected on their actions. This thesis is central to his representation of Constance Markievicz in his biography of that name, and feeds into his figuration of the fictional Leo Donnel in *A Nest of Simple Folk*.

If Leo is presented as an example of the rebel – and he is an odd example, for it is hard to know the 'immediate injustice' he suffers – the narrator is nonetheless keen to hint at the ways in which he is subsequently mythologized by those who do not know him. Following his release from his first term in prison, Leo joins his uncle Nicholas O'Donnell and follows Parnell in the campaign for Home Rule. Leo and Nicholas are re-named colloquially 'the two Fenians', and are fêted at political meetings where it is said that they 'look[ed] down proudly at the people cheering [them] whenever the speakers made a reference to the men who had fought for the cause of freedom and liberty. But though [Leo] eagerly wished it', the narrator significantly adds, 'they would never let him speak, and as a result the people began to have a profound respect for him as a desperate man who did not believe in wasting time in words' (*NSF* 188). The deliberate silencing of Leo in such scenes is motivated, and results in him being ascribed an identity ('Fenian') without actually being engaged in any way. Although he is put on a pedestal, the narrative indicates that he is simultaneously denied the means of self-representation or critical agency. This is quite unlike the opportunities for speech-making which are afforded his uncle, of whom it is said 'Nicholas, on the other hand, became such a favourite speaker at these meetings that he travelled further and further abroad' (*NSF* 188). This difference in treatment seems to arise from the fact that Nicholas's more orthodox background places him more conveniently in nationalist circles – Nicholas is Catholic, poor and recognizably 'native Irish'.

The narrator further reflects upon this process of mythification when Leo is released from jail for the second time at the end of Book Two. As Leo follows his small family to Cork, it is said:

> So, as he had been before, he became again a familiar figure that people would stop and look back on. Because of his height, his tall black hat, his pale face, and beard combed with care and sweeping his chest, they could see him long before they met him, and they liked to salute him, and receive his lordly salute in return. He was come at last to a place where the people knew nothing of him, except that he was a Fenian and had been in jail for several years because of his beliefs. They looked at him, these quiet, inexperienced people of the half-rural streets of Cork, as if he were some hero left by the tide of another age (*NSF* 305).

Once again, Leo is brought before 'the people' only to be eclipsed from the encounter that is described. He might be 'a familiar figure' to those he meets, but they still know 'nothing of him', and they instead invent a life story that they think is appropriate. Significantly, on this occasion, Leo's speech is regulated by those who seem to champion him – he responds to the people he meets rather than initiates any form of greeting, and whatever conversation he shares with them remains unrecorded. In addition, speech seems less important than perception or sight in this scene. The stress is on Leo's physical appearance here, and the focus of the narrative is on the ways that this is interpreted by the citizens of Cork – they 'see him' before they greet him, and they twice 'look back' and 'look at' him. In such scenes, it is as if the reality of Leo, with all his complications and idiosyncrasies, is translated in other people's minds into an abstraction that they identify as 'Fenian'. This allows them to revise the messiness of his being to fit the pattern of something they believe to be true of the idea of the rebel, something pure and noble ('as if he were some hero'), and removed from the modest reality of their everyday lives. It is entirely fitting, therefore, that the one group of people who do not participate in this act of myth-making are the people who 'know' Leo for the man that he is, the people who hail from 'his own home-parish', and who remember him 'for a boy who had wasted his substance and his strength to no purpose' (*NSF* 188).

As *A Nest of Simple Folk* follows the life story of Leo Donnel, from the mid-nineteenth century through to the early years of the twentieth, it assumes the form of an historical novel and looks to well-established narrative conventions which have their origins in the work of Walter Scott. An ambitious panoramic sweep is combined in the text with a motley cast of characters from contrasting classes and backgrounds. Occasional references to real historical events and figures also provide a frame against which to place various fictional character-types, and it is through the development of these types that the processes or workings of history are conveyed. James Stephens appears briefly in O'Faoláin's novel, and rubs shoulders with a number of fictional characters (including Leo), while mention is also made of the likes of O'Connell, Terence Bellew MacManus, Charles Stewart Parnell and Michael Davitt. The 1916 insurgents Tom Clarke and Constance Markievicz also feed into O'Faoláin's delineation of the character of Leo, although neither is represented in the text. Clarke's bravery and terrible suffering in Chatham and Portland prisons are reflected in Leo's experiences as a Fenian prisoner in English jails, while Markievicz, as a figure of the Anglo-Irish gentry who rebelled against inherited politics and expectations, bears more than passing resemblance to the principal protagonist. According to the Marxist literary critic Georg Lukács, such interests in the workings of history provided the basis for the emergence of the historical novel a century earlier with Scott. Before the *Waverley* novels, Lukács stated, historical works of fiction were 'mere costumery'. What Scott brought to focus was 'the specifically historical, that is, derivation of the individuality of characters from the historical peculiarity of their age'; or, to put it another way, writing individuals within their history and understanding them accordingly, rather than using history merely as an exotic or colourful canvas.[6] In this way, Lukács argued, Scott identified the ways in which lives and cultural ecologies are interwoven and shaped.

This new way of writing about history was linked to a growing interest in the early-nineteenth century in theories of *ethnos* and national character, as well as the desire to communicate ideas of collective identity and shared history amongst disparate groups of peoples. 'The appeal to national independence and national character is necessarily connected with a reawakening of national history,' Lukács observed.[7] As Jerome de Groot recently suggested, the historical novel played an important part in the articulation of this appeal as it became part of 'the typology of nationhood' through which imagined communities of individuals came to identify themselves.[8] O'Faoláin utilized the conventions of the historical novel to further identify with this appeal and to make sense of the history – or rather, to construct a narrative of the history – of the Free State which had recently come into being. In Lukács' eloquent phrase, part of the achievement of Scott's work was the representation of the past as 'the prehistory of the present', as it was understood to give 'poetic licence to those historical, social and human forces which, in the course of a long evolution, have made our present-day life what it is and as we experience it'.[9] Such claims might also be made of *A Nest of Simple Folk*. The forces that motivate O'Faoláin's text, however, are largely restrictive and non-triumphant, and give rise to experiences which are marked by squalor, despair and poverty. Emigration is a grim reality in this novel, with characters repeatedly lost to the larger world. 'What happened' to many of Leo's sisters and cousins who are compelled to emigrate, it is poignantly remarked, 'in the end no one ever knew' (*NSF* 177). And 'slavery' is a keyword which links most of the remaining characters, as they struggle with the direst of material and emotional circumstances.

The history that is represented is also awkward and confused, as political allegiances and class interrelationships prove more complicated than is often supposed. Leo's character resists neat definition, for instance, and his ancestry is uncomfortably hybrid or mixed. What is more, Leo is related by marriage to the RIC Catholic 'spy' Johnny Hussey, and Johnny's relationship to the law he enforces is at times surprisingly ambiguous. 'In land matters, for all his ... years in "the Force"', it is said of this policeman that he was 'still more on the side of the people than the law' (*NSF* 236). While drawing on the form of the historical novel, therefore, O'Faoláin was careful to distance himself from too close an indebtedness to Scott. Indeed, he would later argue that the danger with following a model like *Waverley* too readily was that it could lead to a simplistic reading of history and the 'slavish' exploitation of Ireland 'as a subject'.[10] O'Faoláin sought to avoid this trap by stressing the unexpected in historical ties, and by pointing to the bleakest, and most unromantic, of actualities and experiences.

Destitution, hunger, alcoholism, rape, domestic abuse, abandoned children and enforced migration all feature in this dejected novel. He also departed from this model by playing with the conventions of the historical novel, blurring it with other genres including the *Bildungsroman*, the family chronicle, nineteenth-century realism and autobiography. In addition, as James Cahalan once noted, O'Faoláin broke with expectations of the form by focalizing the experience of historical episodes through the perspective of certain characters (Denis and Leo especially), rather than concentrating on the representation of the events or relying solely on the presence of an omniscient third-person narrator.[11]

O'Faoláin was cautious with his use of other intertexts as well. Like many of his peers he looked to the great Russian writers of the nineteenth century for inspiration, and *A Nest of Simple Folk* takes its title from Ivan Turgenev's early novel *A Nest of Gentlefolk* (1859). O'Faoláin considered his title 'a gesture of adoration' towards Turgenev, who was also a favourite of fellow Cork writers Daniel Corkery and Frank O'Connor, but contended that his novel borrowed little else from the Russian master, who was in turn influenced by Scott (*VM* 254). Critics have generally concurred with this thesis and pointed to the differences which characterize the two texts. The quiet design of Turgenev's story, with its movement towards nostalgia and some measure of acceptance, is quite unlike the note of despondency which runs through *A Nest of Simple Folk*. Notwithstanding O'Faoláin's claims, though, it would be wrong to suggest, as the late Benedict Kiely once did, that the title is 'the only connection' between the two texts.[12] For both novels engage with the structures and divisions of extremely class-conscious societies, even if the two societies are organized quite differently; both texts also depict individuals who are uprooted in their childhood and cut adrift in their formative years. What is more, both novels tell stories which deal with the aftermath of seemingly happier times. Glyn Turton has commented on Turgenev's 'profound sense of the tragic nature of individual destiny', as a love affair is forced to end because of the weight of circumstances, while a recurring refrain in O'Faoláin's text, which interlinks the stories of Leo and Denis, is a quotation from the early Christian philosopher Boethius, '*Fuisse felicem et non esse, omnium est infelicissimum genus*; to have been happy at one time and then to be unhappy after, isn't that the greatest unhappiness in the whole world?' (*NSF* 169, haltingly repeated 386–7).[13] In addition, the central characters in both texts seek to refashion themselves in the course of their lives: Leo through his various incarnations and re-namings; Lavretski, in Turgenev's novel, as he comes to embody the principle that 'man can remake himself'; and Denis, later in O'Faoláin's story, through his fascination with actors, costumes and the theatre.[14] It is hardly incidental, then, although it is usually overlooked by critics, that separate chapter titles in Books One and Three are respectively titled 'Gentlefolk' and 'Simple Folk'.

Whatever the importance of Turgenev and Scott, however, Lennox Robinson's *Patriots* (1912) is perhaps the most revealing of intertexts. It was this play, O'Faoláin later claimed, which made him appreciate for the first time that art could be local and literature could describe the familiar. In his memoir *Vive Moi!*, O'Faoláin sought to recall the precise moment of this realization as he imagined his response to seeing the play performed, at a young age, in the nearby Cork Opera House. 'On the lighted stage,' he reminisced, 'I beheld, with an astonishment never before or since equalled for me by any theatrical spectacle, the parlour of a house in an Irish country town':

> I saw other familiars talking on the stage as naturally as if they were in my aunt's cottage in Rathkeale ... This parlour on the stage – But why do I say stage? It was Reality itself – was over a shop, all its anti-macassarish details tenderly, delightfully, recognisably familiar: a geranium pot in the window, a chenille cloth covering the table, pictures of Robert Emmet and Pius X on the walls, old lace curtains, old padded furniture (*VM* 89).

Against such everyday realities, *Patriots* tells the story of a man who seems out of touch with his time. The play focuses on the figure of James Nugent, a once-celebrated Fenian rebel who returns home after a long prison sentence in England. The home Nugent returns to is a place which has consigned Fenianism to the past, and the people who inhabit it (the people he fought for and lived alongside) have abandoned earlier principles in their pursuit of material gains and personal self-interest. Nugent is welcomed back into this world as a hero, but this welcome soon sours as the townspeople grow embarrassed by his continued commitment to a politics that they have either forgotten or repressed. The play turns on their gradual shunning of Nugent and their transformation of him into an historical anachronism. Although he holds firm to ideas which were once shared, few people listen to him anymore, as most prefer the easy distractions of a bourgeois life and the local cinema. As the play progresses Nugent cuts an increasingly isolated figure, and any sense of communion with the younger generation is lost in the final, dispiriting scene when it is revealed that his commitment to rebellion was indirectly responsible for the maiming of his daughter years earlier. On realizing this, Nugent surrenders to local pressures and abandons the political struggle. 'I have tried – tried as you tried,' he pleads to the ghosts of dead patriots, '– and been broken …'.[15]

Robinson's play is very much a text of its time and was produced in the period immediately preceding the rebellion. *A Nest of Simple Folk* was published two decades later and comes out of a very different context where, with the benefit of hindsight, radical politics is known to have survived, albeit initially and to a limited degree, underground. Johnny Hussey's naive assessment of the situation is exposed in an interview with an RIC officer when he reiterates the depressed logic of *Patriots*, that the Fenians are 'all done and finished with' (*NSF* 239). Johnny's superior convinces him otherwise, hinting at covert reports on the activities of recently revitalized organizations, and this leads Johnny to reflect on whether Leo is all that he has appeared to be. As he mulls over his knowledge of Leo, the policeman is shocked into revising his opinion of the cantankerous but seemingly docile older man, realizing that the latter's apparent obeisance to the law might also be interpreted as an act of mockery and wilful deception. Where Johnny had previously seen 'old Leo Donnel in his black hat, smiling foolishly at him over his pile of yellowing newspapers', and taken no notice, the narrator comments that 'he saw now, as he had never seen before, a cunning in that smile and a secret in those small, peering eyes' (*NSF* 240). Leo appears the epitome of sly civility in such scenes (or at least is made to appear so to Johnny's eyes), performing aspects of a subjugated or comic identity for his brother-in-law, and seeming to be what he is not.

As important as this stress on performance is, though, Leo's open secret remains his commitment to rebellion – he is under police surveillance, after all, and is instantly recognized on the street as 'Fenian'. What is less obvious is that the shape of this rebellion has changed imperceptibly in the course of the novel, and evolved into something more focused and coherent. It is no longer a question of ill-defined gripes and grudges (against his mother, his aunts or the clergy), since Leo has been transformed by the experience of jail and politicized by the discourse of Irish republicanism. This perhaps explains why so many scenes in Books Two and Three allude to the education of Leo, as he is often depicted reading newspapers and books or attending rallies and political meetings. These scenes quietly gain in value as the narrative progresses. At the same time, they are presented with a light touch by the narrator, as the text shies away from recording specific details or providing any information which might prove particularly revealing. The material Leo reads, for instance, such as the 'yellowing newspapers' mentioned above, remains unidentified, and the meetings he attends take place off the page, with their proceedings left unrecorded.

Reading against the grain, the absence of such details might be considered calculated on the part of the narrator, who chooses not to inform on Leo to his peers or the reader. The novel is full of informers, after all: Julie Keene testifies against her future husband, Leo, in court; their abandoned son, the weakly-imagined Johno, talks too much when he drinks; frightened prisoners inform on comrades and fellow inmates; and Johnny spies on his elderly uncle for the police files. However, this lack of information is also in line with the narrator's engagement with politics and historical events more generally. For if seminal events from across a sixty-year period contribute to the structure of this novel (the Fenian rebellion, the Land Wars, the Home Rule campaigns, the First World War), these events barely intrude upon the actual narrative, and in many ways provide little more than context for the development of the central characters. Ironically, recalling Lukács, O'Faoláin's decision to write like this might be thought to undo the historical significance of his story, as the past is occluded to the degree that it becomes little more than background or 'mere costumery'. Conversely, though, it might be argued that the text's interest is less on the events themselves, and more on the forces that motivated those events and impacted on the ecology of a community. O'Faoláin's primary focus, that is to say, is on the pressures experienced by a 'nest' of ordinary people who have been conditioned by a past that they have inherited and that they partially inhabit. In addition, however, this strategy might be considered a further instance of the technique of perspectivalism that was used to such effect in *Midsummer Night Madness*, as the text elects to represent only those events that are directly experienced by the people it depicts. Either way, the novel ends with another event which it simultaneously declines to represent, as Leo sets off on a final journey, this time to Dublin, to participate in the Easter Rising. By this point in the story Denis has replaced Leo as the principal character, so the narrative remains with the younger man in Cork.

The concluding chapters of *A Nest of Simple Folk* are focalized through the figure of Denis and concentrate on his incipient revolt against the world of his parents. The reasons behind this revolt are not fully articulated (indeed, they are only beginning to be understood by Denis at the close of the novel), but what is clear is that they are directed against values which his parents hold dear. Denis's mother, Bid Keene, is characterized by her devotion to the Church and her desire for social respectability, while of her husband's ambitions for their children it is solemnly stated that 'all he ever thought of was to bring them up respecting the law, and to make them look up to the respectable merchants of the city … [and] above all, to instil into them the love and fear of the good God who made them' (*NSF* 320). These are the values that Denis pitches himself against, but his rebellion is anxious and, at best, only partially realized. By the end of the novel it is not certain what direction his rebellion will take, or what it might give rise to, even if the clues are plentiful and the path seems obvious. Denis looks very like the young John Whelan whose imperialist sympathies were shocked by the Rising, and who subsequently joined the Irish Volunteers; indeed, key scenes in Book Three are repeated almost verbatim in *Vive Moi!*. Denis also resembles some of the volunteers from *Midsummer Night Madness*, such as John in the title story and his namesake Denis in 'The Small Lady' – each is Cork-born, each has a policeman for a father, and each rebels against inherited loyalties to fight in the Troubles. This sense of relative uncertainty is compounded by the decision to close *A Nest of Simple Folk* just before news of the Rising fully breaks, with the ominous image of 'Shandon raising its black finger against the last ray of day, and far away a faint, faint crackling of rifle fire' being heard. Against these signs of foreboding, which look forward to guerrilla activity and curfews as well as the imminent Rising, Denis peers out over a city which seems to anticipate its later terrors, 'listening and holding its breath in a silence of fear' (*NSF* 413). It is crucial that the novel concludes at this point and that its last word is the heavily-weighted word 'fear'.

Denis's rebellion is related to his interest in the theatre, a world with which he comes into contact when his mother takes in lodgers to help secure the family's finances. Theatre is associated with forbidden thoughts and sensations for the young man, and comes to signify a plethora of possibilities. These possibilities are otherwise impossible to conceptualize or speak about, and relate to a world of sexuality, self-fashioning, exoticism, liberation and the body. In a word, they are understood as being representative of 'a life that nobody ever spoke of, or spoke of only as the life of a world and of people whom he and his likes would, should, and need never know' (*NSF* 367). Denis's rebellion is borne of excitement with this world and boredom with 'the dull circle of days' which constitutes the reality of his life, revolving as it does around the fixed poles of study, food and prayer (*NSF* 366). It is also a consequence of the poisonous cocktail of inhibition, shame and snobbery which he has inherited and internalized from his parents. Most importantly, though, it is generational, as he turns his back on his father's loyalties to embrace the politics of resurgent nationalism. By the end of the novel, Denis has not yet joined these forces, despite what his father says or what a reader might be tempted to think, and a vivid scene in 'Interlude', in Book Three, shows how difficult this step will ultimately be, as it describes his reactions to witnessing a group of volunteers drilling on the streets of Cork.

Appalled by the group's poor equipment and their 'absurd costumes' (the reference to theatre resonates), Denis is depicted 'burn[ing] with shame' (*NSF* 351). The narrator skilfully interweaves this shame with an earlier memory of Denis's, when, accompanied by his father, he watched the Sherwood Foresters on parade at Victoria barracks and was swept along by the pageantry of the occasion, and felt 'the thrill of the power and pomp of empire' (*NSF* 352). 'With a groan, almost of pain,' Denis turns from the 'odd company' assembled before him:

> grimacing like a person who has seen something mean or humiliating. 'Bog-trotters!' he called them, 'corner-boys, blackguards.' In and out of the darkness he ran, swifter and swifter, as if to leave pursuing shame behind. How awful if any English person saw them and said, 'Are all the Irish like that?' ... But this rout of the back quays of Cork shambling in the dark through their awkward paces in their rags of uniform! He had to lean against his door to recover from the sight of them, and for a week after he felt as humbled as if he had been caught doing something disgusting in the public street (*NSF* 352–3).

The visceral quality of Denis's response, and the sheer force of its representation, speaks to the powerful mesh of attitudes that he has inherited from his parents. Class prejudices and urban biases are writ large across this passage ('back quays', 'corner-boys', 'bog-trotters'), as are parochial inhibitions and feelings of inferiority. Colonial sensibilities also provide an idiom through which the narrator chooses to represent the encounter (Denis is worried about what '*any* English person' might say), and this is inflected with a moralistic impulse ('darkness', 'humiliating', 'disgusting') and an overarching sense of neurosis and shame. 'Blackguards' is particularly weighted as a term of abuse, since it is explicitly related to his father and covers a multitude of miscreants and sinners who are despised by the Hussey family. 'Nobody minded the word "blackguard"' in the house, it is observed; 'that household used it every day. To the Husseys street hawkers, newsboys, militiamen, corner-boys were all blackguards, because they were, as Johnny once said … "without pride of ancestry, hope of posterity, or desire for place"' (*NSF* 353). Lest the reader forget, social structures are of critical importance to the class-conscious Johnny Hussey, who takes pride in the fact that whatever else people may say of him he can always claim that 'I know my place' (*NSF* 322). This is the world that Denis has been born into, and it is a worldview from which he must strive to break free.

It is not the only outlook that Denis has inherited, however, and in the climactic Oedipal struggle the narrator suggests other forces that he has also, perhaps unknowingly, imbibed. 'From some hidden well of memory all the stored hate of centuries jetted into his mind,' the narrator comments, when Denis clashes with his father over news of the insurrection, 'words fallen from his mother, spoken even by his father, by the monks, by his school companions, read in his history books, they fountained in him like the blood that surges to the head and blinds the eyes with rage' (*NSF* 409). This well of inherited or collective memory provides the source for many of the connections which interlink the generations in *A Nest of Simple Folk*, and comprises a complex legacy of perspectives, allegiances and loyalties which is difficult to explain or entirely escape. (It is notable that Denis has learnt some of these unspoken words from his parents – 'even' his father.) It is this inherited memory which links Denis to Leo, and which characterizes the latter's influence in the final sections of the story. This influence is all the greater given that the two characters barely meet or communicate in the novel. Apart from one accidental encounter which is briefly described, and where little is spoken or shared (other than a vague memory of Latin verse and a sketchy interest in the thoughts of Boethius), the narrative actually works to keep Leo and Denis apart. At no other point are they represented on the same page, and on the few occasions when they happen to meet the narrator skips over the encounter, simply stating that 'the old man never stopped, and never spoke to him except to say, "Good night, Denis"'. Indeed, the two characters are placed so far apart that by the time of the Rising Denis seems to have 'almost forgotten' about Leo (*NSF* 388).

Almost, but not quite, and it is to his uncle's house that Denis finally turns in the closing pages of the novel, after he is thrown out of the family home by his father. There he meets another commanding figure from the past, his aged maternal grandmother Mag Keene. Denis and Mag's conversation is suitably sparse, running to less than a page, and consisting largely of his grandmother's keening for the plight of the male insurgents and their future widows, especially her son-in-law Leo and daughter Julie (*NSF* 412–13). Their conversation is also disjointed, as Mag's mind wanders across subjects and weaves fluidly through time, looking back to the failed Fenian rebellion fifty years earlier, and moving fluently between Irish and English. Mag's use of Irish in this penultimate scene is striking and differs from the narrator's use of the language more generally in the novel. For although Irish-language words and phrases fleck *A Nest of Simple Folk*, especially in the earlier sections of the novel in rural Limerick, these words are usually accompanied by a direct English-language translation which is provided by the characters themselves or by the narrator in parentheses. Such explanations are not always included at the end of the novel, with Mag's words instead left to stand as if they are the remnants of an untranslated, perhaps even an untranslatable, order. As if to stress the point, many of her words are phonetically rendered, which gives her speech a slightly allusive and deliberately oral quality. '*Do cuireag ar an mohar thu*' ('You were put on the road'), she twice says to the recently-evicted Denis, for instance, while she also remarks of Julie, '*Ni 'eadhainn a huille*' ('I could no more for her'), and then falls momentarily into prayer, '*Wirra na grawst*' ('Mary of the Graces') (*NSF* 412–13).

It cannot be known for certain whether Denis, or the reader, follows all that his grandmother says, and this is significant since Mag (like Theo Mor O'Donnell in Book One) represents a link to an older age and culture. Coming so soon after Denis's discovery of a well of memories, Mag's comments complicate or, at the very least, test the bounds of Denis's perceived inheritance, since it is unclear how much he understands or whether he can decode the thoughts of this elderly woman; it is equally uncertain what has been lost by the absence of the middle generation – his parents' generation – in this dialogue. His mother and father are primarily associated with a generation that has tried to break from this past (the past that is embodied by the likes of Mag and Theo), and their interest in the trappings of a modern bourgeois life signifies this. The life that Bid Keene and Johnny Hussey have built for themselves in Cork is a world away from the impoverished circumstances that are described in the early sections of *A Nest of Simple Folk*, and the narrative takes delight in listing the kitsch, pseudo-respectable items that they seem to value and cherish. Uncomfortable chairs, oversized sideboards, empty but expensively-bound family albums, fire-screens with views of Killarney, 'an epergne, with pink and eau-de-Nil vases', cut-glass decanters and decorative gold-framed pictures ('*The Stag at Bay*; *The Doctor's Story*; *His Majesty Edward the Seventh and Her Majesty Queen Alexandra in their Coronation Robes*; *His Holiness Pius the Tenth*; Constable's *Crossing the Brook*; and *Etna Erupting* [in red and silver tinsel]'), are amongst the many possessions coveted and collected by Denis's parents.[16] Each of these items is clearly prized for its status value – a brass plate with the name 'Hussey' is attached to their front door for this very reason – but the family can ill-afford to buy any of these pieces, and their true worthlessness is witnessed by the simple fact that all of the items are placed in a parlour which is locked and never used (*NSF* 317–8).

By the end of the novel the only thing that is clear is that the older generation, and the ways that they embody, will not survive the Rising; according to the book's genealogy, Mag and Leo both die sometime in 1916. Denis's predicament, then, as John Hildebidle has observed, is to learn to 'understand the example' of the older characters that he barely knows or has come into contact with – characters who face imminent death and from whom he has been separated by time, space, narrative and parental ideology.[17] In addition, though, Denis must try to make sense of the conflicting codes that he has inherited from his predecessors, including his parents, and make sense of them for his time.

NOTES

1. Donat O'Donnell (Conor Cruise O'Brien), 'The Parnellism of Seán O'Faoláin', in *Maria Cross: Imaginative Patterns in a Group of Modern Catholic Writers* (London: Chatto & Windus, 1954), pp.96, 101.

2. O'Faoláin, 'De Valera – Rebel or Reformer?', p.173.
3. Seán O'Faoláin, *Come Back to Erin* (London: Jonathan Cape), p.71.
4. O'Faolain, *The Irish*, p.105.
5. Ibid., pp.91, 92.
6. Georg Lukács, *The Historical Novel*, trans. by Hannah and Stanley Mitchell (London: Merlin, 1962), p.19; cf. Ian Ducan 'Introduction' to Walter Scott, *Waverley* ed. by P.D. Garside (1814; London: Penguin, 2011), pp.xvi-ii.
7. Lukács, *The Historical Novel*, p.25.
8. de Groot, *The Historical Novel*, p.94.
9. Lukács, *The Historical Novel*, p.53.
10. O'Faolain, *The Irish*, pp.135–7.
11. James M. Cahalan, 'The Realistic Visions of Seán Ó Faoláin and Francis MacManus', in *Great Hatred, Little Room: The Irish Historical Novel* (Dublin: Gill & Macmillan, 1983), p.116.
12. Benedict Kiely, 'Sean O'Faoláin: A Tiller of Ancient Soil', rprt. in *A Raid into Dark Corners and Other Essays* (Cork: Cork University Press, 1999), p.126.
13. Glyn Turton, *Turgenev, and the Context of English Literature, 1850–1900* (London: Routledge, 1992), p.77.
14. Frank Frederick Seeley, *Turgenev: A Reading of his Fiction* (Cambridge: Cambridge University Press, 1991), p.185.
15. Lennox Robinson, *Patriots*, in Christopher Murray (ed.), *Selected Plays of Lennox Robinson* (Gerrards Cross: Colin Smythe, 1982), p.62 [ellipsis as original].
16. Many of these details are lovingly remembered in O'Faoláin's semi-autobiographical 'The Sugawn Chair'. This short story was first published in *The Bell* 15: 3 (December 1947), pp.22–5; a revised version was included in the collection *I Remember! I Remember!* (London: Rupert Hart-Davis, 1962), pp.23–7.
17. Hildebidle, 'Sean O'Faolain', p.139.

6

FAUST UNDER THE WEATHER-FISH: *BIRD ALONE*

Inheritance is also a central concern in *Bird Alone* (1936). Narrated in the first person by Corney (Cornelius) Crone, the novel provides an extended reminiscence of childhood and early maturity in Cork, in the years surrounding the fall of Charles Stewart Parnell. The choices the narrator makes as a youth – like the decisions Denis appears to reach at the end of *A Nest of Simple Folk* – are largely determined by his associations with another older relative, his grandfather or 'grander', Philip Crone. Under the older man's influence, the young Corney is groomed to become an outcast to his peers. He is also encouraged to rebel against the assumptions and pieties of his parents, and his father especially, in an extension of the Oedipal theme of *A Nest of Simple Folk*. 'The old man is the vital centre [of both novels],' Conor Cruise O'Brien once stated, 'and seems to drag the temporal centre of the story back into the past along with him; the youth receives from him the radiations of history and begins to turn into something like him'.[1] Both novels certainly speak to several temporalities. In *Bird Alone* this includes the Parnellite years in which the novel is set, but also an earlier period of rural penury and Fenian activity which the grander partially embodies, as well as the post-Independence context from which Corney narrates and O'Faoláin writes his story – Corney is in his early sixties at the time of his narration and was born in 1873. However, a crucial difference between the two texts is that *Bird Alone*, unlike *A Nest of Simple Folk*, often brings the old man and the youth together on the same page, and the relationship that they seem to share is intimate and insistent.

An intentionally comic scene, which occurs at a very early stage of the novel, provides an eerie instance of this. Reflecting on his earliest memories of his grander, Corney briefly recreates the experience of hearing the old man read the story of *Faust* to himself and some of his siblings as young children. This peculiar choice of bedtime story is dramatically enacted by the older man, who places an expected stress on the awful pact agreed with the Devil to the delight of his young audience. The children respond to the twists in their grander's narrative by 'div[ing] right under his bedclothes, clutching him in the dark' and 'peep[ing] out, like mice in hay, for the end' (*BA* 20). The story, as it is recalled, is mischievously local, with some scenes relocated to Cork – Faust, it is said, 'lived on the tip-top of Shandon Tower, right under the weather-fish' (*BA* 20) – and central characters afforded a recognizable idiom and accent. 'Faust, me bucko. Yer time is up,' the Devil announces, when he appears 'in a ring of fire, coated with pale-blue flame "like methylated spirits", his tail waving like a cat with a mouse', to claim the soul of the petrified protagonist. And when Faust desperately pleads 'O-o-o … Gimme wan more minute till I say a perfect Act of Contrition', the response of 'the Ould Lad' is delicious, 'Nah … nor half a minute' (*BA* 20). If the story that Corney remembers hearing is told to most of the children in the Crone family, however, the narrative also suggests that it is directed to Corney alone. All of the questions that the grander asks are addressed to him, specifically, by name, and the rest of the children are gradually erased from the recollected scene as Corney depicts himself, and no one else, falling asleep in the old man's bed and 'rest[ing] in his arms until, sleep-drenched and limp-limbed, he carried me in his shirt-tails down the bare stairs into my cot' (*BA* 21).

Of course, Corney's decision to focus exclusively on his interactions with his grander can be explained by the simple fact that it is he who is doing the remembering. As the first-person narrator, Corney is telling the reader what affected him as a child and what was most important to him at that time, or what seems most important in retrospect. In addition, though, the focus is indicative of Corney's attempts to understand something about the older man, as he ascribes his grander traits and characteristics which are subsequently elaborated in the course of the narrative. The Devil's tail is neatly balanced against the grander's shirt tails, it might be noted, and the reference to methylated spirits can be interpreted as an early allusion to the old man's fondness for hard drink; the affectionate moniker 'the Ould Lad', which is used to denote the Devil, could as easily refer to either or both of these characters, while Faust's plea for more time sounds like many a child fighting off the inevitability of bedtime. Corney's identification of his grander with the Devil in this early scene – and the corollary equation of himself with Faust – suggests that Corney sees the old man as a rebellious figure; however, it also implies that he retrospectively views his relationship with the grander as dangerous or in some way insidious. This is complicated by the fact that the grandfather is also perceived as a Faustian figure in *Bird Alone*.

Only a few pages later, in one of the great set-pieces in the novel, Corney recalls the difficulties that his grandfather encountered when he attempted to organize the burial of his late friend, the Fenian Arty Tinsley. Because of clerical opposition to the Fenian movement, Arty is not permitted a Catholic burial; exasperated, the grander turns to a bewildered rabbi for help, before finally calling on the 'cut-'em-ups', or anatomy students, with a view to donating Arty's body to science. 'Maybe it was then,' Corney reminisces:

> for the first time, when a gas-lamp scooped his temples and made caverns of his eyes, that I thought I saw in his face and look the damned look of another Faust. Or perhaps, I often thought after, it was then the souls of those damned ones entered him for the first time when he realized that by the mortality of his friends he was condemned to the sentence of too-long life (*BA* 31).

Beneath the comedy of this extended set-piece lie serious questions concerning the stressed relationship between integrity and obedience, or politics and Church doctrine, epitomized by the conflict between Fenianism and Catholicism in late nineteenth-century Ireland. These stresses are compounded for those who follow their political principles while remaining, to whatever degree, Catholic in sentiment or faith. The older man's distress in his dealings with the Cemetery Committee is evidence of this. 'What I say is, if an unfortunate Fenian isn't left in peace by the clergy when he's alive then they should leave him in peace anyway when he's dead,' he hopelessly pleads to a bureaucratic caretaker, before sobbing 'where will I bury him?' (*BA* 24, 26). The grander's anger, and his anguish, in this exchange is heartfelt, and suggests a genuine fear that his friend will be damned because of the stance of the clergy. His fears are not restricted to this scene. Indeed, it is notable that for all the explicit associations with rebellion, the grander is frequently placed in close proximity with the Church in *Bird Alone*, as Corney depicts the older man at mass, talking to priests and tending the graves of Fenian comrades (on the third Sunday of every month). The implication seems to be that the nonconformist grandfather remains a residual Catholic who is conditioned by his *habitus*, and who is anxious about the choices that he has made. 'We know, Mister Crone, that your knees are crusted from saying secret rosaries,' it is remarked to him elsewhere in jest, and the grandfather is said to 'cackle with joy' in response to the intended 'flattery of simultaneous belief in his wickedness and his goodness' (*BA* 71). In a perverse act of inheritance, the grander bequeaths this same sentence to his grandson on his deathbed: 'All I wish for you is that you may have as long a run as me. And as long a pause … before the hounds catch you' (*BA* 247). This sinister wish is realized when Corney is condemned to play the role of 'another Faust', consigned to an equally-defined 'too-long life' and ostracized by all who know him (*BA* 9).

The decision to focus exclusively on the grander in the aforementioned scene – where Philip Crone is depicted reading *Faust* to his grandchildren – is linked to an attempt by Corney to make sense of the older man. However, the subsequent erasure of any mention of Corney's siblings from this scene also creates space for a disturbing intimacy to be enacted, as the memory of an act erupts from the past and is cautiously replayed in the text. As part of this brief reminiscence, Corney twice alludes to an incident involving his grandfather. On neither occasion is this seemingly innocent act afforded any explanation or substantiation. Indeed, in the first instance it is presented in the form of a momentary flashback which sits awkwardly with the larger memory that is being recalled: 'His rough hand steals under my nightshirt as he speaks on and on,' Corney suddenly declares, almost in *media res*, as he recreates the scene of his grander reading *Faust* to the Crone children, 'stroking my little belly round and round, his bald poll on the pillow, his beard cocked up to the ceiling, his large O of a mouth reciting to the glow of the lamp over our heads' (*BA* 19). The scene might be innocent enough, but it nonetheless carries disquieting undertones, as the implied intimacy of the encounter ('stroking', 'little belly', 'round and round', 'O') is injected with a sense of intrusion and threat ('rough', 'steals', 'cocked'), which is intensified by the apparent exclusion of the rest of the family. The use of the continuous present to describe this scene is striking, not least when it is considered in relation to the larger narrative of *Bird Alone* which is told for the most part in the past tense, and this shift in tense suggests that the encounter continues to be present in Corney's mind and remains to trouble him as an adult narrator. It also jars with the sentences that precede and immediately follow.

The preceding sentence is written in the past tense: 'To us he was simply our grander who would, of nights, let us into his bed, shoving into him, snuggling into him, while he recites the story of that book'; 'recites' sounds a warning note, however, and prepares for the impending shift in tense (*BA* 19). And the sentence that follows switches to the narrative present and the point from which the story is reported, sometime in the mid-1930s: 'I remember only bits, now, of this saga' (*BA* 19–20). This confusion of tenses supports the impression that the adult Corney is anxious about the scene that he has just recounted, and this is reinforced by the narrator's decision to break the thread of his tale, as he claims to recollect only fragments of the story that he is passing on. If Corney appears keen to shift the reader's attention from the encounter that he has just described, stating that what he has disremembered are the finer details of the *Faust* story rather than the specific details of his grander's 'stroking', the pause that is enforced by the double comma (either side of 'now') invites speculation. The delayed inclusion of the words 'of this saga' also seems deliberately placed to wrong-foot the reader, as it initially appears that Corney is only talking about his memory of this particular scene with his grander. Indeed, Corney's subsequent allusions to the Faust myth suggest a far greater familiarity with the saga than he is letting on, and it seems increasingly likely that Corney is hinting at the repression of a memory which is evinced in the withholding of part of his narrative.

The second iteration of this scene occurs on the very next page and although in general terms it reinforces this sense of intimacy, it also gives the encounter greater context while appearing less intrusive or disturbing. In the second instance the narration of the scene is firmly placed in the past, but this is complicated by Corney's double use of the conditional 'would'. The narrative pace is slowed down, the action is broken into several sentences, and more time is given to the description of the encounter. A greater sense of interaction is recorded between the young Corney and his grander, and considerable stress is placed on the relief the child derived, or the adult Corney remembers receiving, from the presence of the older man:

> Then there was that terrible part where Faust was down in the dungeons. '… and one day, as his eyes grew accustomed to the dark he saw a most terrible thing. And, Corney, doyouknowwhatitwashesaw?'
>
> 'Nnnno, Grandaddy?' I'd whisper, glad to feel his hand round and round my belly-button.
>
> His white mouth in his little pointed beard, rising and sinking, would say very slowly and solemnly:
>
> 'A terrible incantation on the wall.' (*BA* 20)

This scene is not revisited at any other point in the narrative. Its importance to the story is considerable, though, as it introduces the Faustian motif to *Bird Alone*. It also supplies one of the earliest recollections in the text concerning Corney's grander.

The scene is carefully folded into the early pages of O'Faoláin's novel and is counterpointed with another memory, which Corney considers one of his most treasured, which relates to his mother, Pidgie Flynn. A couple of pages earlier, Corney asserts: 'I know few things out of my childhood more pleasant to remember than how I used to lie sometimes, as a little shaver, on [my mother's] great bosom, warm as a kitten against a cat's fur, and both of us dozing off by the fire into a deep-breathing snooze after our little sup of winter punch' (*BA* 17). Very little space is given over to this memory, which is presented in the form of a dreamlike, warm and apparently sustaining sketch. The episode is rich in psychoanalytic potential, as Corney returns to consider a complex of images and sensations which he experienced as an infant in close proximity with his mother.[2] Despite the implied nurturance, it soon becomes apparent that things are not idyllic for the young child. The mother's whiskey has been bought on credit; the belated reference to 'our little sup' stands in place of her milk; the fuel for the fire has been lifted from the ailing business stock; the young child is half-listening to local gossip about floods, death and 'the end of the world'; and 'the red glow between the bars of the range' seems to anticipate the imminent story of *Faust* (*BA* 17). Significantly, the memory provides one of the few instances in the text when Corney is depicted in any kind of proximity with his mother, and no comparable scene is imagined between Corney and his father. It is of additional significance that this scene is cut short, and that it is followed by the encounter with the grander, as the older man steps into the formative space that should have been occupied by Corney's parents and thereby assumes the role of the child's intimate.

As if to enforce the point, the grandfather is the first person who is named in the novel (prior to both of these recollections, at the start of Chapter Two), with Corney evidently keen to make sense of his relationship with this older man. As the adult Corney recreates the aforementioned scene with the older man, the onomatopoeic sounds he deploys and the circular images he advances ('round and round', 'on and on', 'pillow', 'poll', 'mouth', 'glow', 'O-o-o') are continuous with the sounds that his grander invokes in his account of Faust's descent into hell. 'The floor opened beneath [him],' the grander warns his assembled audience, 'and the fire glowed and Faust was thrust down for ever … into the pit' (*BA* 21). From one perspective, these long 'o' sounds can be considered expressive of Corney's attempts to tunnel back in time and to put into words a distant and perhaps troubling memory. Such a reading is not as straightforward as it first appears, though, since the memory is only partially reconstructed and reflects back onto the story that Corney recalls being told, with the young protagonist and his grandfather positioned in roles that approximate those occupied by Faust and the Devil respectively. Not only do the grander's shirt tails align the older man with 'the Ould Lad' by such a reckoning, Faust's descent into the pit appears analogous with Corney's incipient rebellion as well as the latter's imaginative immersion into the past.

This correlation runs counter to most interpretations of *Bird Alone*, which take their lead from the work of Maurice Harmon. Comparing the grander in *Bird Alone* with Leo Donnel in *A Nest of Simple Folk*, Harmon suggested in a study of O'Faoláin first published in the mid-1960s, that 'a similar concentration on passion, will, and integrity' could be found in O'Faoláin's figuration of the two elderly men. 'Their nationalism brings out greatness of character and gives direction to their personality,' he contended, 'both men resist the restrictions placed on their lives by society, politics, and religion', and stand as archetypal images of personal honesty and rebellion:

> Both face the consequences – the disapproval of the respectable, the condemnation of the clergy, and/or imprisonment – without self-pity and without losing their self-respect. In their relationship to and their effect upon the boy-figures, Denis Hussey and Corney Crone, they stand as hypnotic embodiments of an almost heroic way of life.[3]

'Almost heroic' sounds rather euphemistic, however, given that Philip Crone more often appears as an exploitative, controlling presence in *Bird Alone*. Corney's relationship with his grandfather is scarcely glamorized by the adult narrator, and the elderly figure is frequently cast in a sinister rather than a valiant or constructive light. When Corney's mother comically scatters holy water on the old man during an argument, for instance, the narrator is sure to invest the scene with a particular (albeit intentionally jocular) resonance, remarking that the grander quickly 'brushed the drops from his chest and face as if he feared it would hiss on him'; and an uncle is also recorded voicing the implied link with the Devil, when he describes Philip Crone as 'weak in the carnalities. And too proud. Proud as Lucifer' (*BA* 40, 183).

'Could they not have let me be a little longer innocent,' Corney asks several pages later, thinking back to his relationship with his parents and his grandfather, and recalling his early days at home and then in school – a school that his grander, tellingly, 'sent me to [though] I thought I chose it for myself'.[4] 'For years I was grateful to my grander who took my side,' he continues:

> but now I know the truth. If [the school] was a place where the innocence of me was forced and pampered, he wanted it pampered only because he could feed on it. You don't believe that? Then why else did he send me there – an old lecher who had long since lost the Faith? … Or is every old man a vampire on youth like the Faustus of George W.M. Reynolds who sold his children to prolong his own life? Or do they all sell themselves for pride and then cheat their children to retain it? (*BA* 47).

The reference to George W.M. Reynolds is as unexpected as it is revealing. A Chartist, publisher and prolific author of many works of non-fiction and fiction in the mid-nineteenth century, Reynolds is perhaps best remembered today as the founder of the radical magazine *Reynolds's Miscellany* in 1846 and the author of the long-running serials *The Mysteries of London* (1844–8) and *The Mysteries of the Court of London* (1848–56). Much of his work was controversial on publication and his 'penny dreadfuls', in particular, seem to have offended many respectable middle-class Victorian readers. If Reynolds's texts were an affront to this particular audience, they were nonetheless also extraordinarily popular amongst a wider working-class readership, and it is reputed that his works outsold and were more widely read than those of any of his peers, including Charles Dickens.[5]

Given *Bird Alone*'s concern with acts of rebellion, along with its exploration of social mores, including Catholic practice and the tabooed subject of sex, Corney's decision to mention this writer is intriguing; interestingly, it is not the only time that Reynolds is referenced in O'Faoláin's text. The grander's choice of bedtime story is also, allegedly, the 'great play of Faust … written by George W.M. Reynolds, M.D.', rather than the more famous versions of the tale that were produced by the Elizabethan playwright Christopher Marlowe or by the German poet and dramatist Johann Wolfgang von Goethe (*BA* 15). O'Faoláin, Corney and the grandfather each take liberties with Reynolds's version of the Faust myth. Reynolds did not relocate any of his story to Ireland, let alone Cork, for instance, although it is possible that the grander's transposition of the scene is simply playfully intended, since it brings the story closer to the world of his young audience. Similar licence is shown, after all, when Corney recalls his grandfather's narration of the works of Jonathan Swift: 'when I came to read *Gulliver's Travels* for myself I noticed that the only part my grander had ever told us was about the horseheaded men and he had called them all by names like Paddy and Shawn and they all lived in Skibbereen,' where the grandfather was born, 'so that it came as a surprise to me to find that the story had nothing at all do with Cork or Ireland' (*BA* 33). In addition, George Reynolds was not a medical doctor (the letters 'M.D.' are not explained), and the grander's claim – or rather, Corney's remembrance of the claim – that he is reading from a play misidentifies the genre in which the Victorian novelist wrote.

Reynolds's *Faust* was first published in serial form in the weekly penny-issue magazine *The London Journal* between October 1845 and July 1846. Consisting of ninety-five chapters with a prologue, it was printed in forty-two issues, with many of the instalments accompanied by dramatic woodcuts or visual images. It was subsequently collected and published under the title *Faust: A Romance of the Secret Tribunals* in 1847. Set principally in late-medieval Germany, the story is populated with two-dimensional character-types (the grotesque rich, the suffering poor, hyper-sexualised vamps, angelic maidens, chivalric heroes, mad monks and a corrupt pope), and makes heavy use of standard Gothic tropes and motifs, including dungeons, castles, dark forests, acts of torture, living corpses, mysterious doubles and Orientalist fantasies. The tale is sensationalist, derivative and often digressive; it is also driven by an incongruous moralistic impulse. This is clear from a footnote that is inserted into an advanced issue of the story, where Reynolds intervenes in his increasingly wayward tale to direct his audience towards a specific interpretation of his narrative:

> The author hopes that the real object and aim of his tale are thoroughly understood. This is not – at least it is not intended to be – a mere romance without any particular moral in view; but it is written to show the evil consequences of vice and the beauty of virtue. Faust is the type of all evil doing persons, who morally, though not by written compact, *sell themselves to Satan.*[6]

The note is a reminder that Reynolds's work was designed to instruct as well as to entertain, a point Q.D. Leavis observed in her brief assessment of *Reynolds's Miscellany* in *Fiction and the Reading Public.*[7] The 'object and aim' of this version of *Faust* appears entirely conventional, as a man sells himself to the Devil in exchange for wealth and power, only to gradually realize the terrible debt that he has incurred. This is brought home to the reader time and again in the text, and reaches a climax in the final instalment when Faust, the self-proclaimed 'most wretched of men', is set against his narrative double, Otto Pianalla. Otto, despite the many wrongs that he has endured, remains 'all that human virtue and moral goodness can possibly be', and is duly rewarded. Faust, on the other hand, faces eternal damnation, with the narrator unequivocal in his judgment that there could be 'no solace for Satan's Own!'[8]

Reynolds's tale lacks the subtlety and complexity of its literary antecedents, and there is no sense that its protagonist is operating in a world where the fates have conspired against him, or where intellectual daring is cruelly restricted by cosmic forces. In the epilogue to Marlowe's

Doctor Faustus (1588–9), the Chorus famously described Faustus's tragedy as that of one whose curiosity enticed him 'To practice more than heavenly power permits'.[9] It remains an open question in Marlowe's text whether Faustus should consequently be interpreted as an object lesson in hubris and intellectual vanity or as an example of the limitations that are imposed on human enquiry by a ruthlessly restrictive divine order. Goethe's *Faust: Part I* (1808) raises similar questions concerning regulatory relationships between the divine and the humane, and opens with a scene in which Mephistopheles gains permission from God to specifically target Faust as part of a wager between the two powers. No analogous concerns are raised in Reynolds's *Faust*, where issues of intellect and free will are never substantially entertained, and the focus is instead placed on gratuitous scenes of sex and violence. That said, Faust finds himself again placed within a prescribed hierarchical structure in this tale, and his opportunities are determined by a larger order that he has played no part in shaping.

Faust opens in prison, where an impoverished young student, Wilhelm Faust, awaits execution for presuming to fall in love with, and in turn be loved by, a wealthy baron's daughter. Bereft of hope, Faust happens to discover an incantation on a cell wall, and by this means unknowingly summons a mysterious stranger, named 'the Demon', to his aid. With the Demon's assistance he escapes from jail, pledging his soul in exchange for twenty-four years of freedom; his immediate plans extend no further than survival, winning back his beloved, and gaining revenge for a wrong inflicted. Thus, at the outset of Reynolds's text, the reasons for Faust's rebellion are clearly stated: 'the once noble and generous heart of that young man had been tutored by adversity and persecution to entertain and cherish sentiments of deadly vengeance against the powerful lord who had been the cause of his sufferings'.[10] Unlike the protagonists of Marlowe's and Goethe's tales, Faust is neither a learned sage nor a scholar of the black arts; on the contrary, early instalments of this work repeatedly describe him as 'a poor and humble student'.[11] He is vulnerable, easily manipulated and alone, something which is reinforced by the fact that he is represented without pedigree or social standing (there is no reference to any family or friends). The deal that he strikes with the Demon is motivated by an understandable desire to avoid a brutal death (he has been sentenced to death on the wheel), rather than the result of self-conceit or a thirst for divine or forbidden knowledge. Most notably, Faust is young, in his early twenties, and this further distinguishes him from the protagonists of Marlowe's *Doctor Faustus* and Goethe's *Faust*, both of whom are more advanced in age and experience (Goethe's Faust is allowed to seem thirty years younger by means of a magic potion).

Although Reynolds's *Faust* is twice referenced in *Bird Alone*, it is not known whether O'Faoláin ever actually read this text. Some of the details mentioned by the grander, or by Corney thinking back to his grander at a later date, would lead one to believe that he did not. In the aforementioned bedroom scene, for instance, Corney briefly references the older man reflecting on a particular episode – 'how Otto Pienella arranged a meeting between Faust and Beatrice by a canal in Rome' – which is not present in Reynolds's saga (*BA* 20). No character named Beatrice is included in the latter text, no approximate scene unfolds in Italy, at no point does the virtuous Otto pimp for Faust, and Otto's surname is incorrectly given by the grander. The obvious implication is that O'Faoláin did not know the text or, at the very least, that he misremembered it, and that this accounts for the grandfather's description of *Faust* as a play; it also explains his erroneous transposition of certain scenes to Cork, and his tendency to slip between the names Faustus and Faust. Such an explanation seems unduly literalist, however. For one thing, the misspelled reference to Otto Pianalla implies some familiarity with the work of the Victorian novelist, since this character is only present in Reynolds's version of *Faust*. For another, the grander's misattribution of this scene, or Corney's confusion of the scene that the grander narrated (it is not clear which), seems more than a simple mistake, as Corney is quick to gloss over his mis-reference with the seemingly random remark that '– we had a print of that famous picture in the sitting-room –' (*BA* 20). This parenthetical comment suggests that more might be at stake than Corney is letting on, since his memory of his grandfather's reading seems interconnected with his recollection of a particular visual image (Otto, Faust and Beatrice) which carries personal and domestic significance.

The mistaken reference to Beatrice also suggests that O'Faoláin is less concerned with the narration of a specific incident and more with the narrativization of this incident and the way that it is shaped through the process of narrative and the workings of memory. Corney is clearly aware of these distinctions, since he elsewhere talks of how difficult he finds it to talk about the past and to distinguish between things that happened at different points in time, making sense of 'peepshow bits, seen through pinpricks of memory, interrupting me perpetually and uninvited' and 'drag[ging] less sunny things from the well of the past' (*BA* 32). He also repeatedly discloses the narratological dimensions of his story, hinting at experiences which he opts not to share and gesturing towards tales which remain untold. Glimpses are only given of his sister Vicky, for instance, who turns away from a life of religious devotion for a career on the stage (it is never said why), and little is known of his brothers Barty and Michael who emigrate to Canada and London respectively. The brother who remains, Bob, is somehow disabled – he is described as 'a natural' and as 'my idiot brother' (*BA* 15, 283) – but the nature of his illness is not identified and does not seem to be of interest to the narrator. Nor are reasons given to explain why his mother suddenly abandoned her talent as a singer when she returned from a Parisian school after only one night – 'why we never knew,' Corney abruptly states once he brings up the subject with the intriguing comment, 'I should have mentioned before that my mother had "a voice"' (*BA* 61). In addition, Corney chooses not to provide the context for his first meeting with the artist Stella ('how, is of small matter now: all I will say is that ...'), and does not account for the reasons why he was 'very disturbed' at this particular time; indeed, Corney seems anxious to shut down any speculation, as he declares to the imagined reader 'there is no reason why I should tell more' (*BA* 201).

Inclusion of the name Beatrice extends the textual range of reference beyond the story of *Faust* to incorporate another famous literary figure, Beatrice di Folco Portinari, who reputedly inspired Dante's beautiful love poems in *La Vita Nuova*. The choice of name is somewhat ironic given Corney's self-centred treatment of his sweetheart, Elsie Sherlock, in *Bird Alone*. It is also strangely apt, though, since Beatrice served as a guide to Paradise in the last book of *La Divina Commedia*, with the grander describing Faust's converse descent to hell at this very moment in O'Faoláin's story. In addition, mention of Beatrice casts light on the 'famous picture' that Corney is struggling to remember, since similarities can be discerned between the print that he is alluding to and the sumptuous pre-Raphaelite painting *Dante meets Beatrice at Ponte Santa Trinita* (1883) by the contemporary English artist Henry Holiday. Obvious differences remain, including the location and arrangement of the figures in Holiday's painting, where Dante is depicted alone looking on at an accompanied Beatrice in Florence. O'Faoláin declines to labour the point, however, leaving it to the reader to decide whether the references, as well as the slippages and the mistakes, are at all significant.

If some knowledge of Reynolds is implied in the allusion to 'Otto Pienella', many key elements of his *Faust* are also afforded structural or thematic significance in *Bird Alone*. In both texts, for instance, star-crossed lovers are kept apart by interfering fathers, with class difference identified as a key impediment to the sanctioning of youthful relationships. In *Bird Alone*, Elsie's father refuses Corney permission to marry his daughter because the young protagonist has no prospects or capital. What is more, in both works, Faust, or a Faust-like figure, appears as a young man who rebels against an order that imprisons him (literally in Reynolds's case, figuratively in O'Faoláin's), and who is encouraged to do so by a grotesque, older individual. The language of love is deployed in both texts, but in each instance it is debased and made to sound very like the desire to own or erase another. 'I loved her; and I longed to possess her,' Faust succinctly explains of his relationship with Theresa in an early issue of Reynolds's story, with similar sentiments expressed in *Bird Alone*, when Corney rejoices in the suggestion that Elsie 'was losing her identity for me', and links this to the sinister 'satisfaction that comes on a man when he is gradually moulding another mind to his own image and desire' (*BA* 127, 167).[12]

Other interconnections might also be supposed: O'Faoláin's and Reynolds's narratives each include spectral or monstrous characters in their pages (consider the strange figure of old Condoorum in *Bird Alone*, dragging his chains across the sands, or the ghosts of felons gruesomely nailed to London Wall, or the wraithlike Fenian Christy Tinsley after his release from an English jail), and each makes frequent reference to prisons, cells and other types of enclosed structures and spaces. The grander's reference to 'that terrible part where Faust was down in the dungeons' explicitly draws the two texts together – no such scene is set in Marlowe's *Doctor Faustus*, while Goethe's *Faust* only visits prison to briefly re-unite Faust with his captive lover Gretchen. In addition, Corney's reference to 'Faustus … who sold his children to prolong his own life' – which is repeated when Corney describes himself as 'a Faust who had sold his child for his lusts' – partially recalls an incident that is unique to Reynolds's story, where the damned Faust is only allowed to marry Theresa if he condemns his first-born son to the Devil (*BA* 47, 283).[13] Once again, no analogous scene is imagined by either Marlowe or Goethe, even though Corney's confusion of names – the Elizabethan Faustus as well as the Germanic Faust – further complicates the terms of the intertextual reference.

These points are raised not to reduce O'Faoláin's text to some neatly-defined association with a melodramatic nineteenth-century novel. Rather, the intention is to suggest the significance of Faust, and a fluidly-defined Faust at that, to the design of *Bird Alone*. It is a topic that has been overlooked by most critics of the novel. Paul A. Doyle is perhaps the exception, as he briefly touched on the subject in his short study of O'Faoláin, published in the late 1960s. Doyle was dismissive of the Reynolds link, though, dismissing it in an endnote and instead asserting that *Bird Alone* 'follows the more standard Goethe version'. Thus Elsie is read with Gretchen in mind, as she attracts, resists and finally succumbs to temptation; the scene where she visits a London pub with Corney is equated with the famous Auerbach tavern episode in Goethe's drama; and her attempted suicide and subsequent death in childbirth is counterpointed with Gretchen's drowning of her and Faust's child.[14] Conor Cruise O'Brien also alluded to the general subject in his discussion of O'Faoláin's 'parnellism' – a term coined to denote the triple concern with national, spiritual and sexual emancipation in O'Faoláin's work – in his early book *Maria Cross*.

Considering the plights of Denis Hussey and Corney Crone, in *A Nest of Simple Folk* and *Bird Alone* respectively, O'Brien momentarily remarked:

> The Irish rebels of the nineteenth century, so regularly condemned by the hierarchy, were the inevitable heroes for the spirited son of a pious and 'loyal' family. Prometheus and Faust were remote and tenuous symbols, but the Fenian dead to whom, in that treasured episcopal phrase, 'hell was not hot enough nor eternity long enough', lived in people's minds ... And even mightier than theirs was the name of Parnell, whose struggle not only against Church and State but directly against the power of sexual prohibition made him the essential figure of rebellious youth.[15]

The subject of Faust seems to have been of interest to O'Faoláin in the years preceding *Bird Alone*, as he reflected on its importance on a number of occasions. In 1930, for instance, in an article for the journal *Folklore*, O'Faoláin counted 'Faustus' one of several 'legendary heroes' who 'undergo transformation as they progress in popularity'. Such figures evolve and change shape, O'Faoláin noted, as their stories are taken out of context and grafted onto the conditions of other times and places. 'The question,' he asked, 'is when does a legendary hero cease to be himself under this process?'[16] References to Faust were also made in several of O'Faoláin's short stories of the period: Charles Gounod's grand opera, *Faust* (1859), provides part of the back-story of Pat Lenihan and Trixie Flynn's love affair in 'A Born Genius' (1934), as the characters play the parts of Faust and Marguerite respectively; while 'A Broken World' (1937) includes the cryptic closing reference to 'the peasants who held the hand of Faust with their singing one Easter morning' (*PC* 27).[17] Both of these stories were subsequently included in *A Purse of Coppers*. In a contemporaneous essay for *The Virginia Quarterly Review*, O'Faoláin also engaged with the subject of Faust, but considered it from a different angle, as he pressed the need for a new type of fiction that would revisit 'the old drama of Faustus, the drama of sin, the drama old as Eve with the colours of the serpent twinned about her eyes', but that would update this story to speak to an age of uncertainty and technological advance.[18] Similar points were made in 'It No Longer Matters, or the Death of the English Novel' (1935), in *The Criterion*, where O'Faoláin alluded to Faust as part of a general reflection upon perceived shortcomings in the contemporary novel.

In the latter essay, O'Faoláin advanced the case for a new direction in fiction-writing, away from the enervated legacy of French naturalism and the supposed disinterestedness of high modernism. This change of direction would allow for a resuscitation of the novel, he argued, enabling 'the revivifaction of literature by a spiritual view' and the restoration of the idea of 'a great Catholic novel'. Aware of the dangers of such an argument, O'Faoláin was keen to stress that his thesis should not be interpreted as a call for some kind of puritanical or religious zealousness: 'I do not wish to be taken as wishing for or hoping for anything from sectarianism in literature,' he stated, conceding, while at the same time critiquing, the tendency for 'religious feeling [to] more commonly all[y] itself with censorship than creation'. It is a tendency with which he was all-too-familiar, given the context in which he was living and writing. Instead, a case was presented for 'a Catholic novel' that would sensitively engage with questions of physicality and faith, exploring the body as a site of contention, and interpreting 'life' (always a keyword for O'Faoláin) through the conflicting codes of Church doctrine, inherited patterns of belief and changing social ecologies. Such fiction would not be content with the polite avoidance of things deemed taboo; nor would it maintain some kind of Manichean or tightly-patrolled division between the sensual and the spiritual. Rather, it would 'handle manfully the drama of the Seven Deadly Sins' in a contemporary context (the casual use of the gendered adverb is as revealing here as it was in the biographies), and seriously represent topics that might otherwise be dismissed as 'unseemly' or 'immoral'. As part of this argument, O'Faoláin speculated on the 'deeply tragic view of life' exemplified by characters like Oedipus, Macbeth and Faustus, remarking that for such figures 'man in his fall became both more noble and more terrifying for being the antagonist of Heaven'.[19]

According to O'Faoláin, one of the problems facing this thesis was that it could easily be deemed regressive or obsolete in a rapidly-changing world. 'But there is no more reason why it should be so,' he countered, 'than that Marlowe's *Faustus* would be tedious if it were written by some such Marlowe of to-day, as, let us say, Liam O'Flaherty'.[20] It is tempting to consider *Bird Alone* along these lines, reading it as a reworking of aspects of the Faust myth in a specifically Irish Catholic context, exploring complex issues of trespass, guilt, regret and damnation. O'Faoláin himself retrospectively described it as a novel about 'nothing less than sin and salvation in an Irish setting', and many of his contemporaries read the book in this way (*VM* 254). The novelist Forrest Reid, for instance, was struck by the pressures that drove the young lovers, Corney and Elsie, 'into conflict both with the Church and society' in his review of the book. 'Elsie has the beliefs and principles of Catholicism in her blood,' Reid observed, 'she cannot escape from or renounce them. Corney is a rebel, determined to gain freedom. But though she yields to him she remains haunted by the consciousness of sin'.[21] The sensitivity with which *Bird Alone* interrogates these issues, and the seriousness with which it reflects upon questions of sin and faith, helps to account for the outrage that was provoked by the banning of this text. As Peter Martin has shown, the widespread suspicion was that *Bird Alone* was placed on the banned list because of clerical interference, and was a direct consequence of O'Faoláin's strained associations with the Catholic Church in Ireland. The Censorship Board claimed otherwise, defending its decision by perversely arguing that *Bird Alone* was 'an immoral and dangerous book, the more so because there is some good writing in it'. Not surprisingly, the Board focused its attention on a few erotic passages in the text, contending that the book posed a particular danger to young or impressionable readers since 'the writer seems rather to gloat over the sexual incidents he presents'. Despite the Board's claim that the novel was 'immoral', at no point did it reflect upon O'Faoláin's engagement with questions of religion or faith.[22]

O'Faoláin's response to the ban took several forms, including, most famously, the essay 'The Dangers of Censorship' (1936) for the journal *Ireland To-Day*. This damning essay was also occasioned by the contemporaneous banning of Francis Hackett's *The Green Lion*, the story of the illegitimate child of a seminarian, and Austin Clarke's *The Singing-*

Men at Cashel, a romance of religious orthodoxy and personal freedom set in medieval Ireland. O'Faoláin's primary focus in this piece was the abuse of the Censorship Act and the impact of censorship on intellectual health and freedom of expression in the emerging state: 'The chief results of the Censorship are to debase the public conscience,' he argued, 'to bring the law into disrepute, and to limit, not the growth of the author, but the growth of the nation'. The work of the censors was characterized as hypocritical, myopic and pernicious, and their ambition was seen as nothing more than a concerted attempt to reduce Irish people to 'a condition of moral slavery under the pretence of "helping" it to "obey" the moral law'. By keeping the reading public 'in a state of perpetual adolescence', O'Faoláin suggested that the censors hoped to impose a protectionist ideology that would, theoretically, defend the state from 'all the influences that must, in spite of it, pour in from an adult world'. To this end, they were said to have the support of a powerful concatenation of political groups and forces. O'Faoláin was unambiguous in his assertion that 'the combination of forces which is at present most active here in supporting such prohibitory ordinances as the Censorship Act is a combination of the Gaelic Revivalist who fears the influence of European, and especially English, literature (for nationalist reasons) and the Catholic Activist who fears the same influences (for pious reasons)'.[23] He was equally clear about what was needed to counteract the work of these parties.

Writing to a 'learned' section of Irish society ('University professors, professional men, private students, journalists, and so forth'), in an impassioned and characteristically elitist vein, O'Faoláin called on his readers 'either to affect by penetration the prejudices of their associates', who might be in support of the Censorship Board, 'or to dissociate themselves from their present methods by forming an independent Catholic – if necessary even a politically active – wedge; not a new Front, indeed, for they are not numerous enough, but a spear-head into the dullness of the mass'. Such a response was deemed necessary if the state was to avoid the otherwise 'inevitable collapse into a moral pit'. The formation of such a group would provide 'the sole bulwark between the national character and the disintegrating influences of the Censorial mind'; it would also arrest the deterioration of cultural and intellectual life in Ireland.[24] As critics have noted, this plea for a liberal 'spear-head' carries traces of George Russell's thinking in *The Irish Statesman* a decade earlier; it also anticipates ideas that would come to dominate O'Faoláin's editorials in *The Bell* a few years later.[25] The stress on 'an independent Catholic wedge' is particularly relevant in the context of *Bird Alone*, though, and gains added significance when it is considered alongside O'Faoláin's contemporaneous interest in the need for a rejuvenated Catholic novel.

In *Bird Alone,* a sixty-something year-old Corney thinks back to his relationship with Elsie Sherlock forty years earlier. His memories are intertwined with the concurrent split in Irish politics in the late nineteenth century, following public revelations over Charles Stewart Parnell's long affair with the married Katharine O'Shea; they are also interleaved with a series of recollections concerning his grander, a Fenian supporter and a devoted Parnellite, who exerted considerable influence over the narrator as a youth. The turbulent events of the period help to define Elsie's and Corney's tragedy and provide context for his reminiscence of their story. The world that is recreated is supposedly long-distant. 'That Ireland is gone,' Corney insists at the outset of his tale, with many of its anxieties and concerns consigned to a time that 'youngsters hardly even hear of' anymore (*BA* 11–12). 'Those dead years in which I lived, the years after Parnell ... [were years when] the shore of Ireland was empty,' he subsequently explains, and were years that 'would remain empty for a long time'; Corney accordingly identifies himself as part of a remaindered generation, 'merely one of many left stranded after the storm' (*BA* 197). However, the world that he describes also retains a 1930's resonance, as his relationship with Elsie is declared illicit by the repressive mores of Catholic society, and the young lovers are separated, and then ostracized, once it is known that they have transgressed the laws of community and Church. 'It was only necessary that the girl should sin once,' O'Faoláin commented a number of years later, as he reflected on the central action of *Bird Alone*. Indeed, 'it was necessary that she should sin only once – to underline the horror of the idea of eternal damnation for a single sin. It was with the greatest difficulty that I made it seem plausible that she should allow herself to be seduced at all, so powerful are the religious beliefs and social conventions of modern Ireland'.[26] It is not just Elsie who 'sins', of course; and the ways that the two lovers respond to this sin, and the society that casts judgment on them, provide much of the focus of the narrative. For Corney, for the most part, sex is understood as an act of gratification and seen in terms of rebellion, as it is pitched against ideas of conformity, respectability and parental piety. For the pregnant and increasingly distraught Elsie, by contrast, it is a wrong for which she cannot be absolved. 'It *was* a sin, Corney,' she insists, just before she attempts suicide. 'All the time, for both of us, it *was* a sin' (*BA* 268 [emphasis as original]).

The strength of these beliefs is encapsulated in Elsie's anxieties in the latter stages of *Bird Alone*. Elsie's worries recall those of Ophelia in *Hamlet*, as well as Gretchen in *Faust*, with the Shakespearean heroine ghosting *Bird Alone* initially through references to one of Corney's aunts and latterly through Elsie's breakdown and ideations of suicide. Elsie's fears are historically specific, though, and evolve out of the complex body of ethical, moral and social thinking that was Irish Catholicism in the post-Famine period. This 'all-embracing value-system', in the words of Gearóid Ó Tuathaigh, was founded upon an ideology of fear and self-discipline, and exerted immense control over the ways a people thought about themselves and others.[27] This value-system leads Elsie to believe that she will be damned because of her involvement in their affair – 'she was not afraid of the child' that she had conceived, Corney comes to realize, 'only of the sin' (*BA* 228). It also, by chance, results in her dying without the sacraments, in a cruel reversal of the grander's almost leisurely death. Despite the latter's heterodoxies, the old man is allowed to make a kind of confession on his deathbed to the most understanding of priests; Elsie, by contrast, dies slowly and in great anguish, pleading in vain for a confessor. The strength of this system also explains why tropes of circularity, containment and restraint are used to such effect throughout *Bird Alone*. The prevalence of 'o' sounds in the grander's reading of *Faust* is but one subtle instance of this, as the visual image of the enclosed circle is advanced; the recurring mention of prisons, convents, coffins, roundabouts and other types of controlled or circular spaces provides other, more obvious, examples.

The structure of the novel reinforces this sense of circularity, as Corney enters into exile in the penultimate chapter of the book, only to return home years later, in the final chapter, and to the point from which he begins his narrative in Chapter One; what is more, the story is told in retrospect, after everything has already been decided, in a form approximating the confessional. In many ways, Corney is trapped within the parameters of his story, as he is condemned to revisit painful memories and narrate his tale without ever being allowed to move on (shades of Samuel Taylor Coleridge's 'Rime of the Ancient Mariner', perhaps). If the structure of *Bird Alone* indicates that Corney is confessing all to an imagined reader, it also suggests that he might be telling the story to himself – he is the self-professed 'Inspector of Isolations', after all, the eponymous 'Bird Alone', appellations which further impress the link with the eternally-alienated Faust (*BA* 196).[28] It remains unclear whether Corney is compelled to narrate his story, over and again, as a result, because he is haunted by everything that has happened, or because he is seeking to justify his actions to others, or because he is trying to make sense of things for himself. '*Je souffre tant, O Jésus*' is the never-explained 'strange' entry that was inscribed into the grander's prized copy of *Faust*, and some of the words that the old man added to the book's flyleaf are equally reflective of the plight of the mature narrator: '*labyrinth*' might be taken to hint at Corney's figurative entrapment, while '*homologation*' suggests an implied link or measure of correspondence between the two characters (*BA* 19 [emphasis as original]).

Not only is Irish Catholicism associated with an internalized, all-encompassing value-system in *Bird Alone*, it is also presented as a physical force that defines the space that the central characters inhabit. Cork is described as a city 'girt by praying spires', for instance, and the Crone family home is repeatedly placed in proximity to churches, a convent and the city's North Cathedral (*BA* 146). It is not without significance that the first building mentioned in Corney's narrative is the cathedral, nor is it inconsequential that this building is used as a reference point by the narrator to fix the place where he lives. As he walks out of the city in the early morning, in the opening scene in the book, Corney describes the view 'look[ing] up the stinking river at the cold chimneys of the city, where two spires of a triad – broken trident of a cathedral – catch the light. They mark my house' (*BA* 7). The sounds of the city are also associated with the Church. When Corney is not invoking 'a lonely heel-click on a pavement', a cock crowing or a milk-churn rattling, he is summoning to mind 'the little rondo of the angelus-bell kept up for a few minutes between the three churches – the Capuchins, the Dominicans, the Friars' (*BA* 8). The Cork that Corney portrays is over-populated by members of the clergy, as episodes are frequently represented which include mention of 'the usual stray Franciscan or Dominican priest'; such characters might be of marginal importance to the events described, but they nonetheless remain in the background, attending, advising, observing or directing (*BA* 98). What is more, the Church that is depicted is a key player in the organization of the local economy, as it grants valuable contracts to some, withholds employment from others, and decides who should receive preferential treatment or support. Corney's parents are keenly aware of this influence, and crave the status, as well as the wealth, that might be gained through respectable connections with the clergy. 'This is a tight little city,' Corney is pithily advised, 'and a tidy, small little place, where them that knows how to do it can make good money, and them that doesn't know how to do it might as well be trying to sell crucifixes in Jerusalem' (*BA* 292).

The advice dispensed to Corney speaks to the material muscle of the Catholic Church, as money and religion are interlinked and few opportunities are afforded to those who choose not to play by the rules. However, it also indicates the Church's conceptual power, as the advice is articulated in a language that draws upon a specifically religious set of signs and images; unsurprisingly, this idiom is used by many characters in the text to make sense of their world. Significantly, though, it is not just the preserve of those who are obviously aligned with orthodox religious practice – Corney's father, who is nicknamed 'Christ-on-the-Cross Crone', as well as Elsie, her conservatively-minded father, and the rest of the Sherlock family – since religious language is also used by characters who otherwise appear nonconformist (*BA* 14). When Corney recalls a scene he part-witnessed as a youth, involving a bad-tempered dispute at dinner about Parnell, the description he gives of his grander is richly revealing: 'My grandfather rose in his seat like the Resurrection of Lazarus,' he states, as the old man prepared to respond to a slur against his beloved Chief (*BA* 108). The image deployed indicates not only the curious death-in-life status of the grander – something that is repeated over and again in the text, as he lives a 'too-long life' and feels 'the damp of the grave in his bones' – but also Corney's tendency to use a religious idiom to aid in the narration of his story (*BA* 97). It is a tendency that is repeated on other occasions in *Bird Alone*, such as when Corney depicts his father ironically, in a Christ-like mode, struggling to hold his patience 'as if he were asking God to let this chalice pass over him', or when he provides the context for a particular disagreement with Elsie by remarking that 'outside was the cold wintry wind and the falling sea – that cry of water and wind that is, they tell us, the cry of the lost souls of the world' (*BA* 120, 234). Elsewhere, the Sherlock family's treatment of Elsie is described in acutely religious terms ('I hated the way she let her family crucify her'), and an almost apocalyptic scene is presented when Corney attempts to re-envisage the night that Elsie died: 'I was in terror. The night was like the Deluge. I thought hell was opening' (*BA* 161, 272). The prevalence of such images suggests that Corney's rebellion is not as complete as is often supposed. That is to say, recalling – but gently revising – Forrest Reid's initial comments on *Bird Alone*, it seems that Corney, like Elsie, cannot fully escape from or renounce the principles that he has inherited. In this respect, the novel declares the influence of an additional intertext, James Joyce's *A Portrait of the Artist as a Young Man* (1916).

Critics have long since noted O'Faoláin's debt to Joyce, pointing to similarities between the aforementioned dinner scene in *Bird Alone* and the celebrated Christmas episode in *A Portrait of the Artist*, where arguments are staged over the betrayal of Parnell. Attention has also been paid to the '*non serviam*' stance that is adopted by the protagonists of both texts, the claustrophobic conditions described in turn-of-the-century Cork and Dublin respectively, and the stress that is placed on common themes including education, family and exile.[29] This is only part of the story, however, for it could equally be argued that the most important link between the two texts is the power of religion in the interpellation of its young subjects. 'It is a curious thing,' Cranly says to Stephen, late in *A Portrait of the Artist*, 'how your mind is supersaturated with the religion in which you say you disbelieve'.[30] Similar observations might be made of O'Faoláin's protagonist, as the artist Stella astutely notes:

> There are some prisons you can never break. You Irish don't know, and you will never know, the ones you can break and the ones you can't break. I believe you don't want to know. You remind me of Dante's people in hell who 'lived wilfully in sadness'! ... But I do know that you, Cornelius, don't and never will know, because your mind is a core on core of prisons. It's an onion of them (*BA* 213–14).

'You are a good little Catholic,' Stella twice goads an outraged Corney, unknowingly repeating the Sherlock family's earlier teasing of the iconoclastic grandfather for saying 'secret rosaries' (*BA* 220, 221). In many ways, the structure of *Bird Alone* reinforces Stella's charge, as the story is framed by references to the Bible: the title is a quotation from Psalm 102, the lament of an afflicted man to the Lord ('I have become like a bird alone on a roof'); while the epigraph, which is taken from Psalm 87 ('I am become as a man without help, a freeman among the dead'), is repeated at the end of the novel, and reinforces the sense of a circle. The implication is that Corney remains trapped within the codes that he has inherited, and the final revolt that is staged in the novel provides further, depressing evidence of this.

Corney's sudden epiphany, in the penultimate chapter of the book, that 'it was not that I did not believe in men, but that I could not believe in what men believed...', is realized within the confines of a church and is dated in accordance with the liturgical calendar, as it takes place during the Easter services on Spy Wednesday (*BA* 296 [ellipsis as original]). Leaving the church, Corney looks out on his native city, leaning with his hands on a wall 'like a priest on a pulpit', before entering into his period of exile (*BA* 298). The recourse to religious images and similes, at this climatic moment of rebellion, signifies the extent to which these codes have been internalized by the narrator. They are, perhaps, the prisons alluded to by Stella, whose mention of Dante implicitly recalls the earlier reference to Beatrice and the picture on display in Corney's family home. It also accounts for Corney's attempts to make sense of his perceived punishment, as he places himself in an almost purgatorial state, outside time ('Time's wheel is stopped for me' [*BA* 10]) and beyond the limits of the natural order ('I was a living corpse' [*BA* 225]). Not only does Corney become a Faust-like figure in consequence, doomed to eternally reflect upon a short-lived period of happiness, he also morphs into the semblance of his long-dead grandfather. The walks he takes in the early morning in Chapter One, along the River Lee, follow the path that is later charted by the older man; while the 'green-globed lamp' by which he reads in the concluding chapter of the book, in the attic of the Crone home (evocatively named 'the Red House'), is the same light by which the grander told the story of *Faust* to the Crone children years earlier (*BA* 303, 14). Corney's rebellion is always incomplete, the novel seems to suggest, and for all the stress that Corney places on defiance and nonconformity, he remains bound by the beliefs that he has inherited – from his grander, certainly, but also from those against whom he appears to be in revolt.

NOTES

1. O'Donnell (O'Brien), 'The Parnellism of O'Faoláin', pp.101–2.
2. While Pidgie Flynn's chest might seem of appropriate interest to her infant child, it also recalls Evelyn Conlon's amusing criticism of O'Faoláin as a writer for whom 'the bosom loomed large'. In *Midsummer Night Madness*, for example, the narrative gaze is often voyeuristically directed towards the breasts of female characters, including Bella Browne in 'The Small Lady', the unnamed woman in 'Fugue', Norah in 'The Bombshop', and Gypsy Gammle in the title story. Conlon, 'A Flawed Portrayal', p.74.
3. Harmon, *O'Faolain: A Critical Introduction*, p.143.
4. The school is the same 'Lancasterian National School' that O'Faoláin attended as a child, with descriptions of the building and its teachers repeated with little alteration in *Vive Moi!* (*VM* 40–50).

5. Louis James, 'George William MacArthur Reynolds', in *The Oxford Dictionary of National Biography* (Oxford: Oxford University Press, 2004–11); see also Anne Humpherys and Louis James (eds), *G.W.M. Reynolds: Nineteenth-Century Fiction, Politics, and the Press* (Aldershot: Ashgate, 2008).
6. George W.M. Reynolds, *Faust*, in *The London Journal; and Weekly Record of Literature, Science, and Art* 55: 3 (14 March 1846), p.19 [emphasis as original].
7. Q.D. Leavis, *Fiction and the Reading Public* (London: Chatto & Windus, 1932), pp.175–7.
8. Reynolds, *Faust* 73: 3 (18 July 1846), p.306.
9. Christopher Marlowe, *The Tragical History of Doctor Faustus* V.iii., epilogue, 27, in J.B. Steane (ed.), *Christopher Marlowe: The Complete Plays* (London: Penguin, 1986), p.339.
10. Reynolds, *Faust* 32: 2 (4 October 1845), p.49.
11. Ibid., 36: 2 (1 November 1845), p.113.
12. Ibid., 41: 2 (6 December 1845), p.195.
13. Ibid., 39: 2 (22 November 1845), p.162.
14. Doyle, *Sean O'Faolain*, pp.54, 134 (n.27).
15. O'Donnell (O'Brien), 'The Parnellism of O'Faoláin', p.103. John Hildebidle also briefly observed that '*Faust* (not Marlowe's or Goethe's but, in good Corkonian fashion, a version by "George W. [*sic*] Reynolds, M.D.") is Corney Crone's grandfather's favourite text'. Hildebidle refrained from explaining what is meant by the phrase 'good Corkonian fashion', however; he also declined to elaborate on the significance of this intertext, consigning it to a footnote. Hildebidle, 'Sean O'Faolain', p.143.
16. Seán O'Faoláin, 'The Spurious Fenian Tale', *Folklore* 41: 2 (30 June 1930), p.154.
17. Sean O'Faolain, 'A Born Genius', *Lovat Dickson's Magazine* (April 1934), pp.468–98; reprinted as Seán O'Faoláin, *The Born Genius: A Short Story* (Detroit: Schuman's, 1936). 'A Broken World' was first published in *The London Mercury*, in late 1936, under a different title, 'Broken World?'. This version of the story is shorter than the one included in *A Purse of Coppers*, and concludes with the image of the farmer leaving the train and being swallowed up by the dark. It does not include any reference to Faust. Seán O'Faoláin, 'Broken World?', *The London Mercury* 35: 206 (December 1936), pp.123–32.
18. O'Faolain, 'The Modern Novel', p.351.
19. O'Faolain, 'It No Longer Matters', pp.52–3, 54.
20. Ibid., p.55. The same point is made in *The Virginia Quarterly Review*, where O'Faoláin argued that 'to find a counterpart to what the Catholic novelist is striving to create we must go to such work as Marlowe's "Faustus", imaging [*sic*] it as treated in the naturalistic mode … and as treated by people of infinitely more refined sensibilities living in a much more mechanical and complicated age'. O'Faolain, 'The Modern Novel', p.344.

21. Forrest Reid, review of *Bird Alone*, *Ireland To-Day* 1: 3 (August 1936), p.81.
22. Qtd. in Peter Martin, *Censorship in the Two Irelands, 1922–39* (Dublin: Irish Academic Press, 2006), p.203; see also Michael Adams, *Censorship: The Irish Experience* (Dublin: Scepter Books, 1968), pp.74–5.
23. O'Faolain, 'The Dangers of Censorship', pp.57, 58, 61.
24. Ibid., pp.62–3.
25. Martin, *Censorship in the Two Irelands*, p.206; Matthews, *'The Bell' Magazine*, pp.10–13.
26. O'Faoláin, 'Ireland After Yeats', p.331. According to O'Faoláin, this invited comparisons with the Puritanical world re-created by Nathaniel Hawthorne in *The Scarlet Letter* (1850). 'We are, in effect, very much in the same position as Hawthorne,' he suggested, who also wrote of a society where 'sin was furtive, revolt slight and brief, and convention rigid'. The comparison was extended in *Vive Moi!* (*VM* 255).
27. Gearóid Ó Tuathaigh, 'The Irish People', in Lee and Ó Tuathaigh (eds), *The Age of de Valera*, p.184.
28. In his study of Goethe's *Faust*, Michael Beddow has noted that the eponymous character 'first appears with a monologue, his most characteristic mode of utterance; even when ostensibly speaking to others, he is more often than not talking to himself'. Similar observations might be made of Corney in *Bird Alone*. Michael Beddow, *Goethe: Faust I* (London: Grant & Cutler, 1986), p.35.
29. Harmon, *O'Faolain: A Critical Introduction*, pp.157–9; Doyle, *Sean O'Faolain*, pp.50–2; John Cronin, 'Sean O'Faolain: *Bird Alone*', in *Irish Fiction: 1900–1940* (Belfast: Appletree Press, 1992), pp.153–7.
30. James Joyce, *A Portrait of the Artist as a Young Man*, ed. by Seamus Deane (1916; London: Penguin, 1992), p.261.

7

'It's hard to tell...': *A Purse of Coppers*

'The Church in Ireland works through the people, not through Governments,' O'Faoláin declared in 'The Priests and the People' (1937), 'and depends for its power on its influence over the people'. If this influence is qualified, insofar as it is dependent upon the populace, it is nonetheless all-encompassing, since the Catholic Church is afforded 'as much influence (in Ireland, only, I agree) as if it held direct political power'.[1] Its teachings are part of received opinion, O'Faoláin observed of his contemporary environment, its doctrines inform the discourse through which many people think and speak about their world, its authority is underlined through repeated associations with particular narratives of the past, and its rituals provide distinct reference points in the structure of everyday life. As Tom Inglis has noted, such influences constitute a significant strand in the formation of a collective consciousness and proved crucial in the establishment of an Irish Catholic *habitus*. Drawing upon the work of the sociologist Pierre Bourdieu, Inglis has explained this point by remarking that 'it is helpful to think of *habitus* as an intuitive way of being religious or (what feels like) a deeply natural way of reading and interpreting one's life and the world'.[2] These 'ways of being' are not simply 'natural', of course. Instead, they evolve out of complex processes of socialization and interpellation, gaining authority by seeming to be obvious, and so foreclosing discussion about practices which have been legitimized because they are considered God-ordained or self-evident. Such practices are never easily formulated and are infused with social, economic and political value: 'The influence of the Church to-day appears to be as great as ever,' O'Faoláin reasoned. '*Appears*. For can one be sure?'[3]

The argument of 'The Priests and the People' suggests some uncertainty on this score – the enforced pause, the stressed repetition of 'appears', and the use of italics, above, all indicate as much – as specific moments in Irish history were identified when the Catholic Church set itself against 'the hard wall of Nationalist tradition', and found its authority and its influence questioned: 'There is in these interruptions of clerical influence a tradition of revolt by Irish left-wing nationalism,' O'Faoláin posited, a tradition meriting serious consideration, which remains alive in some circles resolutely opposed to 'such church-snaffling bodies as the Knights of Columbanus or the Irish Christian Front'. Progressive individuals are invariably branded '"anti-clerical" for daring to differ' with conservative thought. However, 'any man who holds, to-day, unpopular opinions on social or political matters may, I think, feel almost complimented by being called "anti-clerical" by such people'.[4] Part of the reasoning behind 'The Priests and the People' was to see the Catholic Church in Ireland as not simply a monolith, and to draw a distinction between the activities of those reactionary groups who operated with the support of right-wing religious authorities, and who were vociferous in the implementation of censorship, and moderate elements within the Church, amongst the clergy and the laity. O'Faoláin's essay canvassed for support amongst the latter audience, and so echoed his earlier call, also articulated in *Ireland To-Day*, for the formation of 'an independent Catholic wedge' or a liberal, religious-minded intelligentsia.[5] In addition, his essay was intended to warn the Church of the consequences should it succumb to reactionary forces. Any such alignment would be 'most dangerous to the harmony that ought to exist between priests and people,' he concluded, 'and to the ascendancy of religion, which can only be achieved and maintained by both – either working together or working separately in a condition of mutual respect'.[6]

A Purse of Coppers (also 1937) explores some of the nuances in this relationship in an Irish Catholic *habitus*. The book consists of fourteen stories, of unequal length, which are loosely organized into a volume rather than a cycle of short stories. Most of the stories share a contemporary, post-Independence setting, and all are interconnected (though not to the extent of the preceding cycle, *Midsummer Night Madness*) through the use of particular tropes and themes. In this instance, the principal link is the Church, as all of the stories bar one ('A Meeting') either include clerical characters or contain mention of priests, and each carries references to Catholic devotions, symbols, rituals, inhibitions, idioms, spaces or practices. As with the rest of O'Faoláin's short-story collections, *A Purse of Coppers* includes an explanatory subtitle, *Short Stories*, on its title page (all of his collections carry similar subtitles); unusually for O'Faoláin, though, the title does not correspond to the title of any one story in the collection.[7] Instead, it picks up on a line from the story 'My Son Austin', where an unnamed narrator thinks back to a former priest, Father Tom, who told a tale about another man, Dinny Fagan. Dinny's tale seemed to Father Tom, or to the narrator recalling Father Tom (the syntax is deliberately unclear), 'not merely the contents of one life, but the contents of all human life – a tiny purse of it, with all the coins there, well rubbed, much treasured' (*PC* 129). *A Purse of Coppers* draws upon this reference, but replaces the non-distinguished 'coins' with the lowly-denominated 'coppers'. Appropriately, given the power of the Church in the text, the title also carries a likely Christian import, since St. Matthew's Gospel includes mention of a purse of silver awarded to Judas Iscariot for his betrayal of Christ.[8] 'A Purse of Coppers' alludes to this archetypal case of treachery. However, the substitution of coppers for silver invests this tale with a distinctly Yeatsian quality, calling to mind the uncouth Catholic middle class who inspired such indignation in Yeats's *Responsibilities* (1914), and who, according to O'Faoláin, were the principal beneficiaries of the recent revolution. The price of betrayal in Ireland, or rather of the betrayal of Ireland – and of republican hopes and ideals – was paltry, it is inferred.

The dedication in *A Purse of Coppers* further explains this choice of title. In a long tribute to his mentor and friend, Edward Garnett, the book is presented as a 'handful of modest life out of Ireland, much rubbed, perhaps even with the superscription defaced by time and circumstance. You have wished me more passionate and heroic,' O'Faoláin added, 'and I have said, "What can a writer do but gather up the coins and make his own fumbling effort to say to which Caesar each belongs?"' (*PC* np). 'Fumbling' strengthens the implied link with Yeats and the latter's disdain for 'the fumbling wits, the obscure spite / of our old Paudeen in his shop,' as well as for the *petit bourgeoisie* in 'September 1913' who choose to 'fumble in a greasy till / And add the halfpence to the pence'.[9] The embedded quotation also returns the reader to the Bible, since O'Faoláin's reference to Caesar recalls Christ's response to those who questioned him over the payment of taxes to Rome: 'Render unto Caesar the things that are Caesar's, and unto God the things that are God's'.[10] This advice, recorded in three of the four Gospels, has often been interpreted as an argument in favour of the separation of spiritual and secular forms of authority. In the context of the mid-to-late 1930s, when the Church exerted such influence in Ireland, this call was especially timely.

Not only was *A Purse of Coppers* contemporaneous with 'The Priests and the People', it was also published the same year that de Valera's constitution was completed and passed into law. It has been well documented that the drafting of the latter text came under serious pressure from senior figures in the clergy, including Cardinal Joseph MacRory and John Charles McQuaid (the future Archbishop of Dublin), who wanted the constitution to be wholly consonant with Catholic teaching. De Valera, it seems, was against the State being conceived in narrow theocratic terms; however, he simultaneously sought advice from and was influenced by the thoughts of several religious figures, including McQuaid especially. He was also undoubtedly influenced by the larger Catholic context which he inhabited, as well as by his own religious convictions and faith which remained intact despite the Church's joint pastoral of 1922, excommunicating those who fought against the Free State government.[11] In many respects, the 1937 constitution can be considered part of a larger process which had been underway since independence, which sought to enshrine Catholic teaching in the laws of the newly-established State. As the late John Whyte noted, it provided 'the coping-stone' in the gradual conflation of secular and religious principles, differing from the preceding Irish constitution (drafted by William T. Cosgrave's Cumann na nGaedheal party in 1922, and seen by some as an 'imposed' or British-based document) in crucial ways, not least in its replacing of the 'typical liberal-democratic' impulse which informed the earlier text with articles that were 'obviously marked by Catholic thought'.[12] Dermot Keogh has similarly traced the doctrinal influences in the later text, commenting that 'de Valera always worked within a Catholic philosophical context', and that the social legislation drafted by de Valera and his advisors 'was predicated on the principles of the Roman Catholic Church' – even if this did not satisfy the wishes of some of his more zealous co-religionists writing for such papers as the *Catholic Bulletin*.[13] Summarizing this historical process, Patrick Murray has posited, in a carefully-worded assessment, that 'the 1937 constitution may be regarded as a formal expression of de Valera's commitment to the principle of a Catholic Republic'.[14]

Its preamble, for instance, substantially drafted by McQuaid, implies that Irish Catholics – or more specifically, Irish nationalist Catholics – are its intended audience, with its allusion to the Penal Laws, the experience of oppression, and the struggle for political autonomy: 'The 'people of Éire' are represented 'Humbly acknowledging all our obligations to our Divine Lord, Jesus Christ, Who sustained our fathers through centuries of trial', and 'Gratefully remembering their heroic and unremitting struggle to regain the rightful independence of our Nation'.[15] The Catholic colouring of the document was further reflected in its pronouncements on family, property, education and marriage, which are in line with Church teaching, as well as in its passing allusions to vocationalism (inspired by Pope Pius XI's 1931 encyclical *Quadragesimo Anno*) and its controversial recognition of the 'special position' of the Catholic Church in Irish society.[16] Catholicism was not afforded the status of the established religion of the State, however, and de Valera's decision to hold back on this provoked criticism in some quarters, as did his official recognition of the Protestant denominations and the Jewish congregation. De Valera would later claim that this article caused him more anxiety than any other element of the constitution. He also maintained that religious minorities were specifically identified in the constitution to guarantee their protection by the State – a decision which carries particular resonance in the context of the contemporary persecution of European Jews, and which ensured that citizenship was not the preserve of any one religious grouping.[17]

The privileged place afforded the Catholic Church meant that it remained the most powerful interest group in Irish civil society, however. Equally importantly, as Inglis has noted, the influence that it wielded was based on the fact that the majority of people in the Free State saw themselves 'first and foremost as Catholics', an allegiance that 'ranked with, and often surpassed, loyalty to the state, political party, interest group, family or friends'. This allegiance evolved out of a deeply-ingrained way of thinking, permeating institutions at all levels of society, and interweaving with the fabric of everyday life. 'This is what made Ireland an example not so much of a theocratic state, but rather of a theocratic society,' Inglis has argued, as:

> religious identity fused not just with the fulfilment of religious interests, but with economic, political, social and cultural interests ... What makes a society religious rather than secular, and what made Irish society Catholic, was not only the extent to which the church was able to exercise control over the state in particular social fields, and the way the church shaped the vision, goals and policies of the state, but the way a Catholic *habitus* pervaded all aspects of social life.[18]

The prevalence of this *habitus* accounts for Corney's inability to break free from the codes that he has inherited in *Bird Alone*. It also explains the images of enclosure that recur throughout *A Purse of Coppers* (small rooms, narrow lanes, confessional boxes, gossiping circles, train compartments, priests' collars), as the influence of the Church is powerfully felt and lives are determined in accordance with the degree to which individuals conform to accepted practices. 'Sure a person might as well be an animal if they don't go to Mass,' the lonely titular character of 'Kitty the Wren' observes, and her allusion to the importance of this sacrament (from which she has been excluded), and the power of the Church that has ostracized her, is reflected in other stories in the collection (*PC* 109). Protests are organized against an 'immoral play' (in reality, a third-rate touring ballet) in 'The Old Master' because, as one of the protestors concedes, 'it's the way I *couldn't* be seen supporting it. I'm in this all on account of Canon Paul. As you know, what he says goes' (*PC* 38 [emphasis as original]). A poor couple are kept patiently waiting in 'Discord', in the hope of seeing a clergyman about their child's baptism, while rows of penitents queue for hours in 'Sinners', to gain absolution for sins committed. Their faith is gently parodied in 'The Confessional', where young boys are so familiar with the sacrament of confession that they re-enact it as play, showing that it is important enough to them to merit their attention, and also that they are conversant with the practice to be followed, even if they differ about the implications of what they are doing in the sacred space of a church. 'That's a sin,' one of the boys gasps; 'Yerrah! It's all a cod', his pal, the wonderfully-named 'Foxer', replies (*PC* 230, 234). Meanwhile, Father Tom thrice reports to the narrator of 'My Son Austin' that 'a priest knows everything' about the lives of his parishioners, and, as if to bear this out, local 'spies' are depicted keeping him up-to-date with what is happening in the back streets of his parish (*PC* 125, 129, 131).

O'Faoláin is careful not to simplify the matter, however. Thus, the first time Father Tom claims that the priest is all-knowing, he immediately qualifies this by also stating 'And he knows nothing' (*PC* 125). In Father Tom's case, this lack of knowledge can be traced back to his own private frustrations, and to the fact that, despite his best efforts, he is never able to fully understand his parishioners' innermost needs. It seems that Father Tom is especially anxious about the body (in particular the female body, as well as his own sexual self), but this continues to intrude on the margins of his story. The narrator is sure, for example, that Father Tom's vocation was not genuine and that the priest himself 'had known for years that he was a square peg in a round hole'; he is additionally certain that 'he told me himself when I met him in London that his mother had made him become a priest' (*PC* 123). Significantly, Father Tom quits the priesthood once his mother dies – his mother being a likely source of his imbibed 'terror', although it is equally probable that his 'extraordinary ideas' about women are a product of the fearful, chauvinistic society in which he grew up. O'Faoláin stressed this very point in *Vive Moi!*, after all, when he rebuked the Catholic Church in Ireland for policing any discussion of sex, and so contributing to a culture that chose not to speak of the body, sending young men and women 'so sweetly, so virtuously, so loftily and so benevolently … naked to the wolf of life' (*VM* 22).[19]

These codes provide part of the context for 'My Son Austin', and are expressed through the story that Father Tom tells of Dinny, and Dinny's beloved son, Austin. Austin fell in love with and married the 'loose lady of the parish', the beautifully-alliterative Lily Long (*PC* 130). Lily is described in knowing terms by Father Tom as a 'girl of that type', and at first their marriage is greeted with relief by the priest, who had 'for years' been 'crucified running after her', extricating her from various entanglements and trysts (*PC* 136, 130). After a honeymoon period, the marriage proves unsuccessful, as Lily returns to former ways (or at least is reputed to do so, since there is no evidence of this), and Austin spends less and less time at home. Ultimately, this gives way to estrangement, an uneasy reconcilement, emigration and the early death of Dinny. 'She was a warm-blooded piece,' Father Tom nonchalantly confides to the narrator, 'and she liked her bit of gaiety, and on the other side her only anchor was the Church and the priest – and Austin, he derided the Church' (*PC* 136).

Lily's recourse to religion is not evinced at any point in the story, however, and Father Tom's casual comment might conversely be read as code for the supposed power of the Church – that is to say, it is less a case of Lily's 'anchor', rather than Lily being anchored. What is more, it is significant that Father Tom feels the need to include a parenthetical observation at this point, balancing Lily's alleged behaviour with an abrupt reference to Austin's religious dissidence. For the latter's actions are of special concern to the priest, since Austin has declined to join his father's sodality, ceased to attend mass, and intends (but is not permitted) to get married in a registry office: 'Father Tom was so cross at the bare memory of it that I had to smile. He saw me and grew red. He waved his hands

… "You can see, of course", he expostulated, "what a scandal it would be for these poor people. In the end I married them myself"' (*PC* 134). Austin has also developed a taste for heterodoxical reading material which causes Father Tom, and his father Dinny, considerable worries, with one concerned about the state of Austin's soul and the other anxious about the condition of his son's eyes:

> '"Father, I suppose you do be reading a lot at night? I wonder now, could you tell me where I'd get a good lamp cheap? That son of mine is a terror for the books."
>
> 'I knew', added Father Tom, here, 'what books Austin was reading. A priest, as I say, knows everything. Lessing's *Laocoon*, Renan's *Life of Jesus*, the atheistical one. Books from the Rationalist Press, Bob Ingersoll, and such-like.'
>
> '"He's a terror for the books", says Dinny, "and the poor boy do be complaining how he can't come out to the Confraternity with me on account of all the study he wants to do."' (*PC* 128–9)

Despite these concerns, Father Tom is not simply presented as a thinly-veiled representative of an inflexible moral code in 'My Son Austin', and it is striking that on a few occasions he is described performing his duties when he was a priest. His style of praying, for instance, is said to have 'had a great *effect* of piety and impressed every parish he went to' (*PC* 124 [emphasis added]). The narrator's understated choice of words complicates the way Father Tom presents himself to others, and how he should be perceived by others (including the narrator and the reader) in turn; it also adds to the sense that Father Tom's public persona is incompatible with a barely-intimated, perhaps even barely-realized, private life. The allusion to performance also provides a delicate link between the narrator and the priest, for just as the narrator recalls how as a youth he 'used to imitate [Father Tom's] earnest, lugubrious, up-and-down way of saying the prayers', so he marvels that 'Tom was excellent at the sing-song, slender, Cork accent, and he trolled it with delight' (*PC* 124, 131). An implication is that Father Tom has been working to fit the role that is expected of him, and that there is more to the priest than is revealed in this short, multi-layered story. The strength of the *habitus* is such, however, that many months after Father Tom has left the priesthood – indeed, many years after he has died – the narrator is compelled to remark that 'I never could get used to calling him plain Tom' (*PC* 125). The long-dead, former clergyman is instead named 'Father Tom' for the duration of the story (the above incident, where the narrator reflects on 'Tom's' ability to mimic his parishioners, is the only exception to this). The narrator also notes, without ever revealing how he knows, that Father Tom 'never did destroy his black trousseau' after he chose to follow a non-religious life in England (*PC* 123).

Father Tom is not the only priest who is disappointed by choices taken, or not taken, in *A Purse of Coppers*; nor is he the only religious figure who is sensitively described by O'Faoláin. The priest in 'A Broken World' appears a distant, complex, but thoughtful individual, 'silenced' by Church authorities, and unappreciated by his congregation who consider him 'a local "character"' (*PC* 23, 14). An elderly nun in 'Mother Matilda's Book' has likewise become a source of embarrassment to the community she lives within, as she is ridiculed by young novices and 'a constant worry' to successive Reverend Mothers, who are either unable to comprehend her idiosyncratic behaviour or unwilling to accept the harsh realities of the aging process (*PC* 238). Father Peter appears self-confident and assured in 'Discord', but he is also childish and ill-at-ease, 'awkward with the newly-wedded', and bizarrely challenging a young couple to race him up a flight of stairs (*PC* 215). Intriguingly, the omniscient narrator calls Father Peter by his Christian name several times at an advanced stage of this story, recalling a less distant narrator's inability to do the same in 'My Son Austin'. In the middle section of 'Discord', the narrator momentarily refers to him as 'Peter' but reverts back to 'Father Peter' almost as quick; but in the closing phases he is stripped of this title entirely, and thrice named 'Peter' in the final two paragraphs, as the story moves outside the confines of the church where he lives and works (*PC* 222, 225–6). No explanation is given for this narratorial lapse, which is hardly incidental on the part of

O'Faoláin or his narrator. It is notable, however, that this coincides with an increasing sense of Father Peter's vulnerability, to the point where he becomes a figure of amusement for others, 'turned into a fat Punch like the Devil in the play' (*PC* 226). It also seems aligned to his gradual loss of status and power, as the priest appears ill-suited to the context in which he finds himself: 'You'd go off your nut if you took too much notice of things,' is his uncaring response to a young visitor who is alarmed by the poverty that she witnesses in his inner-city parish (*PC* 222).[20]

The priest in 'Admiring the Scenery' is also presented as an individual who has not quite come to terms with lingering thoughts and regrets (despite the narrator's claims to the contrary), as well as the frustrations of the provincial world that he inhabits. Through the eyes of another third-person narrator, he appears as 'a young man, too fat for his years, with drooping lids, puffed lips, and a red face as if he suffered from blood pressure':

> The same features on another man might have suggested a sensual nature, but there was in his heavily-lidded eyes a look that was sometimes whimsical and sometimes sad, and that look, with the gentle turn to his mouth when he smiled, gave him the appearance of a man who had gone through many struggles and finally solved his problems in a spirit of good-humoured regret (*PC* 67–8).

This man is the only one in a group of three who is not named in 'Admiring the Scenery' (the other two are lay teachers in the local Diocesan College, gradually identified by surname only as Hanafan and Governey), and O'Faoláin's decision to withhold the priest's name reinforces the sense that he lacks a degree of individuation, and that he has not fully, or 'finally', resolved those struggles that are in conflict with his calling. It also suggests that the narrator is reluctant to pierce the skin of this particular character. In his critical study *The Short Story*, O'Faoláin argued that such reticence is characteristic of the short-story genre more generally, as the form is better suited to providing Chekhovian-style glimpses or intimations of a life rather than full-scale portraits of complex characters.[21] In 'Admiring the Scenery', this perhaps explains why so little information is disclosed about the priest's companions (even though they are named) as well as the priest himself. The irascible and inquisitive Governey is driven by an anger that is never quite explained – the narrator merely observes that 'the main thing about him was that he did break occasionally into sudden talk, and when he did he banged the hard railings repeatedly or lifted his two fists in the air and slapped his forehead' (*PC* 68). Meanwhile 'the sad man, Hanafan', reflects on a love story that is never fully told (although it would appear that it is already known to his friend, the priest), and is instead pictured 'weeping to himself' in the closing moments of the story, 'the drops creeping through his tightly closed eyes' (*PC* 69, 79). The care with which O'Faoláin sketches such characters adds to the textured quality of the *habitus* that is described in *A Purse of Coppers*, as many lay figures remain bound by codes that are restrictive but reassuringly familiar, and most of the priests are presented as more than one-dimensional, propagandist figures.

That said, although many of the priests appear sensitive and humane in *A Purse of Coppers*, they are nonetheless part of an institution that is repressive and power-driven. Reflecting on this *habitus* years later in *Vive Moi!*, O'Faoláin characterized the period as 'a time when the Catholic Church was felt, feared and courted on all sides as the dominant power' (*VM* 264). That dominance is expressed time and again in *A Purse of Coppers* through social organizations that give structure to individual lives (confraternities, sodalities, charitable societies), the visible architecture of churches and other religious buildings, and the patterns of thought and speech that enable – but also condition – people to make sense of their world. It is also evident in the pressure that the Church exerts on those individuals who choose not to conform. In a deflated economy, contracts are withheld and jobs are secured on the whims of the clergy, while those who are perceived as 'different' are punished or shunned if they are considered a threat to the established order. This is the case for the politically-engaged priest in 'A Broken World'; it is also the situation presented to the pretentious John Aloysius Gonzaga O'Sullivan in 'The Old Master', who is compelled to protest against his own fantasies, and, in the process, is turned into a figure of caricature and abuse. Analogous situations are faced by other characters in the text: an artistic nun with dementia in 'Mother Matilda's Book'; a depressed clerk who dreams of escape but concedes his desires in 'A Born Genius'; a frustrated station master who sings his innermost needs to passing trains in 'Admiring the Scenery'; and an orphaned domestic servant who is subjected to the threats of her mistress in 'Sinners'. Most poignantly, in 'Kitty the Wren', it is the fate of a woman who has had a child outside marriage, and who is expelled by her community as a result.

Misogynistic prejudices and sexist double standards are part of the subject matter of 'Kitty the Wren', as the title character is treated with great cruelty by her former neighbours, and is banished to the remotest of locations as punishment. The world that she is cast out to is described in appropriately purgatorial terms – she is said to 'liv[e] all alone where you wouldn't hear a sound but the stones falling on the mountain' – and is miles from her native village, Croghanbeag, where the principal character, a visiting French sailor, first hears mention of her (*PC* 102). It takes the sailor two hours to cycle to her house, across a desolate Connemara landscape of rock and bog, and, significantly, past 'a railway so covered with weeds and rust that it looked as if it had not been used for fifty years' (*PC* 103). It transpires that Kitty does not live alone, as she cares for her unnamed brother who suffers from an unspecified intellectual disability. 'But what matter?' she sighs, as her brother is scarcely able to communicate, and the man with whom she got pregnant has long since skipped the country (*PC* 107). Most movingly, she does not live with her child, who is only mentioned once in this terribly sad story. It is not known whether the child is still alive, or whether he or she (the gender is not given) was taken away to be housed with those 'boarded-out children' who are briefly mentioned in 'A Broken World' – 'children unwanted by poor parents, or simply illegitimates' (*PC* 17). If so, it is possible that the child will have grown up in an orphanage, like the endearing penitent, Madgie, in 'Sinners', and trained for a life of service to the better-off. However, it is equally possible that the child was drowned at birth by Kitty's father, before he killed himself in perceived disgrace, after a bout of heavy drinking: 'They found the body, God help him, in a bog-hole,' a villager confides to the sailor, but 'the body' in question is not identified by either the gossip or the narrator, and the syntax is deliberately unclear (*PC* 114). Many other things also remain unexplained – what, for instance, of Kitty's mother, who is not mentioned at any point in the story; where are the rest of her brothers; and how did her family lose the land that they are said to have once held – and this lack of information seems increasingly appropriate in a story that turns on hearsay, innuendo and rumour (*PC* 105).

The focus of rumour is Kitty, of course (that is why the story is named for her), but the Frenchman soon realizes that the woman who is discursively constructed by Croghanbeag as 'Kitty the Wren' bears little resemblance to the Kitty Canavan that he actually meets. The latter is a devout, sensitive, desperately lonely, forty-year old woman, with an unfulfilled desire for pretty things and books, not the 'loose woman' he was promised by his drinking companion, Jamesy Dinny John, in the pub. O'Faoláin further complicates this by having each of the characters in the pub play a part (with the exception of the sailor), and by suggesting that the sailor is unable to understand this. Local codes of conduct prove bewildering to the Frenchman, who fails to make sense of a barmaid's flirtatious behaviour and is happy to take a stranger's sudden companionship at face value, even though he is being cadged for free drinks:

> 'But are you a good girl?' [the sailor] asked [the barmaid].
>
> 'I'd be very bad, now, then' (she tossed her head and flicked his cheek lightly with her cloth), 'if I'm not half as good as whoever you left behind where you last drew anchor.'
>
> He could not catch that, so he tried to chuck her under the chin, and as she stalked away haughtily he cried out after her:
>
> 'And, my little one, if you are so good as all that, then I waste the beginning of a good night with you!'

> That sealed the friendship between himself and Jamesy, who roared fit to burst, and slapped the counter, and took another pint (*PC* 101).

As Pierce Butler has observed, the sailor is evidently confused by the barmaid's verbal dexterities.[22] However, he is also being played for a fool by Jamesy Dinny John, who presents Kitty as the promiscuous woman that the Frenchman had hoped – indeed, had expected from the outset – to find. A series of double standards are set in place in O'Faoláin's story, with the sexual exploits of men avowed and the behaviour of 'good girls' carefully regulated. The only reference to Kitty's former lover is a fellow villager's indulgent description of him as 'one of the lads', while the sailor enters the village at the start of the story aroused and ready to declare to the world that 'what he wanted was a girl' (*PC* 104, 99). He subsequently coaxes the desired information out of Jamesy (although it is likely that Jamesy is really in charge of this conversation) by massaging his ego with a bawdy compliment: 'I am certain that many a time you have squeezed a girl under a bush' (*PC* 102). By contrast, no allowance is made for the vilified Kitty.

Kitty's desire for education is shared by her unfortunate brother, who regularly spends nights waiting outside a school because 'he has a wish to be there' (*PC* 107). Neither of the Canavans has received much schooling, however, and Kitty herself is barely literate. Thus, when the sailor promises that he will return with books for Kitty to read, she pitifully replies, 'Oh, God, do! … Books with pictures' (*PC* 111). This adds to the pathos that gathers around one of her most treasured possessions, a primary schoolbook (her only book), which she has learnt by heart, and which she partly recites 'in a high monotone, with rests after each group of words, just as if she were reciting it in the classroom' (*PC* 110). It also explains why Kitty appears 'childish, undeveloped, in spite of her years, immature' to her visitor (*PC* 105). The conversation between Kitty and the sailor speaks to the awful reality of her plight. Crucially, it also enables O'Faoláin to depict Kitty as an articulate, thinking subject, and to set the complexity of her character against the object status that she is at risk of being reduced to by the gossips of Croghanbeag: 'Women like that … should be hunted out of the country,' one of the villagers viciously states, and this poisonous belief is shared by others in the locale (*PC* 114).

The local priest might not endorse this belief; however, he does little to alleviate Kitty's situation. Although he seems 'kind and genial' to the sailor, he is nonetheless also deeply judgmental – his face 'darkens' when Kitty's name is mentioned, and he responds with a 'grunt ... between derision and satisfaction' to the sailor's account of his recent meeting with this much talked-about figure (*PC* 114, 115). 'The poor girl will never enter this village again,' is his ineffective response to the bigotry of Croghanbeag. 'And 'tis better that way,' he adds, claiming that Kitty should instead expect to find some solace from the natural world around her. 'It's a lonely glen, but it can be lovely. God, my child, deals with His little creatures in His own way – a more kindly way than our way. Take her from where she is, and …' he ceases to say (*PC* 116, 117 [ellipsis as original]). The priest's empty platitudes recall the comments of the narrator of 'Fugue', in the earlier collection *Midsummer Night Madness*, and the response of an unnamed woman who confronted the triteness of this type of argument with an acknowledgment of the true cost of rural isolation:

> 'Do you live here?'
> 'Yes.'
> 'But you're not always as desolate as this – surely?'
> 'Desolate, just as you say; this is a lonely district, you know.'
> 'Well, it's not so bad at all now,' I said. 'I shouldn't mind if I lived here – the mountains and the valleys … '
> She halted in her step and faced me: the little mouth was gathered into a hard white button of flesh.
> 'You would soon tire of these mountains!' (*MNM* 109 [ellipsis as original])

This fate is replayed in other stories in *A Purse of Coppers*, where the hypocrisies and sexist practices of post-Independence culture are laid bare, and focus is given to instances of loneliness, female depression and domestic imprisonment. 'This focus on women's lives contributes to the modernity of the collection,' Heather Ingman has argued, and 'anticipates later writing by Irish women'.[23] In 'A Meeting', for instance, a former revolutionary, Sally Dunn, is robbed of her potential, and is left drowning in a world that she can scarcely articulate or comprehend. 'It's hard to tell ... You know, it's ...' is the best Sally can manage, as she tries to partake in a conversation with the narrator (*PC* 211 [ellipses as original]). That conversation is riddled with ellipses and regrets, however, and is punctuated by a series of pauses that neither Sally nor the narrator is able to fill. Likewise, in the last story in the collection, the ambitiously-organized 'There's a Birdie in the Cage' (first published separately in 1935), Helen Black is forced to accept that she has been 'caught in that coil of things from which there is no escape' (*PC* 285).[24] 'She was here and would be here always' is her sombre realization, as she reflects on a love that has been cruelly taken from her, and contemplates her future life as an unmarried daughter in her father's house (*PC* 285).

Appropriately, in the closing pages of this multi-perspectival story, Helen is only called by her given name once, by her father, requesting something of her, and is instead assigned the status of a non-individuated 'she' by the narrator. (Earlier in the story, she is referred to as 'Helena' by her snobbish sister, Lolly; in the middle section, by contrast, she is warmly identified by name, by her lover, Bel.) It seems that Helen's very identity is at risk at this point, as 'she' is presented as an already petrified figure – twice described as a 'statue', and momentarily referred to as 'it' – before 'dissolving into a woman' so that she can 'absently' perform the domestic chores that are demanded of her (*PC* 285–6). Helen's awareness of her situation adds to the poignancy of the story, as the focalized third section stresses her ability to reflect on what has been lost and recognize the limits of her future entrapment. This is encapsulated in the late image of 'the dumb gulls fly[ing] inland over the house and in the harbour the fog breathing on the full water', something Helen herself observes, but significantly at a remove, through a window-pane (*PC* 285). It is an image that is rich in interpretative potential, as it suggests movement, but of a type that is ingrown or stifled (the birds do not fly out to sea), as well as suffocation (the sinister 'breathing' fog), and also hints at pleasures that were once directly experienced by Helen, but that can only be recreated in memory (the reference to 'the full water' recalls that sensually-drawn night in the second section, when Helen was stranded with Bel because the tide was low). It is particularly telling that the gulls are described as 'dumb' by the narrator, since Helen herself barely speaks in the final few pages of the story, either because she cannot or will not talk, or because there is no one left to share her thoughts with. 'Did – what ...?', and 'Oh!', is all that is left to say to her father, as she turns to music to better communicate her heartbreak – 'music that is like the sound of human tears', playing the piano 'gently and slowly, but with more understanding than she had ever played it in her life before' (*PC* 284 [ellipses as original]). This retreat into music, and into an aphasic silence, is all the more powerful in a story that otherwise features so much conversation.

Loss of spirit, fear of entrapment, the desire to escape, failure to communicate, an inability to understand – each of these themes is repeated over and again in *A Purse of Coppers*, as O'Faoláin presents a world of quiet frustration and despair. It is a world with clear Joycean echoes, drawing upon naturalist concerns (determinism, inheritance, the writer as diagnostician), and intertwining this with elements of documentary realism. Stasis and suffocation are identified as the principal conditions of Irish life, and characters routinely struggle with an order that is clerically and chauvinistically defined, and that carries the imprint of a colonialist, but also an anti-colonialist or nationalist, heritage. 'Discord' is a notable example, with its claustral allusions to eighteenth- and nineteenth-century Dublin, and its palpable sense of stilled lives edging around the coffins of those who are not quite dead. Despite the stress on inactivity, though, and the recurrent leitmotif of enclosure, *A Purse of Coppers* is repeatedly drawn towards the act – or, at least, the promise – of movement, with boats and roads mentioned on numerous occasions ('There's a Birdie in the Cage', 'A Born Genius', as well as one of the weakest stories in the collection, 'Egotists', for instance), and trains and railway lines featured to a greater or lesser degree in a number of the stories ('Admiring the Scenery', 'A Broken World', 'A Meeting', as well as the thin parody of de Valera's economic war with Britain, 'Sullivan's Trousers').

Trains, in particular, serve as symbols of modernity in the collection, with carriages providing space for people from very different places to come together to share experiences that are, by definition, transitory. Railway lines also allow remote locations and fragmented communities to be connected and interlinked. The overgrown tracks in 'Kitty the Wren' suggest that this is not always achieved, however, and it is not clear why some stations are placed in the locations where they are found: 'Why on earth is this ten-thousand times accursed station three miles from the village?' the exasperated Governey asks in 'Admiring the Scenery'. 'My God, what a country! What – is – it – for?' (*PC* 68). What is more, the movement that is registered is of a very particular kind, as trains run along predetermined tracks, to specifically chosen locations, in accordance with set timetables and schedules. Carriages are also invested with symbolic value by O'Faoláin, serving as appropriately enclosed locations to explore the psychic patterns of human consciousness, as Denis Sampson once suggested, and to reflect upon the interiorized practices of narrative and memory.[25] In addition, they tacitly acknowledge the influence of some of the great nineteenth-century storytellers, including Maupassant and Chekhov, both of whom repeatedly used trains in their stories, and both of whom are subjects of lengthy analysis by O'Faoláin in *The Short Story*.[26] Trains and train journeys also provide lateral points of interconnection with other short stories of the period, such as Frank O'Connor's dramatic 'In the Train' (1936) and Flann O'Brien's surrealist 'John Duffy's Brother' (1940).

Many of these strands come together in the opening story of the collection, 'A Broken World', where O'Faoláin provides a clear statement of intent and offers a bleak assessment of intellectual activity (or the lack thereof) in post-Independence Ireland. The story is structured in three parts, and presents three characters – a dejected priest, an uncommunicative farmer, and an inquisitive narrator – briefly sharing a journey on a train. The world that is presented is cold and impoverished, and is devoid of any kind of political idealism or civic consciousness. In the judgement of the 'silenced' because once-radical priest, this is a consequence of colonialism, as social ecologies were broken and people were taught to become dependent upon their imperial masters. 'The human dignity of men is always impaired when … they're depending on other people who can make or break them,' he tries to explain to his travelling companions. 'They weren't men. They were servants. That's the whole of it' (*PC* 17). The landscape that the train passes through is consequently described as a series of broken parishes, populated by people who are unable to think for themselves and who are obsequious in their demonstrations of obedience to those in authority. They are a people who have inherited and internalized the 'slave mentality' that is identified in *King of the Beggars* (*KB* 361). In the post-Independence context, the primary source of authority is the Church, and the dependency that is shown to the clergy (structurally, psychologically and physically) is depicted as one of the most insidious legacies of colonial rule. This is clearly illustrated at the end of the first section of the story, when the priest abruptly breaks his narrative and steps from the train when it arrives at his station:

> He got out without even saying 'Good day' to us, and his face was coldly composed. A manservant, touching his cap, took the bags. The station-master touched his cap to him. The porter receiving the tickets touched his cap to him. The jarvey, who was waiting for him, bowed as he received the bags from the manservant. Black, tall, thin, and straight as a lamp-post, he left the lit, snow-bright station with every down-looking lounger there bowing and hat-touching as he passed (*PC* 22).

The deferential behaviour of the men at the station exemplifies the point that the priest had previously tried to make about his former parishioners in another part of the country, that they were 'too respectful – tipping their hats to everybody. They were always making what we call "the poor mouth" – a mendicant habit of centuries' (*PC* 16). However, the studied posture of the priest as he departs the train suggests that he is also involved in some kind of performance, as he adopts a mask and assumes the 'coldly composed' role that is expected of him. The narrator's account of 'bowing and hat-touching' captures the infinitesimally hierarchical nature of Irish society, with its minute gradations of status (from station-master to jarvey), and its clear division of labour, and it seems that the society that is being glimpsed is organized along the lines cherished by Johnny Hussey in *A Nest of Simple Folk* – where people can say, whatever else, 'I know my place' (*NSF* 322). The slow-paced organization of this scene, with each man paying his respects to the priest separately, reinforces the sense that the community that these men inhabit is atomized, and this reception contrasts with the lack of attention paid to the famer, when he arrives at his destination at the end of the second section:

> I was just wondering if I should wake him when suddenly, at a station, identical with every other station, as if some animal magnetism in the place stirred him, he rose and stumbled out. He did not speak, he did not raise his head to see if it was his station. He saluted no one. Anyway, there was no one there but a muffled porter who silently waved a lantern over his head. As we moved off he was trudging in the middle of a road that glimmered with its own strange afterglow ... He was exactly like an old black mongrel loping home (*PC* 25–6).

The narrator's double description of the farmer as animal-like betrays his own prejudices (the narrator is city-born, and frequently appears aloof and patronizing), but also reinforces the explicitly unromantic image of rural life that O'Faoláin is keen to present, as the story refers to isolation, emigration and destitution, and criticizes a culture of docility and mute acceptance. 'His mind had gone to sleep,' the narrator declares of the farmer, as he tries to engage his companion in what is being said, and 'to shake him from his lethargic mood – possibly, most likely indeed, the mood in which he spent the greater part of his life' (*PC* 23, 24). As the narrator grows increasingly frustrated with this inability, or unwillingness, to talk, he feels compelled to assault the farmer, if only to provoke a response. He resists the temptation, however, snidely commenting 'that if I did he would only moo' (*PC* 25). This remark further impresses the equation of farmer with animal, recalling Liam O'Flaherty's brutal exposé of the valorization of 'the peasant' in *A Tourist's Guide to Ireland* (1929) – a figure traditionally celebrated as the essence of simplicity and the embodiment of all things 'Irish' – as well as anticipating Patrick Kavanagh's savage indictment of the romanticization of rural Ireland in his long poem 'The Great Hunger' (1942).[27]

The keywords in 'A Broken World' are 'lonely' and 'silent', as three characters are brought together from different walks of life but find themselves unable to communicate. Significantly, all three characters are figured as representative types (almost to the point of cliché), with none named and each barely realized or described. The tripartite structure of the story reinforces this sense of non-understanding, as each of the characters dominates a section but is effectively framed by that section, leaving their respective narratorial compartments without achieving any sense of coherence. The priest, for instance, who is presented as a seemingly compulsive talker (even though he has been 'silenced'), simply ceases to talk at a critical point in his narrative, with his final comments ending in ellipsis rather than a full stop: 'I mean to say, it was two halves of a world …' (*PC* 21 [ellipsis as original]). The narrator's requests for further information are ignored, and for the remainder of the first section of the story the priest only communicates by nonverbal shakes, shrugs and half-gestures: 'Then he actually began to laugh, a cold, cackling laugh, an extraordinary, inhuman, kind of laugh that ended in a noise like a little groan' (*PC* 22). Similarly, the exhausted farmer completes his fractured attempts at conversation with a double, non-committal 'Aye!', and 'I suppose 'tis quiet', before 'relaps[ing] into indifference' and falling asleep (*PC* 24). As the narrator pulls back from offering any explanation, the reader is challenged to make sense of these comments and actions, and to look beyond that which is recorded to discern patterns, resonances and possible meanings.

'A Broken World' ends with the clearest of these resonances, to Joyce's *Dubliners* (1914), with the narrator reaching his destination alone, and looking out on a snow-clad scene.[28] 'I could not deny to the wintry moment its own truth,' he reflects, 'and that under that white shroud, covering the whole of Ireland, life was lying broken and hardly breathing'

(*PC* 27). The narrator longs for some inspiring thought or ideal that might galvanize his fellow citizens and wake them from the inertia that has been registered throughout the story. 'What image of life … would fuse and fire us all,' he asks, 'what music bursting from the spring, what triumph, what engendering love' (*PC* 27). It is doubtful whether any such image can be found, as the revolutionary spirit of the early 1920s has been lost, and the country brought to a point where it must recognize the conditions in which it finds itself. In this respect, it is telling that 'A Broken World' was produced in the period between the publication of O'Faoláin's two biographies of Eamon de Valera, with *De Valera* charting a loss of faith in leadership that the *Life Story* had once advanced. It is also significant that an earlier version of 'A Broken World' did not include the narrator's final reflections, concluding instead with an image of the farmer departing from the train and becoming 'lost in the dark'. ('No one saluted him. He saluted no one.') This version, published in late 1936, was granted the more equivocal title, 'Broken World?', with the indefinite article dropped and a question mark instead added.[29]

With an adjusted title, and the inclusion of the brief third section, 'A Broken World' offers little hope. Despair is mollified by the narrator's reference to 'the peasants who held the hand of Faust with their singing one Easter morning' (Easter being the time of Christian renewal, and also the occasion of the 1916 Rising), alongside his admission that 'perhaps it was foolish to wish for such an image – so magnificent that it would have the power of a resurrection call?' (*PC* 27–8). The qualifying adverb 'perhaps', together with the lingering question mark and reference to resurrection, suggests that the narrator has not quite given up on the prospect of rebirth – although it is again revealing that this is expressed within, and thereby contained by, the language of the Church. This sense of possibility, remote and deferred, is mapped into the final sentence of the story: 'In the morning, Ireland, under its snow, would be silent as a perpetual dawn' (*PC* 28). The narrator seems neither convinced nor convincing, however (the vaguely-romantic 'dawn' is weighed against the much-repeated lodestone 'silent'), and his despondency serves as prologue for the collection that follows.

NOTES

1. Sean O'Faolain, 'The Priests and the People', *Ireland To-Day* 2: 7 (July 1937), pp.31, 36.
2. Tom Inglis, 'Religion, identity, state and society', in Joe Cleary and Claire Connolly (eds), *The Cambridge Companion to Modern Irish Culture* (Cambridge: Cambridge University Press, 2005), p.62; see also Tom Inglis, *Moral Monopoly: The Rise and Fall of the Catholic Church in Modern Ireland*, second edition (Dublin: University College Dublin Press, 1998).
3. O'Faolain, 'The Priests and the People', p.37 [emphasis as original].
4. Ibid., pp.36, 37.
5. O'Faolain, 'The Dangers of Censorship', p.63.
6. O'Faolain, 'The Priests and the People', p.38.
7. Six of O'Faoláin's other seven collections are named for a signature story: *Midsummer Night Madness and other stories* (London: Jonathan Cape, 1932); *Teresa and other stories* (London: Jonathan Cape, 1947); *I Remember! I Remember!: Stories by Sean O'Faolain* (London: Rupert Hart-Davis, 1962); *The Heat of the Sun: Stories and Tales by Sean O'Faolain* (London: Rupert Hart-Davis, 1966); *The Talking Trees and other stories* (London: Jonathan Cape, 1971); and *Foreign Affairs and other stories* (London: Constable, 1976). The exception is *The Stories of Sean O'Faolain* (London: Rupert-Hart Davis, 1958). *A Purse of Coppers* only includes *Short Stories* on its title page; this subtitle is not included on either the cover or the spine.
8. *The Gospel According to St. Matthew* 26: 14–16. In St. Matthew's Gospel, a despondent Judas subsequently returns his thirty pieces of silver to the high priests before committing suicide (27: 3-10). In *The Acts of the Apostles*, Judas instead buys a plot of land 'with the reward of his wickedness', but dies gruesomely in that field, which is thereafter named the 'Field of Blood' (1: 16–19). The Gospels of St. Mark (14: 10–11) and St. Luke (22: 2–6) also include reference to the 'blood money' given to Judas, but neither specify what was received.
9. Yeats, 'Paudeen', 'September 1913', first published in *Responsibilities*, rprt. in *Yeats's Poems*, pp.210, 211.
10. *Matthew* 22: 21; *Mark* 12: 17; *Luke* 20: 25.
11. See Dermot Keogh, 'Church, State and Society', in Farrell (ed.), *De Valera's Constitution and Ours*, pp.103–22; see also Ferriter, *Judging Dev*, pp.198–9; Brown, *Ireland: A Social and Cultural History*, pp.164–6; Lee, *Ireland 1912–1985*, pp.201–6. For a full account of McQuaid's involvement in the drafting of the constitution, see John Cooney, *John Charles McQuaid: Ruler of Catholic Ireland* (Dublin: O'Brien Press, 1999), pp.94–106.

12. J.H. Whyte, *Church and State in Modern Ireland, 1923–1979*, second edition (Dublin: Gill & Macmillan, 1980), pp.50, 51.
13. Keogh, 'Church, State and Society', p.118.
14. Patrick Murray, *Oracles of God: The Roman Catholic Church and Irish Politics, 1922–37* (Dublin: University College Dublin Press, 2000), p.291.
15. 'Preamble' to *Bunreacht na hÉireann (Dréacht)* (Dublin: The Stationery Office, 1937), p.4.
16. Articles 40 to 44 of the 1937 Constitution were collected together under the general heading 'Fundamental Rights', and covered the subjects 'Personal Rights', 'The Family', 'Education', 'Private Property' and 'Religion', respectively. *Bunreacht na hÉireann*, pp.82–93.
17. Longford and O'Neill, *Eamon de Valera*, pp.297–8; Murray, *Oracles of God*, pp.292–3.
18. Inglis, 'Religion, identity, state', pp.68, 69.
19. In *Vive Moi!* O'Faoláin angrily commented that this was the 'one thing I do blame, I must blame', about the society he was born into, 'because it caused me so much suffering as a boy – the delicate-mindedness, or over-protectiveness, or mealy-mouthedness, whichever it was, of the Irish Church, and the sentimentalized picture of life, especially in relation to sex, that it presented to us ... as if it believed that if nobody mentioned sex organs we would not notice that we had them, or if they had decided that in all such matters as the flesh, familiarity breeds desire, or as if they considered that God, in creating desire for woman in man, had been guilty of a lapse of taste about which the least said the better' (*VM* 21).
20. Various details in 'Discord' indicate that the story is set in what was St. Michael and St. John's Church, in Dublin's south inner city. Most revealingly, Father Peter remarks to the young couple in the story that the church is located on the site of the old Smock Alley Theatre, where the celebrated eighteenth-century Irish actress Peg Woffington 'used to foot it one time' (*PC* 223). He also alludes to the proximity of Thomas Street, Lord Edward Street and Dublin Castle, while looking across the river to several landmarks on the north inner city, such as St. Michan's Church and St. Mary's Abbey. O'Faoláin draws the story into the crypt of the church, so that his characters can be presented before the vault of one of the great villains of Irish history, Leonard MacNally. 'MacNally the spy. The scrubby lawyer who was the friend of the Earl of Clare, the traitor who used to eat his nails and was so dirty the bar-mess would not admit him. The friend of Tone. The friend of Emmet. He had defended him and betrayed him. Not until he was dead did the people discover it' (*PC* 221). These unattributed comments compound the weight of history that is powerfully felt throughout

the story, and accord with the larger theme of betrayal which runs through *A Purse of Coppers*. Although St. Michael and St. John's Church included a crypt, the detail is factually incorrect, since Leonard MacNally was actually buried in Donnybrook Church, on the south side of Dublin. St. Michael and St. John's Church was deconsecrated in 1989; in the summer of 2012, it reopened as the Smock Alley Theatre.

21. O'Faolain, *The Short Story*, p.191.
22. Butler, *Sean O'Faolain*, pp.31–2.
23. Ingman, *History of Irish Short Story*, p.140.
24. Seán O'Fáolain [*sic*], *There's a Birdie in the Cage*, with illustrations by Joy Lloyd (London: Grayson & Grayson, 1935).
25. Denis Sampson, '"Admiring the Scenery": Sean O'Faolain's Fable of the Artist', *Canadian Journal of Irish Studies* 3: 1 (June 1977), p.73.
26. For discussion of Chekhov and Maupassant respectively, see O'Faolain, *The Short Story*, pp.76–100, pp.101–31.
27. 'Seeing [the peasant] with a cow, his slow gait and his downcast head strike no jarring note', O'Flaherty wrote, with more than a pinch of sarcasm. 'Even his jaws moving slowly as they chew a wisp of straw move in unison with those of the cow that is chewing her cud'. Liam O'Flaherty, *A Tourist's Guide to Ireland* (1929; Dublin: Wolfhound Press, 1998), p.71. 'Let us salute him without irony / The peasant ploughman who is half a vegetable.' Kavanagh, 'The Great Hunger', *The Complete Poems*, p.101.
28. In the preface to a later selection of his short stories, O'Faoláin partially acknowledged this influence. 'A friend suggested to me that "A Broken World" was my unconscious reply to Joyce's wonderful story, "The Dead". I certainly did not consciously mean any such thing; but I can agree that what with the snow over Dublin, and the suggestion that Ireland is not dead but sleeping, as against Joyce's feeling that Ireland is paralysed by its past, one could, I suppose, say that the stories contrast the attitudes of two different generations. After all, Joyce grew up with a strong distaste for Ireland'. O'Faolain, 'Foreword' to *Finest Stories*, p.x.
29. O'Faoláin, 'Broken World?', p.132.

POSTSCRIPT

She Had to Do Something

O'Faoláin's only play, *She Had to Do Something*, was performed at the Abbey Theatre in late 1937. Directed by Hugh Hunt, with a cast of actors that included the talented Shelah Richards and a young Cyril Cusack, it had a short run before being replaced by George Shiels's *Neal Maquade* in January 1938. When the script was published six months later, O'Faoláin included a lengthy preface in which he attempted to account for some of the play's shortcomings – it is flat and ponderous, despite his wish that it be considered 'a light-hearted thing … which should ripple along on a series of chuckles'. He also recalled its mixed reception on opening night, when polite applause was drowned out by heckles and boos. O'Faoláin diagnosed the central concern of this feeble comedy as a 'contrast between Poetry and Puritanism', a contrast re-enacted by 'the angry portion of the crowd [who] proved the veracity of the play by continuing its theme, after 11pm, on their side of the footlights'.[1] The play the audience objected to is partly based on incidents that took place in Cork in 1931, when local priests spoke out against the visit of the Anna Pavlova Company to the Opera House. It also carries traces of Lennox Robinson's masterful comedy *Drama at Inish* (1933), while returning to a topic that O'Faoláin had explored a few months earlier, in the story 'The Old Master', where protests are organized against a touring ballet group whose performances are deemed 'indecent' by callow bigots and an intolerant Church. 'I want there to be poetry in life', the play's central character, Maxine Arnold, explains to her antagonist, the canon, as she justifies her invitation to the Russian ballet to come to their unnamed provincial town. 'And I want good behaviour', the canon pithily responds.[2]

She Had to Do Something has never been revived and is seldom engaged with in discussions of O'Faoláin's *oeuvre*. Paul A. Doyle captured the critical consensus half a century ago, when he expressed the opinion that 'this play is a very superficial, flimsy comedy that does absolutely nothing to enhance O'Faolain's literary reputation'.[3] Nor is the play mentioned in most surveys of Irish theatre in the 1930s, with focus instead deservedly given to the work of Teresa Deevy, Paul Vincent Carroll and George Shiels at the Abbey, as well as to innovations carried out at the Gate Theatre, under the stewardship of Micheal Mac Líammóir and Hilton Edwards. If the play was not a success – and it is telling that O'Faoláin declined to write for the stage again – it nonetheless granted him an opportunity to represent in visual form issues that were central to this phase of his writing life. These include his commitment to the arts and to imaginative expression, his struggle against censorship and social hypocrisy, his belief in diversity and international patterns of influence, and his anxiety over the shape of a Catholic *habitus* in post-Independence Ireland. 'I just want to sit here quietly and smoke my cigarette and read my Lamartine,' Maxine exclaims late in the play. 'But that is not the way people live in this country. There are canons to the right of you and canons to the left of you. And you just sit in the middle while they volley and folly and whatever it is. It pleases them and it is good for you'.[4] In addition, writing for the stage gave O'Faoláin the chance to experiment with a form that he had deployed, in other ways, in his prose writings of this period – as his extended use of the idiom of the theatre suggests, in his biographies and fiction of the 1930s, along with his exploration of the ways that people perform aspects of their identity in private and in public.

'We artists, in modern Ireland, are few in number, and we are harassed on every side.' So O'Faoláin declared in the closing lines of the preface to *She Had to Do Something*, having summoned the spirit of the young Joyce a few pages before, and Joyce's critique of the early Abbey Theatre in the precocious pamphlet 'The Day of the Rabblement' (1901). O'Faoláin's argument was grounded in a conceptualization of art that was characteristically elitist. 'This is a time, in Ireland, when the artists must unite against the multitude,' he portentously wrote, since drama is in danger of being 'vulgarized', poetry is at risk of being 'dragged down to something very near the mob idea of what poetry should be', and a complex of forces have ensured the need to 'insulat[e] art from the mob-virus'.[5] There is more to this argument than cultural snobbery, however, as O'Faoláin's comments bore witness to the frustrations and pressures that many writers must have felt at this point in Ireland's recent past. These pressures can be exaggerated, of course, to the point of absurdity, particularly when they are set against the appalling treatment of contemporary dissident writers across the European continent. After all, despite its many problems, Ireland in the 1930s was not a totalitarian police state where all dissent was ruthlessly suppressed and no pleasure was to be had. As John Montague sang years later, in the parodic refrain of 'The Siege of Mullingar' (1967), '*Puritan Ireland's dead and gone, / A myth of O'Connor and O'Faoláin*'.[6] However, if it is important not to overstate the case, it is equally important not to underestimate the fact that O'Faoláin was twice banned by this society – his own society – in the 1930s. His strength of purpose deserves serious consideration, therefore, particularly given the impact that censorship must have had on his own writing and thinking. As John Banville has asserted, O'Faoláin 'embarked with great courage and tenacity on the task of re-educating, or perhaps one should just say, educating, the Irish public', and his fearlessness in the fight against bigotry and narrow-mindedness set the standard for subsequent generations of artists and intellectuals. 'We need more O'Faoláin's, and now more than ever'.[7]

Reading O'Faoláin today, his work appears far less confident or certain than he himself intended, or than is often assumed to be. It also seems more valuable, though, as it engages in a sustained way with issues of influence and inheritance, and refuses to take the easy path – of unqualified acceptance, superficial mockery, or outright refusal – instead exploring sensitively the ways that people are imprinted by their past and the societies that they inhabit. O'Faoláin's interpellation as a loyalist then a nationalist subject is an important aspect of this, as is his middle-class Catholic upbringing, since early experiences prove formative and, as he remarked once again in his autobiography, 'no man jumps off his own shadow' (*VM* 125). His work also appears far more sophisticated and self-reflexive than is generally allowed, and O'Faoláin himself emerges as more than the reductively-defined 'Cork realist' who so often appears 'always already read' to cultural commentators and literary critics. There is much more to his work, for instance, than the claim that it was illustrative of a 'cosy, cottage-industry idealism', or that his fiction was 'unwilling, or perhaps unable, to contemplate th[e] reality' of Irish society in the 1930s.[8] For all the differences in perspective and methodology, criticism in the last few years by Joe Cleary, Kelly Matthews and others, suggests the beginnings of a serious reassessment of his work and legacy. Niall Carson's recent observation that O'Faoláin's 'thinking is much too diffuse and elaborate to fit comfortably into any one category', is particularly significant in this respect, pointing to O'Faoláin's interest in the processes of revision, re-interpretation and becoming.[9] 'We all know', O'Faoláin wrote in *King of the Beggars*, 'how men can, and do, live for years in the most equivocal condition of mind about the most vital subjects' (*KB* 86). This equivocation is ultimately the defining feature of O'Faoláin's pre-*Bell* work, and points to the enduring significance of this once towering figure in contemporary Ireland.

NOTES

1. Seán O'Faoláin, 'Preface' to *She Had to Do Something: A Comedy in Three Acts* (London: Jonathan Cape, 1938), pp.7–8, 13.
2. O'Faoláin, *She Had to Do Something*, p.69.
3. Doyle, *Sean O'Faolain*, p.126.
4. O'Faoláin, *She Had to Do Something*, p.145.
5. Ibid., pp.22–3.
6. John Montague, 'The Siege of Mullingar', in *New Selected Poems* (Oldcastle: Gallery Books, 1989), p.29 [emphasis as original].
7. John Banville, 'The Ireland of De Valera and O'Faoláin', *The Irish Review* 17/18 (Winter 1995), pp.149, 151.
8. Keith Hopper, *Flann O'Brien: A Portrait of the Artist as a Young Post-modernist* (Cork: Cork University Press, 1995), p.57; Hand, *History of the Irish Novel*, p.170.
9. Carson, 'The Barbaric Note', p.407.

Bibliography

Selected Primary Texts by O'Faoláin

Midsummer Night Madness and other stories, with an introduction by Edward Garnett (London: Jonathan Cape, 1932)

The Life Story of Eamon De Valera (Dublin: Talbot Press, 1933)

A Nest of Simple Folk (London: Jonathan Cape, 1933)

Constance Markievicz, or The Average Revolutionary, A Biography (London: Jonathan Cape, 1934)

Bird Alone (London: Jonathan Cape, 1936)

A Purse of Coppers: Short Stories (London: Jonathan Cape, 1937)

The Autobiography of Wolfe Tone, abridged and edited by Sean O'Faolain (London: Thomas Nelson & Sons, 1937)

She Had to Do Something: A Comedy in Three Acts (London: Jonathan Cape, 1938)

The Silver Branch: A Collection of the Best Old Irish Lyrics, variously translated and chosen by Seán O'Faoláin (London: Jonathan Cape, 1938)

King of the Beggars: A Life of Daniel O'Connell, the Irish Liberator, in a Study of the Rise of the Modern Irish Democracy (1775–1847) (London: Thomas Nelson & Sons, 1938)

De Valera (Harmondsworth: Penguin, 1939)

Come Back to Erin (London: Jonathan Cape, 1940)

An Irish Journey, specially illustrated by Paul Henry (London: Longmans, Green & Co., 1940)

The Great O'Neill: A Biography of Hugh O'Neill, Earl of Tyrone, 1550–1616 (London: Longmans, Green & Co., 1942)

The Story of Ireland (London: Collins, 1943)

The Irish (London: Penguin, 1947)

The Short Story (London: Collins, 1948)

The Vanishing Hero: Studies in Novelists of the Twenties (London: Eyre and Spottiswoode, 1956)

Vive Moi!: An Autobiography (London: Rupert Hart-Davis, 1965)
The Collected Stories of Sean O'Faolain, Volume 1 (London: Constable, 1980)
The Collected Stories of Sean O'Faolain, Volume 2 (London: Constable, 1981)
The Collected Stories of Sean O'Faolain, Volume 3 (London: Constable, 1982)
Vive Moi!, revised edition, with an afterword by Julia O'Faolain (London: Sinclair-Stevenson, 1993)

Selected Essays, Articles and Short Pieces by O'Faoláin

'Prendergast', *Éarna* 2: 5 (Meitheamh 1924), 12–16
'A Letter to the Editor', *Sinn Féin* (20 September 1924), 7
'Principles versus Progress', *Sinn Féin* (11 October 1924), 2, ctd. 8
'D'fhear eagair "Shinn Féin"', *Sinn Féin* (25 October 1924), 6
'Deich mBliana d'Fhás i mBeatha Fhile, Dáibhidh Ó Bruadair; 1670-1680', *Éarna* 2/3: 7 and 2/4: 8 (Féile Pádraig and Nodlaig 1925), 26–33 and 14–17
'The Best Irish Literature', *The Irish Statesman* 4: 26 (5 September 1925), 816
'A Plea for a New Irish Scholarship', *The Irish Statesman* 5: 10 (14 November 1925), 296–297
'In Lilliput', *The Irish Statesman* 5: 22 (6 February 1926), 680–681
'The Gaoltacht Tradition', *The Irish Statesman* 6: 7 (24 April 1926), 175–176
'The Language Problem 1: Is Irish Worth Reviving?', *The Irish Tribune* (9 July 1926), 20–21
'The Language Problem 2: Irish – An Empty Barrel?', *The Irish Tribune* (16 July 1926), 8–9
'What Does an Irish Speaking Ireland Imply?', *The Irish Tribune* (23 July 1926), 9–10
'The Spirit of the Nation', *The Irish Tribune* (23 July 1926), 23
'The Language Problem 4: Constructive', *The Irish Tribune* (30 July 1926), 13–15
'The Bomb Shop', *The Dial* 82: 3 (March 1927), 197–209
'The Cruelty and Beauty of Words', *The Virginia Quarterly Review* 4 (April 1928), 208–225
'Fugue', *Hound and Horn* 2: 1 (September 1928), 7–28
'Style and the Limitations of Speech', *The Criterion* 8: 30 (September 1928), 67–87
'Censorship in America', *The Irish Statesman* 11: 5 (6 October 1928), 86–89
'Anna Livia Plurabelle', *The Irish Statesman* 11: 18 (5 January 1929), 354–355
'Preface' to *Lyrics and Satires from Tom Moore, selected by Seán O'Faoláin* (Dublin: Cuala Press, 1929), np
Review of *Selected Poems, Lyrical and Narrative* by W.B. Yeats, *The Criterion* 9: 36 (April 1930), 523–528
'The Spurious Fenian Tale', *Folklore* 41: 2 (30 June 1930), 154–168

Review of *Synge and Anglo-Irish Literature* by Daniel Corkery, *The Criterion* 11: 42 (October 1931), 140-142
'The New Irish Revolutionaries', *The Commonweal* 15 (11 November 1931), 39–41
'About Myself', *Now and Then* 41 (Spring 1932), 35–36
'Celts and Irishmen', *New Statesman and Nation* 4: 74 (23 July 1932), 93–94
'Mr. De Valera – Rebel or Reformer?', *New Statesman and Nation* 4: 77 (13 August 1932), 173–174
'Provincialism and Literature', *Motley* 1: 3 (August 1932), 3–4
'New Directions in Irish Literature', *Bookman* 75 (September 1932), 446–448
'Literary Provincialism', *The Commonweal* 17: 8 (21 December 1932), 214–215
'Letter from a Novelist to an Idealist', *Motley* 2: 7 (November 1933), 3–5
'The Emancipation of Irish Writers', *The Yale Review* 23 (Spring 1934), 485–503
'Plea for a New Type of Novel', *The Virginia Quarterly Review* 10 (April 1934), 189–199
'A Born Genius', *Lovat Dickson's Magazine* (April 1934), 468–498
'The Modern Novel: A Catholic Point of View', *The Virginia Quarterly Review* 11 (July 1935), 339–351
'James Joyce and the New Fiction', *The American Mercury* 35: 140 (August 1935), 433–437
'Revamping Ireland', *The Commonweal* 22: 18 (30 August 1935), 417–418
'Irish Letters: To-Day and To-Morrow', *The Fortnightly* 138 (September 1935), 369–371
'The Case of Sean O'Casey', *The Commonweal* 22: 24 (11 October 1935), 577–578
'It No Longer Matters, or the Death of the English Novel', *The Criterion* 15: 58 (October 1935), 49–56
'Pigeon-holing the Modern Novel', *The London Mercury* 33: 194 (December 1935), 159–164
There's a Birdie in the Cage, with illustrations by Joy Lloyd (London: Grayson & Grayson, 1935)
'Daniel Corkery', *The Dublin Magazine* 11: 2 (April-June 1936), 49–61
'Introduction to Book Section', *Ireland To-Day* 1: 2 (July 1936), 69–70
'The Gamut of Irish Fiction', *Saturday Review of Literature* 14 (1 August 1936), 19–20
'Commentary on the Foregoing', *Ireland To-Day* 1: 5 (October 1936), 32
'Guerilla', review of *On Another Man's Wound* by Ernie O'Malley, *Ireland To-Day* 1: 5 (October 1936), 67–68
'The Dangers of Censorship', *Ireland To-Day* 1: 6 (November 1936), 57–63
'Broken World?', *The London Mercury* 35: 206 (December 1936), 123–132
The Born Genius: A Short Story (Detroit: Schuman's, 1936)

Review of *Famine* by Liam O'Flaherty, *Ireland To-Day* 2: 2 (February 1937), 81–82
'The Proletarian Novel', *The London Mercury* 35: 210 (April 1937), 583–589
'The Priests and the People', *Ireland To-Day* 2: 7 (July 1937), 31–38
'Don Quixote O'Flaherty', *The London Mercury* 37: 217 (November 1937), 170–175
'Sean O Faolain replies to Prof. M. Tierney', *The Leader* 76: 22 (6 August 1938), 521–522
'The Gaelic Corpse', *The Leader* 76: 24 (20 August 1938), 565–567
'No. 4', reply to 'Politics and Culture: Daniel O'Connell and the Gaelic Past' by Michael Tierney, *Studies: An Irish Quarterly Review* 27: 107 (September 1938), 378–380
'Irish Gasconade', review of *At Swim-Two-Birds* by Flann O'Brien, *John O'London's Weekly* (24 March 1939), 970
'This is Your Magazine', *The Bell* 1: 1 (October 1940), 5–8
'Ah, Wisha! The Irish Novel', *The Virginia Quarterly Review* 17 (Spring 1941), 265–274
'1916-1941: Tradition and Creation', *The Bell* 2: 1 (April 1941), 5–12
'Yeats and the Younger Generation', *Horizon: A Review of Literature and Art* 5: 25 (January 1942), 43–54
'Ireland and the Modern World', *The Bell* 5: 6 (March 1943), 423–428
'The Stuffed-Shirts', *The Bell* 6: 3 (June 1943), 181–192
'Silent Ireland', *The Bell* 6: 6 (September 1943), 457–466
'The Gaelic Cult', *The Bell* 9: 3 (December 1944), 185–196
'Eamon De Valera', *The Bell* 10: 1 (April 1945), 1–18
'Speech from the Dock', *The Bell* 10: 2 (May 1945), 166–167
'Principles and Propaganda', *The Bell* 10: 3 (June 1945), 189–205
'Rebel by Vocation', *The Bell* 13: 2 (November 1946), 97–114
'The Dilemma of Irish Letters', *The Month* 2: 6 (December 1949), 366–379
'The Dáil and the Bishops', *The Bell* 17: 3 (June 1951), 5–13
'Ireland After Yeats', *Books Abroad* 26: 4 (Autumn 1952), 325–333
'Foreword' to *The Finest Stories of Sean O'Faolain* (Boston: Little, Brown & Co., 1957), vii–xiii
'Fifty Years of Irish Writing', *Studies: An Irish Quarterly Review* 51: 201 (Spring 1962), 93–105
'A Portrait of the Artist as an Old Man', *Irish University Review* 6: 1 (Autumn 1976), 10–18
'Living and Dying in Ireland', *London Review of Books* 3: 14 (August 1981), 3–5

Selected Criticism on O'Faoláin

Arndt, Marie, 'Sean O'Faolain as Biographer and Commentator', in Karl-Heinz Westarp and Michael Böss (eds), *Ireland: Towards New Identities?* (Aarhus: Aarhus University Press, 1998), 56–67

________, 'Building a Nest for a Bird Alone', *The Irish Review* 26 (Autumn 2000), 14–19

________, *A Critical Study of Sean O'Faolain's Life and Work* (Lewiston: Edwin Mellon Press, 2001)

________, 'Sean O'Faolain', in Brian Lalor, general ed. *The Encyclopaedia of Ireland* (Dublin: Gill & Macmillan, 2003), 814–815

Averill, Deborah M., 'Sean O'Faolain', in *The Irish Short Story from George Moore to Frank O'Connor* (New York: University Press of America, 1982), 153–225

Badin, Donatella Abbate, et al (eds), *Sean O'Faolain: A Centenary Celebration* (Torino: Trauben, 2001)

Banville, John, 'The Ireland of De Valera and O'Faoláin', *The Irish Review* 17/18 (Winter 1995), 142–152

Binchy, D.A., 'Comments on the foregoing article', *Studies: An Irish Quarterly Review* 27: 107 (September 1938), 368–372

Bonaccorso, Richard, *Sean O'Faolain's Irish Vision* (New York: State University of New York Press, 1987)

Brown, Terence, 'After the Revival: Seán O Faoláin and Patrick Kavanagh', in *Ireland's Literature: Selected Essays* (Gigginstown: Lilliput Press, 1988), 91–116

________, (ed.), 'The Counter Revival: Provincialism and Censorship', in Seamus Deane, Andrew Carpenter and Jonathan Williams (eds), *The Field Day Anthology of Irish Writing*, 3 vols. (Derry: Field Day, 1991), ii, 89–128

________, 'Sean O'Faolain and the Irish Short Story', in Donatella Abbate Badin, et al (eds), *Sean O'Faolain: A Centenary Celebration* (Torino: Trauben, 2001), 59–66

Butler, Hubert, '*The Bell*: An Anglo-Irish View', *Irish University Review* 6: 1 (Spring 1976), 66–72

Butler, Pierce, *Sean O'Faolain: A Study of the Short Fiction* (New York: Twayne, 1993)

Cahalan, James M., 'The Realistic Visions of Seán Ó Faoláin and Francis MacManus', in *Great Hatred, Little Room: The Irish Historical Novel* (Dublin: Gill & Macmillan, 1983), 109–131

Carson, Niall, 'The Barbaric Note: Seán O'Faoláin's early years at the BBC', *Irish University Review* 43: 2 (Autumn/Winter 2013), 398–413

Cleary, Joe, 'This Thing of Darkness: Conjectures on Irish Naturalism', in *Outrageous Fortune: Capital and Culture in Modern Ireland* (Dublin: Field Day, 2007), 111–179

________, 'Distress Signals: Sean O'Faolain and the Fate of Twentieth-Century Irish Literature', *Field Day Review* 5 (2009), 49–73

Conlon, Evelyn, 'A Flawed Portrayal', *The Cork Review* (1991), 73–74

Cronin, John, 'Sean O'Faolain: *Bird Alone*', in *Irish Fiction: 1900-1940* (Belfast: Appletree Press, 1992), 148–158

Davenport, Gary T., 'Sean O'Faolain's Troubles: Revolution and Provincialism in Modern Ireland', *South Atlantic Quarterly* 75 (1976), 312–322

Delaney, Paul, '"A Marginal Footnote": O'Faoláin, the subaltern, and the Travellers', *Irish Studies Review* 11: 2 (2003), 155–164

________, 'The Desire for Clarity: Seán O'Faoláin's "Lovers of the Lake"', in Cheryl Alexander Malcolm and David Malcolm (eds), *A Companion to the British and Irish Short Story* (Oxford: Blackwell, 2008), 448–455

________, 'Changing Times: Frank O'Connor and Seán O'Faoláin', in Julia M. Wright (ed.), *A Companion to Irish Literature*, 2 vols. (Oxford: Blackwell, 2010), ii, 144–158

Donoghue, Denis, 'Romantic Ireland: The Collected Stories of Sean O'Faolain', *London Review of Books* 4: 2 (February 1982), 18–19

Doyle, Paul A., *Sean O'Faolain* (New York: Twayne, 1968)

Dunne, Fiona, '*King of the Beggars*: "A Perfect Onion of Worlds within Worlds"', *The Irish Review* 26 (Autumn 2000), 30–37

Dunne, Seán (ed.), 'Seán O'Faoláin', special issue, *The Cork Review* (1991)

Fanning, Bryan, 'Hidden Ireland, Silent Irelands: Sean O'Faolain and Frank O'Connor versus Daniel Corkery', *Studies: An Irish Quarterly Review* 95: 379 (Autumn 2006), 251–259

________, 'Out of the Mist: *The Bell*, 1940-45', in *The Quest for Modern Ireland: The Battle of Ideas, 1912–1986* (Dublin: Irish Academic Press, 2008), 41–66

Harmon, Maurice, *Sean O'Faolain: A Critical Introduction* (Notre Dame: University of Notre Dame Press, 1966)

________ (ed.), 'Sean O'Faolain', special issue, *Irish University Review* 6: 1 (Autumn 1976)

________, *Sean O'Faolain: A Critical Introduction*, expanded edition (Dublin: Wolfhound Press, 1984)

________, *Sean O'Faolain: A Life* (London: Constable, 1994)

________, 'Sean O'Faolain', in James McGuire and James Quinn (eds), *The Royal Irish Academy's Dictionary of Irish Biography*, 9 vols. (Cambridge: Cambridge University Press, 2009)

Hildebidle, John, 'Sean O'Faolain: The Cave of Loneliness', in *Five Irish Writers: The Errand of Keeping Alive* (Cambridge, Mass: Harvard University Press, 1989), 129–172

Hughes, George, 'Scandalous Matters: Sean O'Faolain, Elizabeth Bowen and the Art of the Modern Short Story', *The Harp* 12 (1997), 113–121

Hunter, Adrian, 'Frank O'Connor and Sean O'Faolain', in *The Cambridge Introduction to the Short Story in English* (Cambridge: Cambridge University Press, 2007), 99–111

Jolas, Eugene, 'Style and the Limitations of Speech', *The Irish Statesman* 11: 21 (26 January 1929), 414, 416

Kabuto, Yasutaka, 'Chugging to the sea: trains in Seán O'Faoláin's *A Purse of Coppers*', *Journal of Irish Studies* 26 (2011), 97–105

Kennedy, Brian P., '"Better sureshot than scattergun": Eamon de Valera, Seán Ó Faoláin and arts policy', in Gabriel Doherty and Dermot Keogh (eds), *De Valera's Irelands* (Cork: Mercier Press, 2003), 115–131

Kennedy, Thomas E., 'Sean O'Faolain's "The Silence of the Valley"', *Critique: Studies in Contemporary Fiction* 29: 3 (Spring 1998), 188–194

Kent, Brad, 'Sean O'Faolain and Pierre Elliott Trudeau's Midcentury Critiques of Nationalism', *New Hibernia Review* 12: 1 (Spring 2008), 128–145

Kiely, Benedict, 'Sean O'Faoláin: A Tiller of Ancient Soil', in *A Raid into Dark Corners and Other Essays* (Cork: Cork University Press, 1999), 124–133

Kilroy, James F., 'Sean O'Faolain', in Robert Hogan (ed.), *The Macmillan Dictionary of Irish Literature* (Dublin: Gill & Macmillan, 1979), 516–519

——, 'Setting the Standards: Writers of the 1920s and 1930s', in James F. Kilroy (ed.), *The Irish Short Story: A Critical History* (Boston: Twayne, 1984), 95–144

Le Moigne, Guy, 'Sean O'Faolain's short-stories and tales', in Patrick Rafroidi and Terence Brown (eds), *The Irish Short Story* (Gerrards Cross: Colin Smythe, 1979), 205–226

Levander, Marianne, 'Sean O'Faolain and Nationalism', in Heniz Kosok (ed.), *Studies in Anglo-Irish Literature* (Bonn: Bouvier, 1982), 306–313

Lyons, F.S.L., 'Seán O'Faoláin as Biographer', *Irish University Review* 6: 1 (Spring 1976), 95–109

McCaffrey, Laurence, 'Sean O'Faolain and Irish Identity', *New Hibernia Review* 9: 4 (Winter 2005), 144–156

McCartney, Donal, 'Seán O'Faoláin: A Nationalist Right Enough', *Irish University Review* 6: 1 (Spring 1976), 72–86

McMahon, Sean (ed.), *The Best from 'The Bell': Great Irish Writing* (Dublin: O'Brien Press, 1978)

McNally, Mark, 'Countering the hegemony of the Irish national canon: the modernist rhetoric of Seán O'Faoláin (1938–50)', *Nations and Nationalism* 15: 3 (2009), 524–555

Markey, Alfred, 'Revisionisms and the Story of Ireland: From Sean O'Faolain to Roy Foster', *Estudios Irlandeses* 0 (2005), 91–101

Matthews, Kelly, *'The Bell' Magazine and the Representation of Irish Identity: Opening Windows* (Dublin: Four Courts Press, 2012)

Mercier, Vivian, 'The Professionalism of Seán O'Faoláin', *Irish University Review* 6: 1 (Spring 1976), 45–53

Moynahan, Julian, 'God Smiles, the Priest Beams, and the Novelist Groans', *Irish University Review* 6: 1 (Autumn 1976), 19–29

Neary, Michael, 'Whispered presences in Seán O'Faoláin's stories', *Studies in Short Fiction* 32 (1995), 11–19

O'Donnell, Donat (Conor Cruise O'Brien), 'The Parnellism of Seán O'Faoláin', in *Maria Cross: Imaginative Patterns in a Group of Modern Catholic Writers* (London: Chatto & Windus, 1954), 95–115

Rippier, Joseph Storey, *The Short Stories of Sean O'Faolain: A Study in Descriptive Techniques* (New York: Barnes & Noble, 1976)

Room, Adrian, 'Seán O'Faoláin', in *The Oxford Dictionary of National Biography* (Oxford: Oxford University Press, 2004–11)

Sampson, Denis, 'Admiring the Scenery: Sean O'Faolain's Fable of the Artist', *The Canadian Journal of Irish Studies* 3: 1 (June 1977), 72–79

________, 'The Big House in Seán O'Faoláin's Fiction', in Jacqueline Genet (ed.), *The Big House in Ireland: Reality and Representation* (Dingle: Brandon Books, 1991), 179–190

Sherry, Ruth, 'Sean O'Faolain', in W.J. McCormack (ed.), *The Blackwell Companion to Modern Irish Culture* (Oxford: Blackwell, 1999), 441

Shovlin, Frank, 'The Struggle for Form: Seán O'Faoláin's Autobiographies', *The Yearbook of English Studies* 35 (2005), 161–170

Storey, Michael, 'Postcolonialism and Stories of the Irish Troubles', *New Hibernia Review* 2: 3 (Autumn 1998), 63–77

Tierney, Michael, 'O'Connell and Irish Democracy', *The Leader* 76: 21 (30 July 1938), 492–493

________, 'Prof. Tierney replies to Sean O Faolain', *The Leader* 76: 23 (13 August 1938), 538–539

________, 'A Corpse that Came Alive', *The Leader* 76: 25 (27 August 1938), 595–596

________, 'Politics and Culture: Daniel O'Connell and the Gaelic Past', *Studies: An Irish Quarterly Review* 27: 107 (September 1938), 353–368

Walsh, Patrick, 'Sean O'Faolain's *Midsummer Night Madness and Other Stories*: Contexts for Revisionism', in Kathleen Devine (ed.), *Modern Irish Writers and the Wars* (Gerrards Cross: Colin Smythe, 1999), 132–146

Walshe, Eibhear (ed.), 'Sean O'Faolain: Reassessments', *The Irish Review* 26 (Autumn 2000), 1–59

Whelan, Diarmuid, 'Seán O'Faoláin', in *Conor Cruise O'Brien: Violent Notions* (Dublin: Irish Academic Press, 2009), 57–66

Critical, Historical and Theoretical Texts

Adams, Michael, *Censorship: The Irish Experience* (Dublin: Scepter Books, 1968)

Allen, Nicholas, *George Russell (Æ) and the New Ireland, 1905–30* (Dublin: Four Courts Press, 2003)

________, *Modernism, Ireland and Civil War* (Cambridge: Cambridge University Press, 2009)

Allen, Walter, *The Short Story in English* (Oxford: Clarendon Press, 1981)

Anderson, Benedict, *Imagined Communities: Reflections on the Origins and Spread of Nationalism* (London: Verso, 1983)

Anderson, Linda, *Autobiography*, second edition (London: Routledge, 2011)

Augusteijn, Joost (ed.), *Ireland in the 1930s: New Perspectives* (Dublin: Four Courts Press, 1999)

Backscheider, Paula R., *Reflections on Biography* (Oxford: Oxford University Press, 1999)

Baines, Phil, *Penguin by Design: A Cover Story, 1935–2005* (London: Allen Lane, 2005)

Ballin, Malcolm, *Irish Periodical Culture, 1937–1972: Genre in Ireland, Wales and Scotland* (Basingstoke: Palgrave Macmillan, 2008)

Bartlett, Thomas, 'Introduction', to *Life of Theobald Wolfe Tone: Compiled and arranged by William Theobald Wolfe Tone* (Dublin: Lilliput Press, 1998), vii–lii

Béaslaí, Piaras, *Michael Collins: Soldier and Statesman* (Dublin: Talbot Press, 1937)

Beddow, Michael, *Goethe: Faust I* (London: Grant & Cutler, 1986)

Bhabha, Homi K. (ed.), *Nation and Narration* (London: Routledge, 1990)

________, *The Location of Culture* (London: Routledge, 1994)

Bowen, Elizabeth, 'Introduction: The Short Story', to *The Faber Book of Modern Stories* (London: Faber and Faber, 1937), 7–19

Brady, Ciaran (ed.), *Interpreting Irish History: The Debate on Historical Revisionism* (Dublin: Irish Academic Press, 1994)

Brown, Terence, *Ireland: A Social and Cultural History, 1922–1985*, second edition (London: Fontana, 1985)

Butler, Judith, *Gender Trouble: Feminism and the Subversion of Identity* (New York: Routledge, 1990)

Caine, Barbara, *Biography and History* (London: Palgrave Macmillan, 2010)

Cairns, David and Shaun Richards, *Writing Ireland: Colonialism, Nationalism and Culture* (Manchester: Manchester University Press, 1988)

Carlson, Julia (ed.), *Banned in Ireland: Censorship and the Irish Writer* (London: Routledge, 1990)

Carlyle, Thomas, *On Heroes, Hero-Worship, and the Heroic in History*, with notes by Michael K. Goldberg (1841; Berkeley: University of California Press, 1993)

Caulfield, Max, *The Easter Rebellion* (London: Muller, 1964)

Clarkson, J. Dunsmore, *Labour and Nationalism in Ireland* (New York: Columbia University, 1925)

Clear, Caitriona, 'Women in de Valera's Ireland, 1932–48: a reappraisal', in Gabriel Doherty and Dermot Keogh (eds), *De Valera's Irelands* (Cork: Mercier Press, 2003), 104–114

Clyde, Tom, *Irish Literary Magazines: An Outline History and Descriptive Bibliography* (Dublin: Irish Academic Press, 2003)

Comerford, R.V., 'Daniel O'Connell', in *The Oxford Dictionary of National Biography* (Oxford: Oxford University Press, 2004–11)

Coogan, Tim Pat, *De Valera: Long Fellow, Long Shadow* (London: Hutchinson, 1993)

Cooney, John, *John Charles McQuaid: Ruler of Catholic Ireland* (Dublin: O'Brien Press, 1999)

Corcoran, Neil, *After Yeats and Joyce: Reading Modern Irish Literature* (Oxford: Oxford University Press, 1997)

Corkery, Daniel, *The Hidden Ireland: A Study of Gaelic Munster in the Eighteenth Century* (Dublin: M.H. Gill & Son, 1924)

________, 'Love Songs in Irish', *The Irish Statesman* 4: 24 (22 August 1925), 761–762

________, 'Mediaeval Irish Poetry', *The Irish Tribune* (27 August 1926), 22

_______, *Synge and Anglo-Irish Literature* (Cork: Cork University Press, 1931)

Coxhead, Elizabeth, *Daughters of Erin: Five Women of the Irish Renascence* (London: Secker & Warburg, 1965)

Cronin, Mike and John Regan (eds), *Ireland: The Politics of Independence, 1922–49* (London: Macmillan, 2000)

Daly, Mary E., *Women and Work in Ireland* (Dundalk: Dundalgan Press/The Economic and Social History Society of Ireland, 1997)

Deane, Seamus, *A Short History of Irish Literature* (London: Hutchinson, 1986)

_______, *Strange Country: Modernity and Nationhood in Irish Writing since 1790* (Oxford: Clarendon Press, 1997)

de Blacam, Aodh, 'Have we a literature?', *The Irish Tribune* (30 July 1926), 17–18

de Groot, Jerome, *The Historical Novel* (London: Routledge, 2010)

Dudley Edwards, Ruth, 'Mrs Markievicz', in Myles Dungan (ed.), *Speaking Ill of the Dead* (Dublin: New Island Books, 2007), 86–105

Dwane, David T., *Early Life of Eamonn de Valera* (Dublin: Talbot Press, 1922)

Eakin, Paul John, *How Our Lives Become Stories: Making Selves* (Ithaca: Cornell University Press, 1999)

Elliott, Marianne, *Wolfe Tone: Prophet of Irish Independence* (New Haven: Yale University Press, 1989)

Ellmann, Richard, *James Joyce*, second edition (Oxford: Oxford University Press, 1982)

Enright, Anne, 'Introduction' to *The Granta Book of the Irish Short Story* (London: Granta, 2010), ix-xviii

Fanning, Ronan, 'Éamon de Valera ("Dev")', in James McGuire and James Quinn (eds), *The Royal Irish Academy's Dictionary of Irish Biography*, 9 vols. (Cambridge: Cambridge University Press, 2009)

Ferriter, Diarmaid, *The Transformation of Ireland, 1900–2000* (London: Profile, 2004)

_______, *Judging Dev: A Reassessment of the Life and Legacy of Eamon de Valera* (Dublin: Royal Irish Academy/RTÉ, 2007)

_______, *Occasions of Sin: Sex and Society in Modern Ireland* (London: Profile, 2009)

Foster, R.F., *Modern Ireland 1600–1972* (London: Allen Lane, 1988)

_______, *The Irish Story: Telling Tales and Making It Up in Ireland* (London: Allen Lane, 2001)

_______, *W.B. Yeats: A Life, Volume 2: The Arch-Poet* (Oxford: Oxford University Press, 2003)

Geertz, Clifford, 'After the Revolution: The Fate of Nationalism in the New States', in *The Interpretation of Cultures* (London: Hutchinson, 1975), 234–254

Geoghegan, Patrick M., *King Dan: The Rise of Daniel O'Connell, 1775–1829* (Dublin: Gill & Macmillan, 2008)

_______, *Liberator: The Life and Death of Daniel O'Connell, 1830–1847* (Dublin: Gill & Macmillan, 2010)

Gibbons, Luke (ed.), 'Constructing the Canon: Versions of National Identity', in Seamus Deane, Andrew Carpenter and Jonathan Williams (eds), *The Field Day Anthology of Irish Writing*, 3 vols. (Derry: Field Day, 1991), ii, 950–1020

_______ (ed.), 'Challenging the Canon: Revisionism and Cultural Criticism', in Seamus Deane, Andrew Carpenter and Jonathan Williams (eds), *The Field Day Anthology of Irish Writing*, 3 vols. (Derry: Field Day, 1991), iii, 561–680

_______, *Transformations in Irish Culture* (Cork: Cork University Press, in association with Field Day, 1996)

Gillis, Alan, *Irish Poetry of the 1930s* (Oxford: Oxford University Press, 2005)

Gittings, Robert, *The Nature of Biography* (London: Heinemann, 1978)

Glendinning, Victoria, *Elizabeth Bowen: Portrait of a Writer* (London: Weidenfeld & Nicolson, 1977)

Griffin-Wilson, Margo, 'Dáibhidh (Dáibhí) Ó Bruadair', in James McGuire and James Quinn (eds), *The Royal Irish Academy's Dictionary of Irish Biography*, 9 vols. (Cambridge: Cambridge University Press, 2009)

Hall, Stuart, 'Cultural Identity and Diaspora', in Jonathan Rutherford (ed.), *Identity, Community, Culture, Difference* (London: Lawrence and Wishart, 1990), 222–237

Hand, Derek, *A History of the Irish Novel* (Cambridge: Cambridge University Press, 2011)

Hanson, Clare (ed.), *Re-reading the Short Story* (London: Macmillan, 1989)

Hart, Peter, *The IRA and Its Enemies: Violence and Community in Cork, 1916–1923* (Oxford: Clarendon Press, 1998)

_______, *Mick: The Real Michael Collins* (London: Macmillan, 2005)

Haverty, Anne, *Constance Markievicz: An Independent Life* (London: Pandora, 1988)

Hegarty, Neil, *Story of Ireland: In Search of a New National Memory*, with an introduction by Fergal Keane (London: BBC Books, 2011)

Hegarty, Peter, *Peadar O'Donnell* (Cork: Mercier Press, 1999)

Hirsch, Edward, 'The Imaginary Irish Peasant', *PMLA* 106: 5 (October 1991), 1116–1133

Hobsbawm, Eric and Terence Ranger (eds), *The Invention of Tradition* (Cambridge: Cambridge University Press, 1983)

Hopper, Keith, *Flann O'Brien: A Portrait of the Artist as a Young Post-modernist* (Cork: Cork University Press, 1995)

Inglis, Tom, *Moral Monopoly: The Rise and Fall of the Catholic Church in Modern Ireland*, second edition (Dublin: University College Dublin Press, 1998)

_______, 'Religion, identity, state and society', in Joe Cleary and Claire Connolly (eds), *The Cambridge Companion to Modern Irish Culture* (Cambridge: Cambridge University Press, 2005), 59–77

Ingman, Heather, *A History of the Irish Short Story* (Cambridge: Cambridge University Press, 2009)

Innes, C.L., *Woman and Nation in Irish Literature and Society, 1880–1935* (Hemel Hempstead: Harvester Wheatsheaf, 1993)

Jameson, Fredric, *The Political Unconscious: Narrative as a Socially Symbolic Act* (London: Methuen, 1981)

Joyce, James, *A Portrait of the Artist as a Young Man*, ed. by Seamus Deane (1916; London: Penguin, 1992)

Kavanagh, Patrick, *The Complete Poems*, ed. by Peter Kavanagh (Newbridge: The Goldsmith Press, 1984)

Kearney, Colbert, 'The Short Story: 1900–1945', in Augustine Martin (ed.), *The Genius of Irish Prose* (Cork: Mercier Press, 1985), 32–41

Kearney, Richard, *Postnationalist Ireland: Politics, Culture, Philosophy* (London: Routledge, 1997)

Kelly, Aaron, *Twentieth-Century Irish Literature* (Basingstoke: Palgrave Macmillan, 2008)

Keogh, Dermot, 'Church, State and Society', in Brian Farrell (ed.), *De Valera's Constitution and Ours* (Dublin: Gill & Macmillan, in association with RTÉ, 1988), 103–122

_______, *Twentieth-Century Ireland: Nation and State* (Dublin: Gill & Macmillan, 1994)

_______, 'Eamon de Valera and the Civil War in Ireland, 1922-1923', in Gabriel Doherty and Dermot Keogh (eds), *De Valera's Irelands* (Cork: Mercier Press, 2003), 45–73

Kiberd, Declan, *Inventing Ireland: The Literature of the Modern Nation* (London: Jonathan Cape, 1995)

_______, *Irish Classics* (London: Granta, 2000)

_______, *The Irish Writer and the World* (Cambridge: Cambridge University Press, 2005)

Lanters, José, *The 'Tinkers' in Irish Literature* (Dublin: Irish Academic Press, 2008)

Leavis, Q.D., *Fiction and the Reading Public* (London: Chatto & Windus, 1932)

Lee, Joseph and Gearóid Ó Tuathaigh, *The Age of de Valera* (Dublin: Ward River Press, in association with RTÉ, 1982)

Lee, J.J., *Ireland 1912–1985: Politics and Society* (Cambridge: Cambridge University Press, 1989)

Lennon, Hilary (ed.), *Frank O'Connor: Critical Essays* (Dublin: Four Courts Press, 2007)

Lennon, Peter, director, *The Rocky Road to Dublin* (Victor Herbert Productions, 1968)

The Earl of Longford and Thomas P. O'Neill, *Eamon de Valera* (London: Hutchinson, 1970)

Lukács, Georg, *The Historical Novel*, trans. by Hannah and Stanley Mitchell (London: Merlin, 1962)

Lyons, F.S.L., *Culture and Anarchy in Ireland, 1890–1939* (Oxford: Clarendon Press, 1979)

Macardle, Dorothy, *The Irish Republic: A documented chronicle of the Anglo-Irish conflict and the partition of Ireland, with a detailed account of the period 1916–1923, with a preface by Eamon de Valéra* (London: Victor Gollancz, 1937)

McCartney, Donal, 'The Changing Image of O'Connell', in Kevin B. Nowlan and Maurice R. O'Connell (eds), *Daniel O'Connell: Portrait of a Radical* (Belfast: Appletree Press, in association with RTÉ, 1984), 19–31

MacDonagh, Oliver, *The Hereditary Bondsman: Daniel O'Connell, 1775–1829* (London: Weidenfeld & Nicolson, 1988)

_______, *The Emancipist: Daniel O'Connell, 1830–1847* (London: Weidenfeld & Nicolson, 1989)

MacManus, M.J., *Eamon de Valera: A Biography* (Dublin: Talbot Press, 1944)

Maher, Eamon and Eugene O'Brien, 'Introduction' to *Breaking the Mould: Literary Representations of Irish Catholicism* (Oxford: Peter Lang, 2011), 1–9

Mann, Susan Garland, *The Short Story Cycle: A Genre Companion and Reference Guide* (Westport, CT: Greenwood, 1989)

Marlowe, Christopher, *Christopher Marlowe: The Complete Plays*, ed. by J.B. Steane (London: Penguin, 1986)

Marreco, Anne, *The Rebel Countess: The Life and Times of Constance Markievicz* (London: Weidenfeld & Nicolson, 1967)

Martin, Augustine, *Exploring English 1: An Anthology of Short Stories for the Intermediate Certificate* (Dublin: Gill & Macmillan, 1967)

Martin, Peter, *Censorship in the Two Irelands, 1922–39* (Dublin: Irish Academic Press, 2006)

Matthews, James, *Voices: A Life of Frank O'Connor* (Dublin: Gill & Macmillan, 1983)

Maume, Patrick, *'Life that is Exile': Daniel Corkery and the Search for Irish Ireland* (Belfast: Institute of Irish Studies, 1993)

May, Charles E. (ed.), *The New Short Story Theories* (Ohio: Ohio University Press, 1994)

Montague, John, *New Selected Poems* (Oldcastle: Gallery Books, 1989)

Morris, Pam, *Realism* (London: Routledge, 2003)
Murray, Patrick, *Oracles of God: The Roman Catholic Church and Irish Politics, 1922–37* (Dublin: University College Dublin Press, 2000)
________, 'Obsessive Historian: Eamon de Valera and the Policing of His Reputation', *Proceedings of the Royal Irish Academy* 101C: 2 (2001), 37–65
Nagel, James, *The Contemporary American Short-Story Cycle: The Ethnic Resonance of Genre* (Baton Rouge: Louisiana University Press, 2001)
Norman, Diana, *Terrible Beauty: A Life of Constance Markievicz, 1868–1927* (London: Hodder & Stoughton, 1987)
Novarr, David, *The Lines of Life: Theories of Biography, 1880–1970* (West Lafayette: Purdue University Press, 1986)
O'Brien, George, 'Contemporary prose in English: 1940–2000', in Margaret Kelleher and Philip O'Leary (eds), *The Cambridge History of Irish Literature: Volume 2, 1890–2000* (Cambridge: Cambridge University Press, 2006), 421–77
O'Brien, William, *The Irish Revolution and how it came about* (Dublin: Maunsel & Roberts, 1923)
O'Casey, Sean (P. O Cathasaigh), *The Story of the Irish Citizen Army* (Dublin: Maunsel & Co., 1919)
________, *Drums Under the Windows* (London: Macmillan, 1945)
O'Connor, Frank, untitled letter, *The Irish Tribune* (13 August 1926), 23
________, *Guests of the Nation* (London: Macmillan, 1931)
________, 'A Boy in Prison', *Life and Letters* 10: 56 (August 1934), 525–535
________, 'The Gaelic Tradition in Literature: Part I', *Ireland To-Day* 1: 1 (June 1936), 41–48
________, 'The Gaelic Tradition in Literature: Part II', *Ireland To-Day* 1: 2 (July 1936), 31–40
________, 'The Future of Irish Literature', *Horizon: A Review of Literature and Art* 5: 25 (January 1942), 55–63
________ (ed.), *Modern Irish Short Stories* (London: Oxford University Press, 1957)
_______, *An Only Child* (London: Macmillan, 1961)
_______, *The Lonely Voice: A Study of the Short Story* (London: Macmillan, 1963)
_______, *The Backward Look: A Survey of Irish Literature* (London: Macmillan, 1967)
_______, *My Father's Son* (London: Macmillan, 1968)
O'Dowd, Mary, 'From Morgan to MacCurtain: Women Historians in Ireland from the 1790s to the 1990s', in Maryann Gialanella Valiulis and Mary O'Dowd (eds), *Women and Irish History: Essays in Honour of Margaret MacCurtain* (Dublin: Wolfhound Press, 1997), 38–58
Ó Drisceoil, Donal, *Censorship in Ireland, 1939–1945: Neutrality, Politics and Society* (Cork: Cork University Press, 1996)

_______, *Peadar O'Donnell* (Cork: Cork University Press, 2001)

O'Faolain, Julia, *Trespassers: A Memoir* (London: Faber and Faber, 2013)

O'Flaherty, Liam, *A Tourist's Guide to Ireland* (1929; Dublin: Wolfhound Press, 1998)

O'Hegarty, P.S., *The Victory of Sinn Féin: How it won it, and how it used it* (Dublin: Talbot Press, 1924)

O'Leary, Philip, *Gaelic Prose in the Irish Free State, 1922–1939* (Dublin: University College Dublin Press, 2004)

O'Malley, Cormac K.H., 'The Publication History of *On Another Man's Wound*', *New Hibernia Review* 7: 3 (Autumn 2003), 136–139

O'Malley, Ernie, *On Another Man's Wound* (London: Rich & Cowan, 1936)

Ó Tuama, Seán, 'Daniel Corkery, Cultural Philosopher, Literary Critic: A Memoir', in *Repossessions: Selected Essays on the Irish Literary Heritage* (Cork: Cork University Press, 1995), 234–247

Ó Tuathaigh, Gearóid, 'Cultural visions and the new state: embedding and embalming', in Gabriel Doherty and Dermot Keogh (eds), *De Valera's Irelands* (Cork: Mercier Press, 2003), 166–184

_______, 'Daniel O'Connell', in James McGuire and James Quinn (eds), *The Royal Irish Academy's Dictionary of Irish Biography*, 9 vols. (Cambridge: Cambridge University Press, 2009)

Paseta, Senia, 'Constance Georgine Markievicz', in James McGuire and James Quinn (eds), *The Royal Irish Academy's Dictionary of Irish Biography*, 9 vols. (Cambridge: Cambridge University Press, 2009)

Pierce, David (ed.), *Irish Writing in the Twentieth Century* (Cork: Cork University Press, 2000)

Reid, Ian, *The Short Story* (London: Methuen, 1977)

Reynolds, George W.M., *Faust*, in *The London Journal; and Weekly Record of Literature, Science, and Art*, 42 issues (4 October 1845 – 18 July 1846)

Robinson, Lennox, *Curtain Up: An Autobiography* (London: Michael Joseph, 1942)

________, *Selected Plays of Lennox Robinson*, ed. by Christopher Murray (Gerrards Cross: Colin Smythe, 1982)

Ryan, Louise, '"Drunken Tans": Representations of Sex and Violence in the Anglo-Irish War (1919–21)', *Feminist Review* 66 (Autumn 2000), 73–94

Said, Edward W., *Beginnings: Intention and Method* (New York: Basic Books, 1975)

________, *Orientalism* (London: Routledge & Kegan Paul, 1978)

Scannell, Yvonne, 'The Constitution and the Role of Women', in Brian Farrell (ed.), *De Valera's Constitution and Ours* (Dublin: Gill & Macmillan, in association with RTÉ, 1988), 123–136

Seeley, Frank Frederick, *Turgenev: A Reading of his Fiction* (Cambridge: Cambridge University Press, 1991)

Shakespeare, William, *The Norton Shakespeare*, ed. by Stephen Greenblatt et al (New York: W.W. Norton, 1997)

Shaw, Valerie, *The Short Story: A Critical Introduction* (London: Longman, 1983)

Shovlin, Frank, *The Irish Literary Periodical 1923–1958* (Oxford: Clarendon Press, 2003)

Smith, Nadia Clare, *Dorothy Macardle: A Life* (Dublin: The Woodfield Press, 2007)

Steele, Karen, 'Constance Markievicz's Allegorical Garden: Femininity, Militancy, and the Press, 1909–1915', *Women's Studies* 29 (2000), 423–447

Taaffe, Carol, *Ireland Through the Looking-Glass: Flann O'Brien, Myles na gCopaleen and Irish cultural debate* (Cork: Cork University Press, 2008)

Tamplin, Ronald, '*Troubles* and the Irish Tradition', in Ralph J. Crane (ed.), *J.G. Farrell: The Critical Grip* (Dublin: Four Courts Press, 1999), 48–63

Townshend, Charles, *Easter 1916: The Irish Rebellion* (London: Allen Lane, 2005)

Travers, Pauric, *Eamon de Valera* (Dundalk: Dundalgan Press/Historical Association of Ireland, 1994)

Turton, Glyn, *Turgenev and the Context of English Literature, 1850–1900* (London: Routledge, 1992)

Van Vorris, Jacqueline, *Constance de Markievicz: In the Cause of Ireland* (Amherst: University of Massachusetts Press, 1967)

Ward, Margaret, *Unmanageable Revolutionaries: Women and Irish Nationalism* (London: Pluto Press, 1983)

Whelan, Kevin, 'The Revisionist Debate in Ireland', *boundary 2* 31: 1 (Spring 2004), 179–205

Whyte, J.H., *Church and State in Modern Ireland, 1923–1979*, second edition (Dublin: Gill & Macmillan, 1980)

Wills, Clair, *That Neutral Isle: A Cultural History of Ireland During the Second World War* (London: Faber and Faber, 2007)

________, *Dublin 1916: The Siege of the GPO* (London: Profile, 2010)

Wilson Foster, John, *Fictions of the Irish Literary Revival: A Changeling Art* (Dublin: Gill & Macmillan, 1987)

________, *Irish Novels 1890–1940: New Bearings in Culture and Fiction* (Oxford: Oxford University Press, 2008)

Wordsworth, William, *The Prelude: 1799, 1805, 1850*, ed. by Jonathan Wordsworth, M.H. Abrams and Stephen Gill (New York: W.W. Norton, 1979)

Yeats, W.B., *Yeats's Poems*, ed. by Norman Jeffares with an appendix by Warwick Gould (Dublin: Gill & Macmillan, 1989)

________, *The Collected Works of W.B. Yeats: Vol. X, Later Articles and Reviews: Uncollected Articles, Reviews and Radio Broadcasts*, ed. by Colton Johnson (New York: Scribner, 2000)

Index

Note: Entries in italics refer to publications and literary works. Entries in italics with a qualifier in brackets refer to newspapers and journals, as well as literary works by Seán O'Faoláin.